A CHILD AT ARMS

Echoes of War

A CHILD
AT ARMS

PATRICK DAVIS

BUCHAN & ENRIGHT, PUBLISHERS
LONDON

First published in 1970 by Hutchinson & Co (Publishers)

This edition published in 1985 by
Buchan & Enright, Publishers, Limited
53 Fleet Street, London EC4Y 1BE

British Library Cataloguing in Publication Data

Davis, Patrick, *1925*–
   A child at arms.
   1. Great Britain, *Army, Gurkha Rifles, 4/8th*
   2. World War, 1939–1945—Campaigns, Burma
   3. World War, 1939–1945—Personal narratives,
   British
   I. Title
   940.54'25'0924   D760.G/
   ISBN 0–907675–54–9

For
my mother and father
who at intervals fed me
and who probably worried

Printed in Great Britain by
Redwood Burn Limited, Trowbridge, Wiltshire and
bound by Pegasus Bookbinding, Melksham, Wiltshire
Cover printed by The Furnival Press, London

CONTENTS

MAPS

ACKNOWLEDGEMENTS

Dick Allen saw an early draft of this book, when it was about twice as long, and made numerous valuable suggestions. Succeeding versions have been read and criticised by Bob Findlay, Peter Wickham, Peter Myers, Scott Gilmore, and by Denis Sheil-Small, who lent me an unpublished typescript giving his account of our battles. My parents and my wife read early drafts. None of these can be blamed for the final job, for none of them have seen it, but I am most grateful for their help. I am grateful also to Ronald Lewin, who took the risk of recommending publication.

For drawing the maps I am much indebted to Miss M. Maureen Evans.

The past is a foreign country:
they do things differently there

L. P. Hartley *The Go-Between*

I

TRANSIT

The little rooms to which we climbed, four storeys up on the west face, their former decoration much abused, seemed barren despite a crush of trestle beds and the washbasin in a corner. The walls were innocent of cupboards and the floors of carpets. Feet clumped along the corridor. Smells and rumours drifted in and out. People shouted. From our room the three of us, Ian Crew, Barry Davies and myself, listened to everything, for everything is important to the novitiate. In this sudden intimacy, proceeding from the hazards of the alphabet, we exchanged stories with half of our attention outside, watching, sorting, analysing, hoarding the signs and symbols and each building his own map of this new country.

I was nervous and excited. It was good to launch oneself from childhood and school into this male, adult world. Growing up is a strange process, often rather shattering. It is better to complete it away from home, away from the people we know too well and who perhaps love us too much. Like the rites of initiation of primitives, joining the army at eighteen was a shedding of adolescence for manhood. Although an army is a closed society with absolute rules and narrow conventions, backed then by the moral and legal approval of a nation at war, yet since I believed in the war and wanted to be in the army this was for me also a kind of freedom: freedom from the past, from the labels that begin to strangle as years accumulate and people assign to you a character and a place in society that have grown on to you and into you mostly through the mystery of birth and choices made by others. Here no one knew anything significant about me. It was a fresh beginning, a new birth.

I was side-stepping the mandatory months in the ranks of
the British Army. I felt guilty about this. For part of me shrank
from responsibility, did not much want to lead anyone, and
identified with the 'ranks'. There was enough to look after, I
felt, in looking after oneself and I had never been at ease with
the privileges of my own social stratum. But another part of
me, since I had to join some army, wanted to join the Indian
Army.

To be brief about a matter that is peripheral just here, my
family had several generations of relatives with service in
India. Many had been with the army. My own early childhood
had been spent among the forests of the United Provinces
(Uttar Pradesh). My father and mother and two sisters were
there now. My maternal grandmother and grandfather, with
whom I had lived since I was five, had spent their adult lives
in the same province. All my days I had listened to stories of
India, of the Indian Army, of the Gurkhas. Through my
grandmother in particular I had been indoctrinated: her father
had been a general in the Indian Army, he had won a V.C.
as a young captain with a Gurkha battalion in Malaya, he
was her hero, and so mine. I had to experience this distant
land and its peoples for myself. I wanted to serve with the
Gurkhas. It was close to compulsion.

So I volunteered for a cadetship under a scheme that
operated around the public schools. We were supposed to be
'the officer class'. An Empire-building colonel from the
Indian Army came to lecture and left behind him a sheaf of
forms. Despite the red face, the white moustache and the
clichés, I filled one up. So here I was, Private 3067357 of the
Royal Scots, a volunteer on 2s. 6d. a day, and soon to be an
officer cadet somewhere in India. It was 1 February 1943. The
war proceeded indefatigably, three years and four months old,
with almost three more years to come. Every day people died
violently, but distantly, and for me abstractly. I was content.

Those three weeks at the Great Central Hotel, Marylebone,
were deflationary. We were treated as human beings! Nobody
bullied us. Nobody's reputation was at ransom for our training.
We had expected to be overworked, trampled on, insulted.
Everyone knew that the life of a recruit was hell. That ours

was not was a relief, but relief mixed with a dash of disappointment: to find that a mountain is a molehill robs the ascent of glory. Even Ian Crew, my well-meaning, uncomplaining, unsoldierly room-companion from the Argentine, even he survived those weeks without attracting trouble. Ian was a 'British Latin-American Volunteer', and was entitled to have the initials B.L.A.V. sewn across the shoulders of his battle-dress. He was not a 'leader' either, but one had to admire a person who travels from the Argentine to London in order to join the Army of India.

Our batch of cadets was in two groups. My lot, about sixty of us, was from school. The others had come from notorious Wrotham, the pre-O.C.T.U., where it was always winter, and where no one slept, or sat, or gently walked. Before that they had already served some months in the army. They were older, sophisticated, and we did not mix closely, though we learned from them.

On the second day we were issued with our kit, home service in the morning and overseas tropical in the afternoon. It totalled eighty-two items, together with a rifle, bayonet and fifty rounds of ammunition.

1 Helmet Steel w/cover camouflage
1 Respirator Anti-Gas
1 Tins Mess Rectangular T.P.
1 Bag Kit Universal
1 Comb Hair
2 Discs Identity
2 Drawers Woollen Long Prs
2 Shirts Angola Drab
2 Shirts Tropical Cellular
1 Fork Table N.S. Small and so on and so on.

We were vaccinated and inoculated, all in a morning, in a form of endless belt which revolved us past the doctor three times, speculating on who would be the lucky bastards to benefit from the rare change of needle. After that they gave us forty-eight hours of compulsory rest. Then we took to drill parades and P.T. on the roof. We ran through the draughty streets. We had gas-mask practice, trying to believe that we

B

were efficient fighters as we peered vaguely at each other and at our instructor through the thickening mist that always came to obscure the eye-piece. We marched to Regent's Park for squad drill. We went by underground to a dentist in Chelsea barracks. We attended lectures on the war, on India, on venereal disease, on weapons, on discipline and hygiene. One cryptic entry in my pocket diary for that year reads under Sunday, 14 February: 'Church Parade. Lecture by Brigadier. Heard it all before.'

And we grew practised in the army's answer to every problem, the queue. We queued for food, we queued for pay, for equipment, for the canteen, for the lavatories. If there was no queue we were suspicious.

That 1943 pocket diary, after Watch No., Season Ticket No., Telephone, Weight, Height, and size in gloves, has a line for Identity Card No. How remote that suddenly makes it! Identity cards. Another era. Yet once that time was mine, and I lived through it from hour to hour when it was now, and all that has followed was unknown.

In the evenings and on Sundays there was London to explore. London was new to me. She was the heroine of the blitz. London could take it. London was mysterious and romantic to a provincial fed on newspapers and the nine o'clock news. Barrage balloons glittered above us in the winter sunlight. Broken buildings gaped, sliced in half and still displaying at inaccessible heights poignant relics of someone's castle. Doorways and windows were sandbagged, and glass criss-crossed with thick strips of brown paper. Everywhere there were signposts to air-raid shelters. People still carried gas-mask cases, but in them were probably sandwiches and a clean handkerchief. This was that uneasy interregnum between the night raids of the earlier winters and the flying bombs to come. London was quiet and the streets were full of troops, perhaps veterans of Dunkirk, North Africa, Greece and Crete. I stepped among them, almost their facsimile in that common carapace of thick khaki cloth. But I had the white bands of the officer cadet conspicuous on my shoulders, and was on the watch for officers, too green to be cynical. I wanted to do my salutes.

I was also too green for the prostitutes: lusting in the imagination only, nervous of the flesh. For me adolescent inhibitions and that fear of young women customarily bequeathed by our monastic boarding schools were reinforced by the Christian embargo on fornication. Sex was no problem, despite the new flow of increasingly dirty stories.

So the final days in England slipped by. I had no regrets. I was aware of my luck and am aware of it now. I was on a voyage of exploration, a physical and a spiritual voyage. Soon I would be sailing for India, in the middle of a great war, in a role approved by everyone I knew, and approved by myself. Present demands upon intelligence were minimal. I had only to be me, clean, reasonably smart, willing to fall in with the army's peculiar routines. The mind was free to absorb sights, sounds and feelings. I was just ripe for the experience.

And we who had come together for the first time in the Great Central Hotel, with a shared experience lengthening behind us we started to become a unit of soldiers instead of a collection of schoolboys: not an efficient unit, nor a knowledge-able one, yet a corporate body. Men close-herded knit together with remarkable speed. And if conditions are not too severe they will scratch one another's backs amiably enough, tolerant of foibles in the face of an instinctive hostility to all outside the group. We tried to keep Ian within the bounds of good order and military discipline.

II

MHOW

It is difficult now to recapture that complete uncertainty about the future which accompanies the solder in time of war; difficult also to recall how little it mattered. This ignorance was a kind of release sometimes, a liberation of the spirit. Adolescence had been a conforming to programmes devised by elders. So was the army. But in the army conditions were so novel and the programme susceptible to such sudden twists that there was often a sense of freedom. There were four Officers Training Schools in India, each hundreds of miles from the others, and after two months of voyaging we arrived at Bombay still ignorant of which was to receive us. When the word circulated that the blow had fallen upon Mhow (rhymes, more or less, with cow), at the end of a day and night of railway-training across the drouth of central India, no one could be found who knew anything of the place.

The contrast between Mhow and our life at sea was at first almost bewildering. We had been cargo to be shipped east round the Cape in a minimum of space, sleeping packed in hammocks down below or, in the tropics, on the hard planks of the open deck; rationed until Durban to a monotonous and unappetising diet; restricted to salt water for washing and showers; never able to move without stepping round or over other bodies. Here in India officer cadets appeared to be regarded as gentlemen. In the Mess we sat at long cloth-covered tables, knives and forks and spoons in banquet profusion, waited on by Indian mess-servants, constrained to moderate rough troopship manners and to retrieve a measure of civilised behaviour. I can recall vividly the pleasure of those early meals, particularly the breakfasts, for which I arrived genuinely hungry after P.T. and drill, and before heat drained the appetite. But soon we were accustomed to this and other luxuries, and began to think them normal, and to grumble at the food.

The Mess was in one of those long cool solid buildings preferred by the earlier generations of British in India: thick stone walls, plenty of windows to let in the breeze, and encased inside a deep arcaded verandah that kept off the sun. Of an afternoon in the hot weather one might cross an open square battered and blinded by the sun, rivulets of sweat trickling and tickling down chest, ribs and back, eyes squinting against the glare of reflected light. Then to enter one of these old buildings was to join another world: forest after the open field, under-water pools after the dazzling sea-surface, subdued, cool, restful.

In temperate climates, and especially in England, the weather changes quickly and is seldom at extremes. In the tropics a man must cultivate his patience to a slower rhythm. For weeks on end, for months, the sun will burn the earth, or the rain will flood it. At Mhow there was no escape save through this slow progress of the seasons.

The heat during our first six weeks or more was so pervasive, so huge, so inescapable, that one could not ignore it at the time and should not forget it now. I cannot quote temperatures and am not trying to compete with anybody in the matter of degrees. It just was hot. No doubt we felt it the more acutely as rookies from wintery England. We sweated and sweated all day and all night. You learn to live with this, but it never grows to be comfortable.

Our sleeping quarters, bed-sitting-rooms you might call them, were arranged in rows, perhaps six rooms to a row, single-storeyed, two bodies to a room, connected by a communal verandah, each room with a small separate cubicle for the tin bath tub, and each with a back porch where the bearers gossiped away their lives, scrubbing, polishing, perhaps stitching, but often just squatting in a kind of detached harmony with their surroundings that was both wonderful, enviable and infuriating. I shared a room with Ian Crew, and our bearer was called Kishan.

Our day began at 5.30 with a cup of tea and two biscuits brought by Kishan. P.T. and drill before breakfast disposed of the energetic part of the programme early. We dashed back after the P.T. with just time to swill off the sweat and dust in a tub of cold water and to change into khaki for the drill. The morning was devoted to Urdu, weapon training, lectures, demonstrations and field exercises. In the middle of the day during the hot weather there were two hours of compulsory rest which had to be taken prone on our beds. We might not sit at the table to write-up notes, nor wander over to the Mess for a cool drink. During the rains and after I think this regime was relaxed; by then it was not only less warm, but we had begun to acclimatise.

After the midday break there might be more Urdu, or driving and vehicle maintenance instruction, or more lectures, until around 4.30 p.m. Then finish. Ian and I collapsed on our beds, mosquito nets rolled up for the day, and waited for Kishan to bring our pot of tea, with some biscuits or cake, and for the afternoon to become evening and a little cooler. When the rains had reduced the heat I played squash or tennis in the late afternoon. After dinner we might wander into Mhow to look at the bazaar, or to see a film. There would be 'home-work' most evenings. Wednesdays and Saturdays were half-days, and Sundays free. That was the rhythm, more or less, for six months. It was a gentlemanly rhythm, busy but not frantic. It was also a rhythm inside which it was easy to spend our limited leisure in frivolous relaxation; the mind addled itself with military knowledge all day and was reluctant to function by evening.

I remember that we reached and left a good many parades on hired bicycles. We did not do so, of course, like an ungoverned rush of undergraduates changing lectures. We moved in formation, mounting and setting off to crisp orders. There was something lightly comic in our bicycle squads, capped by pith helmets, and never without a rich quota of wobbling. Bicycles cannot be disciplined so well as feet. We were not required to salute while in the saddle. When called to attention on the move one simply stiffened the arms, straightened the back, and stared stonily full ahead.

I cannot differentiate Mhow bazaar from the others I went into later. Memory suggests a narrow street of smells, scents and colour, lined on both sides with low ramshackle shops, each filled to confusion with goods among which somewhere the proprietor sits on a rickety chair and calls to the drifting crowd.

'Ah, Officer Sahib, silk for your wife. Cloth for you, sir. Every wife is too anxious for silk.' He sees from our age that by the curious customs of Europe we are certainly without wives. 'Look at the lovely colours. Send home to Liverpool, Sahib, and win finest lady. Simply each and every one is at your foot.'

'Sahib, Sahib, you buy carpet. Come. Look, look. Fine Persian carpet, very cheap. Doubtless you take and sell in England, Sahib, and grow rich.'

Doubtless. Some people did.

After the hot weather came the rains, and these gave me the only proof I received that I had been in India before. As the first thousands of drops hit the fine dust outside our quarters, forming a pointilliste pattern of increasing density before merging into spreading pools, then streams, then lakes, a smell of newly moistened earth arose that I immediately recognised, and knew that I had not smelled for fourteen years. It was unmistakable, and it was of India.

The rains turned our dry rolling plateau green, so that we hardly recognised it; they cooled the air a little; but we soon tired of them and longed for a break in the overcast sky.

Then halfway through the course we were asked to give in order of preference our choice of regiments in which to serve. The choice was wide. Among the infantry, for which most of us were destined, were the Sikhs, Rajputs, Dogras, Gurkhas and Jats; there were the regiments of mixed class such as the Frontier Force, the Punjab and Baluch regiments, and many others. Each had its own tradition. Most could tell of a hundred years or more of fighting history. All, so far as I knew, were equally admirable.

For me there was no hesitation. We react publicly from within our private histories. I wanted to join the infantry. I believed with General Wavell that all battles and all wars

are won in the end by the infantryman. And of all the infantry
I wanted the Gurkhas; and of the ten Gurkha regiments I
wanted the 3rd Gurkhas in which my cousin Bruce Kinloch
was serving, and with whose first battalion he had won an
M.C. during the retreat through Burma in 1942.

There were other possibilities. My great-great-grandfather
had been a colonel in the Bengal Artillery of the old East
India Company. His son, my great-grandfather, I have
mentioned: George Nicholas Channer joined the 1st Gurkhas,
and with them as a captain won his Victoria Cross in Malaya
in 1875. He soldiered on through several of the frontier campaigns of the next twenty years to retire as a general. Perhaps
I ought to have followed him.

The General was the father of Kendall Channer, my great
uncle, who had for a time commanded the 3/3rd Gurkhas in
the 1914–18 war. Then there was a nephew of the General,
George de Renzy Channer, who had joined the 7th Gurkhas.
He was captured by the Turks at Kut in 1916. Despite this
setback he survived to become a general himself. Another
nephew whom I knew well, Guy Channer, had served with the
14th Sikhs. A cousin, David Anderson, was with the 9th
Gurkhas. The women of this large family had mostly been
born in India, and had married men working in India. Through
them I could trace connections with the Indian Medical
Service, the Indian Police, the Indian Forest Service (my
grandfather and father) and the Indian Public Works Department. These last were not choices before me now, and I had
left behind the possibilities in the British Army, where a range
of other connections might have been considered. In fact, on
my mother's side, I was one of the latest units of a typical
nineteenth-century middle-class family. Most of three generations of men had been in government service, with a strong
bias towards India and the military. The few who were not
were dotty or became parsons.

My father's family had no previous connection with India,
and his service there was due to a liking for the country first
contracted as a young officer in the 1/7th Hampshires, a
territorial battalion posted to India in October 1914. His
father was a Unitarian minister, and so was his father's father.

The family on that side were merchants and non-conformists, with a strain of Welsh poetry in them. Probably they disapproved of military gentlemen.

I did not pay much attention to family history as a boy, and did not see a family tree until after the war; I was but vaguely aware of its ramifications. I had nothing against the British Army or the rest of the Indian Army. I wanted the 3rd Gurkhas because I knew and admired my cousin Bruce. He was only a few years older, almost of my generation. So 3rd Gurkhas it was, first, second and third choice. I wrote a note to accompany the official form, and wrote to Bruce. Before the war regiments had interviewed candidates. This was not now possible, which was maybe just as well. I trusted to nepotism. It worked.

On 10 September Ian Crew, my unfortunate room companion from the Argentine, was 'Returned to Unit' for six months. In plain English, he was found to be, temporarily at least, below the standards required of a future officer, whatever these might be. The army succeeds in giving a military veneer to perhaps 99 per cent of the civilians fed to it. Ian was among that obstinate 1 per cent who are resistant to the machine. It was not for want of anxious trying. Ian wanted to be a soldier. But he never looked one. I heard of him later as a sergeant in some British administrative unit, but did not meet him again. The marvel is that more of us were not turned away. There was only one other, though some were put back to the next course and commissioned later. This led us to suppose that the Indian Army must be desperate, for we all thought that many of us were incompetent.

There was one death. On 16 September Jack Jones died of complications following typhoid. We were paraded to be told the news, which shocked us, and I was picked to be a coffin-bearer. That evening we carried Jack, a tall heavy cheerful fellow, down a winding path to the graveyard. We moved slowly, and before we reached the new hole my shoulders and back were buckling. But relieved of the load I stood stiff and awed for the short service, for the filling-in of the grave, the

salute of rifle fire, and for 'Last Post' on the bugle. A military
funeral is a brief but very poignant business. That same
evening we set off on a three-day jungle-training scheme down
in the rift of the Narbada river, where it rained for so much
of the time that they broke it off early, and we forgot the
immediacy of Jack's vanished life in fatigue and discomfort
and work.

I lost a religion at Mhow. One hot afternoon, without
dramatic soul-searching, without convulsions, visions or
subsequent regret, faith in the Christian dogma vanished.
Looking back now it is disappointing that so basic a change
should have arrived so quietly. For nineteen centuries men
and women had died for and against the Christian faith. I had
been a conscientious and regular Anglican communicant even
in the army, had thought of becoming a parson. The fall from
grace should have generated some heat. I can report none of it.
No one had been arguing with me. There was no external
pressure. Like the bath water, belief just drained away, seemed
suddenly unreal, a mental delusion kept going from the
weight of its historical past. I never went to another church
service in the army. And I do not believe that my behaviour
was much changed. I was aware of only one difference at the
time: a multitude of spiritual problems vanished quite magic-
ally. No longer did I have to examine myself microscopically,
a depressing and rather self-centred business. I came to a rough
compromise with my imperfections, and there we have since
rested, more or less equably.

And if I lost a religion, I did not gain much. Mhow was
soft, or at any rate not hard. We were kept busy, we sweated
gallons, yet there was an absence of tension or true seriousness
about what we did. This was India and officers were gentlemen.
Gentlemen should not be more than one night out in the rain.
We did not object, but I was touched from time to time by a
vague dissatisfaction, a sense of being unfulfilled; I had been
taught that good cannot come save from discomfort and hard
labour. Mhow is symbolised for me, perhaps unfairly, by an
elderly colonel (re-employed) who lectured to us on some pre-
war skirmishing among the north-east frontier tracts, where the
principal weapon of both sides was the bow and arrow.

Much of our weapon-training was devoted to the rifle, with which we were familiar after years in school training corps and Home Guard units. The other weapons of an infantry battalion about which we knew less, and which as officers concerned us more closely, were worshipped from an immense distance.

On field exercises we carried dummies—awkward, heavy unpopular bits of wood and metal shaped as rough replicas to the originals. No one wanted to lug them around the Indian countryside. Who could get serious about the siting of a dummy? A functioning weapon is a live and terrible object which has to be lived with day and night before a man becomes its master. How could one learn from a dummy and a training manual?

As I remember we never fired, or saw fired, 2 in. and 3 in. mortars, because there were none. I did once fire the bren-gun, some single shots and two or three bursts. This was a memorable occasion, but inadequate as grounding in the weapon that provided the chief fire-power for every infantry section. I do not recall seeing tommy-guns or sten-guns. Nor can I remember revolver practice; the revolver was regulation issue as an officer's personal weapon.

In our final grading I got an 'A' for Morse Code. I never used the Code again. As a system for communicating within an infantry battalion it was dead, killed by the new wireless that allowed direct speech. Of such wirelesses we saw none, and the world of wireless remained a mystery to me for ever.

Mhow taught me nothing new about infantry tactics at the section level and we had few chances to practise with a platoon or company. I could have learned about the internal combustion engine, but failed to. I did learn to drive. We bucketed around a course that included a water-filled dip, a humped mound, and mud slides. I did learn also to speak a humped and muddy sort of Urdu. Most of it I forgot when I had passed the examination that enabled one to be considered for promotion to captaincy. Within two weeks of leaving Mhow I had to start on Gurkhali and, except on railway stations, scarcely used Urdu again. Now I have forgotten both.

We must have had instruction on many other matters.

Little of it comes to mind at this distance. No, I mildly enjoyed those six months at Mhow, and memory, perhaps, has skipped much and twisted more. Very possibly I am unfair to the place. Perhaps if the course had been tougher, too many of us would have dropped back from illnesses for which climate and newness to the tropics rather than our basic constitutions would have been responsible. Perhaps there were revolvers and 2 in. mortars.* Moreover, I know now of the long negligence by the withholding of finance that was the fate of the Indian Army up to 1939, for most peacetime governments hate to impose the taxes needed to maintain military efficiency, and the Indian Government had also to pay for half the British Army in India. Even so, I am left with a conviction that much of the instruction was unnecessarily out of date and some of it near to comedy.

Mhow began a vulgarisation of the sensibilities. It may be wrong to blame the place for a process that must have started under any permutation of service life. But I had expected to be stretched, to be taught by men who were competent and backed by the latest equipment and techniques. We were not so stretched nor taught by such men (with a few honourable exceptions), so there was an erosion of confidence in authority, fate, luck, or whatever, and the birth of scepticism. Mhow was neither romantic nor efficient. Mhow was a chrysalis in which we had to vegetate before being allowed to hatch out and fly the world. It provided for us a period of familiarisation in a strange country. Since leaving I have hardly thought of the place until I came to write these words.

Mhow in turn seems to me typical of much of India at this time. Perhaps for the European with pre-war experience there had been changes that were obvious enough. But to a young and undiscerning amateur soldier from England it did not seem that the war was near or urgent. There was no shortage of food at our level, although in Bengal that autumn

* Dick Allen is the only fellow cadet with whom I am in contact and he says that we once watched 2 in. mortars firing, that sten-guns arrived near the end of our course, and that some of the cadets knew how the latter worked but the staff did not. He does not remember 3 in. mortars or revolvers.

and winter over a million are estimated to have died from
starvation and the diseases that follow. There was no black-out
of lights, there were no bombers overhead night after night
with that nervous throbbing of heavy engines familiar to half
Europe. There were no searchlights to pencil the black sky,
no barrage balloons, no gas-masks, no ruined buildings, no
concrete pill-boxes discreetly knitted into town and countryside, no air-raid sirens wailing at the nerves, no fire-watching
on lonely roof-tops, no Home Guard parades after a day of
work, no rationing of petrol and clothes. To us India was very
like a country at peace, both in the obvious outward signs just
mentioned, which nobody could help, but also in the feel of
life, in the things people said, the way they behaved, in a lack
of urgency about anything. Yet in 1943 the Japanese were at
the peak of their triumphs in Burma, and little had come to
relieve the story of repeated defeat.

Perhaps this is not too surprising. The Indians had not
declared for war. The English in India had done it for them.
Some Indians were enthusiastically with the English. Many
were actively hostile. A large number were indifferent, wholly
occupied in their grind for survival. The feel of total war, so
apparent in England, could not be reproduced in the vast
uncommitted spaces of India.

I still have the scrap of paper on which I scribbled down
a copy of my final report from Mhow.

A good average cadet, tall and smart, who has worked hard
and well throughout the course. After a mediocre start he
has improved rapidly, and is continuing to show improve-
ment all round. He has a pleasant manner, and with very
little more experience should make a good officer. Personality—average; leadership—average; intelligence—slightly
above average; general behaviour—good.

In particular subjects they graded me 'B', or average, for
drill, physical training and endurance, games, organisation
and administration, military law, field craft, and platoon
training. I got an 'A' for map-reading and Morse, and a 'C'
for weapon-training. This seems a fair assessment.

With it I left Mhow for the last time on Saturday, 16 October,

for ten days' leave in the hills with my parents. At midnight
we became second-lieutenants. As we awoke next morning on
the trains that were distributing us about India, we put up our
single 'pips' and assumed the responsibilities and privileges of
an officer of His Majesty's Army of India. I took several weeks
to grow accustomed to being saluted.

III

ON APPROVAL

Unless thick-headed, a man must be haunted by a suspicion that it is his own fault if there are periods of his life when he is unhappy, off balance, unable to adjust to his surroundings. The first months I spent with the Gurkha Brigade, at the 3rd Gurkha Regimental Centre, Dehra Dun, were such a period. The day I left the Centre was a day more significant than the day that finished the war; it was the end of winter, the promise of spring, rain after drought.

Partly this was caused by boredom. I was bored to indifference, bored to hatred, bored almost to rebellion. It was not the momentary boredom of a blank evening. This was a deep-seated tedium. I arrived, and for day after day stood on those wide parade grounds, shifting uneasily beneath the tilt of a new 'Gurkha' hat, the strap tight round the chin. I was to watch the training of the Gurkha recruits, but was unable to talk to them or their instructors for they knew no English, was unable to talk to the British officers for they were busy, unperceptive men whose chief energies were for turning unsophisticated young hillmen into modern infantry; they had no time for green second-lieutenants.

There must also have been the new-boy-at-school element. And I missed the camaraderie of cadet life. More significant, the 3rd Centre was an unwelcoming place. The emphasis for everyone was on formal discipline: turn-out must not be merely smart, it must be the smartest; saluting must be more than prompt, must reflect a man's burning desire to assist the 3rd Centre to be the top depot of the Gurkha Brigade and of the Indian Army; the 'lines' had to be everywhere and always spotless, the whitewash the whitest, the rows of tents the straightest, the creases on shorts and trousers the sharpest. The Commandant, from whom this compulsion originated, strode about his domain like Jehovah, and like Jehovah had a sharp eye for the smallest irregularity. His permanent staff of British officers took their colour from him. They were not martinets, but they were men obsessed with form and appearance.

Perhaps training centres attract a particular type of officer. Perhaps the 3rd Gurkha Centre was an extreme case, its staff transformed into mirrors of the Commandant by the strength of his particular vision. As I reconstruct my mentors in prejudiced memory, they were hard-working, efficient, but rigid in thought, formal in behaviour, hostile where they sensed nonconformity, and in thrall to their master. I no longer recall their names or faces, but I have not forgotten how much I disliked some of them.

There is nothing so demoralising as inactivity. A young man wants to be doing and learning, he wants to end the day exhausted but wiser. I took little exercise, seemed to learn almost nothing; there were just those hot hours of impotently watching, without responsibility, in linguistic isolation, hours through which one had to maintain the soldier's marionette walk, to appear alert, interested. I tried to adapt, although this approach to army life was the one I most disliked. But the line of hills to the north was like a broken promise; they reminded me too sharply of the days I had just spent with my parents in their house above the lake at Naini Tal, days that now seemed like paradise. I longed to get away, to be back among the mountains around Naini, to be free to walk and run in the pine-scented air, to gaze at the snow peaks on the horizon and dream of exploration.

So here at Dehra Dun there was further disillusion, a further scarring and hardening of the Davis spirit, like the thickened skin of a cicatriced apple. Neither at Mhow nor here could a man respect authority. The romantic vision took another knock.

There seemed nothing to do about it. Rebellion was no answer, not yet. Rebellion would have meant removal from the Gurkha Brigade. I wanted to reach an active battalion, and although even to hint at this was apt to be taken as a personal

insult by that majority of the staff who had seen no action and
who were perhaps thin-skinned on the subject, it was these
men who could get me to my battalion and who would only
send 'good' officers.

Why was I anxious to reach a fighting battalion? This is
not a rhetorical question: I ask it of myself. No one wants to
be killed. Most of us are not heroes. Someone has to do these
jobs behind the lines, and among the people doing them were
hundreds of admirable and courageous men. Using hindsight,
I believe that sometimes, and especially while young, we need
to point ourselves at the heroic. Life most often presents the
squalid, the belittling, the prosaic. One's young self does not
accept this and the image of the heroic is an anodyne. I might
not have admitted so at the time, but battle and preparation
for battle did seem to provide for the heroic element. There
was this need to find out, to be probed and proved, to set
oneself against that most real of realities, death, unable to
predict whether the ending would be happy or not.

This is not an endorsement of war, which I feared then and
hate now. But given the war as inescapably there, in its fifth
year, a monster on the horizon, almost a way of life, certainly
a way of thought, I was drawn towards it as surely as driftwood
to the centre of a whirlpool. And I would do nothing at Dehra
to endanger my passage.

What now surprises me about this period at the 3rd Gurkha
Centre, which I disliked so much, is its brevity. I was on the
Centre's strength for about four months. In that period I was
away on Christmas leave for ten days, and on a 3 in. mortar
course for three weeks; for nine days I was on a jungle warfare
camp, and for another three a courier to Lucknow and back.
Yet I do not exaggerate my dislike. When later in my military
career I returned to Dehra to pick up the luggage I had
stored at the Centre, I stayed with the 9th Gurkhas nearby,
and spent less than an hour recovering the luggage. If I think
of the 3rd there is still the bite of emotion.

Meanwhile, in addition to absence, there were some reliefs.
I was not the only victim. There were three or four of us.
Gradually we came to admit what we all felt in varying
degrees, and to wonder despondently how soon we might

c

escape. Off duty we were company for one another. And over
in the 9th Gurkha lines a mile away there was Dick Allen, my
companion cadet from Mhow. Together Dick and I might
bicycle the five miles into Dehra for an evening at the cinema
or for drinks in the club. Dick took a detached and amused
view of my loves and hates, which was good for me. He was a
better fit in his niche than I in mine, a very competent
administrator behind the black moustache; and the 9th
Gurkha Centre was evidently a more relaxed place.

Most afternoons there was a language lesson, the constructive element in the day. We had to learn Gurkhali, and learn
it fast. Without it we could not talk to the men we had been
commissioned to command and should never have responsibility. Without it there could be no release. I enjoyed those
lessons. Gurkhali (or Khaskura, or Nepali) is from the same
Indo-Aryan language group as Urdu and Hindi, which made
it easier for us to learn. It is a bastard language, the lingua
franca of Nepal. Most of our Gurkhas also spoke their own
tribal languages, whose structure and roots were from very
different sources, from the Tibeto–Burman tongues. For them
as for me Gurkhali was a second language.

Learning a new language is enlarging and liberating. Every
language has its own way of going about things. To learn a
new language is to embrace, partly at least, a different world, a
different way of looking at familiar things and a way of looking
at things that are not familiar. You are being initiated into
another people's birthright.

We now began to penetrate the Gurkha way of thinking,
and even at the beginner's level this was absorbing. Few wartime British officers got much beyond a fluent form of military
Gurkhali. I was no exception. The grammar and vocabulary
needed in order to fight are not extensive, and one tends to
master only what experience proves to be necessary. There was
no necessity for a discussion on farming, or marriage customs,
or the system of clans. In those days no British officer could
travel to the homeland of his men. Few Europeans had been
even to Khatmandu, Nepal's capital; into the hilly country
east and west practically none had travelled.

But if we were ignorant of the domestic background of our

men, we had one advantage over officers in British regiments. The language we learned was demotic, the language of the troops: it was not the language of a ruling class. No turn of phrase, no subtle inflexion, no curiosities of pronunciation, no unconscious use of a larger vocabulary automatically signalled us as men apart, an officer corps. The linguistic oddities we perpetrated in Gurkhali were oddities of ignorance, which is a very different matter, and this was well understood. The men would correct them with great good humour.

Our Gurkhali was rough, simple, often coarse. We knew that polite forms existed. Our Indian teacher at Dehra Dun (who invited me to tea at his home and was a nice man) took pains to explain the differences. 'You will meet a prince, Mr. Davis, and you must be respectful.' But away from our hopeful tutor princes seemed rare. We lapsed into uninhibited imitation of what we heard.

And as I began to master this language, so I was able to break the isolation of those dreadful parades and talk with Gurkhas, for of course the real value of my time in Dehra was happening from my first day to my last, and was happening despite boredom, stuffy officers, language difficulties or any other obstacle. I was meeting Gurkhas, watching them, listening to them, observing their reactions to praise and to blame and the way that others handled them, unconsciously absorbing little by little knowledge of their habits, temperaments, conventions.

The recruits I used to watch looked extraordinarily young. In those days Gurkha soldiers had their heads close cropped, save for the tupi, the scalplock by which they would be drawn to heaven when they died. Their faces were round and smooth, innocent of hair, with high cheekbones and the epicanthic fold that gives that characteristic slant-eyed look to the Mongolian races. Their bodies were ill-developed from poor food, and generally worm-ridden. This changed after a few months of army food and army training. But from the beginning they had well-developed leg and thigh muscles, for in Nepal everything was carried up and down the steep hills upon the backs of people. Mechanical aids did not exist and transport animals were rare. Probably this is still so over most of the country.

If the recruits were young, and at first bewildered, they were
also an independent and light-hearted lot, properly unawed
by a young and almost as bewildered new officer. I never
knew a Gurkha with an inferiority complex. Most of those I
saw came from central and western Nepal, and in 1943 were
collected first at the Recruiting Depot at Kunraghat, just
inside the Indian border. There were no recruiting officers in
the hills. Nor were British officers permitted to tour in Nepal.
Instead army pensioners were used, men with good records
and now in retirement to their homes. According to the needs
of each year they were told how many recruits to bring in and
when to bring them. During the Second World War, as in the
First, there was an enormous expansion of the Gurkha Brigade,
and almost anyone could join who had two legs, two arms and
sound lungs.

I found that our recruits were gently handled. There was
none of that cataclysmal conditioning of young soldiers common
in Europe and America. The Commandant might demand the
highest standards, but he followed the tradition of the Indian
Army by refusing to obtain them through bullying. Toughness
was not equated with cruelty. Learning to be a soldier was a
matter for co-operation and hard work. To each squad of
Gurkha recruits was assigned an N.C.O. who looked after them
from early morning until late at night; it was his job to trans-
form them from anarchic individuals into disciplined soldiers,
from boys into men. His weapons were humour, example,
persuasion and patience; the guard-room was very seldom
necessary.

My first close contact with our recruits came one cold
November morning ten days after I joined. Every new officer
was required to spend a working day with a squad, in theory
with one recruit in the squad, doing with him everything that
he did. It was a valuable but embarrassing experience: embarrassing because I hate to be conspicuous, and a ruddy-skinned,
six-foot, shy and ignorant Englishman is apt to stand out from
a bunch of brown-skinned stocky Gurkhas; and when he does
not understand the language, is apt to make mistakes. I had to
use much resolution to make the dawn entry into the barrack-
room of my squad, shivering in my shorts as much from nerves

as from cold. (Those shorts were so thickly starched that they stood of their own accord: we stepped into them and thereafter sat down rarely and with care to avoid disturbing the knife-edge crease.)

The long day passed. During breaks there was little relaxation: both sides felt that some sort of social communication was demanded; bad Urdu or worse Gurkhali were my only media. I remember sitting on a recruit's string bed trying to explain to a havildar* about service in the Home Guard in England, and having to simplify grotesquely. I was always making fearful simplifications to fit thought to a limited vocabulary and deficient grammar. An un-English use of gesture was helpful. But towards the end of the day, when the blur of friendly brown faces had partly resolved into individuals, and when from sheer nervous and physical fatigue I no longer cared about mistakes, I enjoyed myself. Gurkhas are extraordinarily direct and human humans. Life is an amusing business to be taken as it comes. It would not have occurred to these recruits, nor to their instructors, to make things difficult for me. Their instinct was to help. If I went wrong they laughed, but it was kindly laughter, unconcealed and genuine amusement which anaesthetised embarrassment.

Soon after this there was an attestation parade, a ceremony that was moving because of what it meant to those recruits who at this parade, their preliminary training complete, became riflemen. They were no longer apprentices, but workmen. Two at a time the stiff and impeccably dressed young men marched before the Commandant, saluted, and were presented with their own kukris. When the original recruit is considered, the transformation was surprising. The recruits arrived from the hills barefoot, dirty, ignorant and proud. For the Gurkhas on their hillside farms there was none of the background of Western civilisation that gives to even the poorest and most stupid of Western children the rudiments of reading, writing and how things work. A Gurkha might not have seen taps. He would not have seen a train or a car. He had to master boots as well as marching, to learn of hygiene as well as the machine-gun.

* See page 24 for ranks in the Gurkha Brigade.

At the time of which I write he would not have seen a wireless, a telephone, a cinema, electric light, a compass, a map, a key, a clock, probably not a bicycle. One of the lighter sights of an afternoon at Dehra was young recruits learning to ride bicycles. These boys within six months were turned into riflemen, and after a few months more into signallers, muleteers, mortarmen, drivers, medical assistants, cooks, carpenters. Most of them by then had learned to write and read Urdu. Although little was being done for me and I almost lost heart from the neglect, I could see how much was done for the recruit. The change in them was almost magical.

I must here interpolate an explanation of the ranks used in the Gurkha Brigade, since some of them were peculiar to the Indian Army, and a vague appreciation of their order is necessary to the rest of this story.

Gurkha Brigade (until 1947)	British Army Equivalent
Rifleman	Private
Lance-Naik	Lance-Corporal
Naik	Corporal
Havildar	Sergeant
Havildar-Major	Sergeant-Major
Jemadar ⎫	
Subadar ⎬ Gurkha officers	No equivalent
Subadar-Major ⎭	

The Gurkha officers, or Viceroy's Commissioned Officers, were always promoted from the ranks and were always Gurkhas. What they may have lacked in education they more than made up in experience. They were platoon commanders and seconds-in-command of companies, posts which in British battalions were held by British officers. Thus in a Gurkha battalion there were fewer British officers holding the King's commission, and a junior British officer was given larger responsibilities at an earlier age. Gurkha officers were full officers, entitled to receive salutes, to wear belts and swords on occasions of peace-time ceremony, to be addressed as 'Sahib' ('sir') by their juniors.

They ran their own Mess. They were a vital link in the chain of command, perhaps the most vital. A rifle company with good Gurkha officers had no trouble with discipline or morale.

The British officer commanding a company was the link between his hundred or more Gurkhas and the military structure above that was largely British. He was not a figurehead; he was the Commander, with full responsibility for his men and all they did or did not do. He supplied education and a trained intelligence.

The Subadar-Major commanded nothing and everything. He was the senior Gurkha officer in the unit, and if good, a man of immeasurable influence. For example, it was upon the Subadar-Major that the Colonel relied for advice as to whether or not proposed actions would affect the men in ways unconnected with simple soldiering: on matters of religion, or family welfare. The Subadar-Major was second only to the Colonel in his real powers, and we junior British officers paid to him every respect, and were careful not to cross him.

This order of ranks was common to the whole of the Indian Army, though the names of the ranks varied.

The Gurkha Brigade at that time consisted of ten Gurkha regiments. Before the 1939 war each regiment had two battalions. During the war two more battalions per regiment were raised, depots founded and various specialised units came into existence. But until 1947, when India became independent and four of the Gurkha regiments went to the British Army and six to the Army of India, no Gurkha in them received the King's commission, and thus none could fill the higher posts held by British officers. In theory the most junior British second-lieutenant was senior to the most senior Gurkha officer, even to a subadar-major. This should have led to friction. I never heard that it did, and this must have been due partly to the apparent immutability of the system, which had existed since Gurkha regiments were first formed in 1815, and partly because every new British officer was taught never to pull his rank. If he did so more than once he did not stay long with his unit.

Since 1947, in both the British and Indian Gurkha regiments, Gurkhas have been trained and commissioned for higher posts.

So far as I know they have done well, and it is hard to see why they were not so trained years before.

At the 3rd Centre I had quarters to myself. This was some compensation for the unpleasantness of most days. 'Quarters' was a large square hut, roofed with thatch, walled with canvas, on a brick foundation and with a brick chimney. It could be put up cheaply and scrapped easily. I was comfortable enough. The sides could be rolled back to that beautiful winter sunshine on a Sunday morning. In the evening they were closed to keep in a sufficient warmth. No one bothered me. There were a dozen such huts spread around a couple of grass fields, nicely distant from the Mess and the quarters of the regular staff. There was nothing regimental between my hut and the hills two miles off.

I had an elderly Mohammedan bearer, a man who could speak some English, and who had spent a lifetime meeting the demands of a long succession of officers. He was resigned to short tempers and rough affection, and to the peculiar whims of his masters. Like so many Indian servants, his capacity for loyalty survived the worst of English ignorance and lack of manners. He himself might cheat you in a small way, but by the Prophet's beard no one else should.

Beside our fields a footpath led on through the woods and past a farmer's hut or two until it crossed the Nun river at the base of the hills. Sometimes at weekends I set off down this path and others into which it branched. I had no object except the joy of movement, the pleasure of exploration, and the wish to be alone. Everything was new, different. To turn a corner among the trees, to see another corner ahead luring one on, to come suddenly to the banks of the wide sandy river bed with its enlargement of vision and in it somewhere a fast cold stream; to see a hill and immediately to climb it; to find obscure hamlets in which lived people about whom I knew nothing, who knew nothing of me, who wanted nothing and returned a simple greeting simply; to run because I felt like running, to turn left or right, climb up or down, to be silent, still and listening, as I pleased, all this was to me an enlarging freedom that helped to combat the waste of regimented spirit suffered on parade. I had a passion for solitary walking. There are patches of remote countryside all over South-East Asia that once I knew intimately.

I scarcely remember the Officers' Mess at the 3rd Centre. I seem to see it surrounded by shrubs and trees, the ante-room full of animals' heads, portraits, dark wood and chairs covered in brown leather. The animals' heads may have been else-where; they were almost universal, staring down with their glass eyes for year after year as young men grew old and new young men arrived to make the same mistakes and find the same wisdom. The portraits were equally universal, and the men they represented often had the same glass-eyed stare as the stags and bears. I ate in the Mess, but did not feel at home. The atmosphere was not for juniors. I was nervous of breaking some unexplained convention. Occasionally there were formal guest nights, with toasts to the King Emperor, and pipers piping and port circulating and deafened guests. Only Scots-men and elderly ears bludgeoned by tradition or shell-fire can derive pleasure from bagpipes so close.

Then there was 'Beating the Retreat'. It was an occasion at which the 3rd Gurkha Centre excelled, and it happened frequently during my short time. Officers, wives and guests lined one side of the great parade ground (chairs and benches to sit on), and Gurkhas the other side (they stood). Long shadows striped the earth. The chiselled hills looked wonder-fully close in the sharp evening air, lit by the setting sun and more like a *tromp d'œil* painted backdrop than live mountains. In the open, and not too close, massed bagpipes are another matter. They grip the heart. Gurkhas take to them easily and play them well. For the finale, with the whole audience at attention, buglers rang out 'Last Post' into the gathering dusk, and down came the flag. Although I was often sceptical of tradition, for it seemed sometimes to overwhelm us, to suffocate the present for the sake of the past, I could not be so at that moment.

We emergency-commissioned officers were welcomed by some, resented by others. We were, inevitably, a dilution of the original Indian Army brew. My experience was that the resentment was strongest in those parts of the organisation furthest from the war, and the welcome most genuine in the fighting battalions. But whatever some of us suffered from our reception in the training establishments—and it is fair to add that many of my contemporaries did not feel as I did—we all suffered from a shortage of time: time to learn techniques and traditions so thoroughly that they became instinctive. The army has an answer to everything, but the soldier needs time to absorb these answers. Books and lectures impart knowledge. The use to which you put this knowledge, adapted automatically to the circumstances of your own shifting experience, larded with the wisdom which you personally have acquired, can come only with time, time measured in months and years rather than weeks. We did not have this. And at my age there was something else you do not have which only time can give you—knowledge of people.

Yet I ought not to complain. The subalterns of the First World War might find themselves in the trenches three weeks after commissioning, and a high proportion dead after three months. My fate, by comparison, approached most gently. I had now been in India a year, and had been commissioned six months. Under wartime regulations I could put up the second star of a full lieutenant.

I will end on a different note, and one that lilts through the background of all those unsatisfactory days around Dehra Dun. To Hindus and Muslims the profession of arms is an honourable profession. In India the army had never been the last resort for the indigent, as it was apt to be for so long in Europe. In India joining the army could be a family tradition, a way of life, son following father into the same regiment. Between these soldiers and their officers, still mostly British in my day, but with increasing numbers of Indians in the Indian regiments, there was a close bond. It was a bond built of mutual respect, of agreement over ends and means, of pride in the regiment to which both belonged and in their own contribution to that regiment's well-being, of a knowledge of the regiment's history and of the pressure which this engendered to give only the best, of self-discipline, sincerity, straight dealing, loyalty, hard work and courage. These qualities were

expected of a man, and by and large were found in him; and
if he had them in reasonable measure but lacked a little of
intelligence or experience, this was forgiven him.

Though I have grumbled at the inadequacy of Mhow, and
was unhappy at the 3rd Gurkha Regimental Centre, I never
wavered in my hope that these were temporary blocks to the
felicity I might inherit when I could speak Gurkhali and was
safely inside a battalion of my own. Then I would add my
own mite to the Regiment's traditions and would myself be
enlarged by them.

IV

JUNGLE TRAINING

My escape from the Centre came on 28 February 1944, a fine day, a red-letter day. I left in company with a draft of 160 men, another more senior British officer, and the unexpired portion of the day's rations. We paraded on Roberts Lines Football Ground for the Commanding Officer's inspection, and were played to our motor transport by the Pipe Band. After a morning of such ceremonial it was a slight anticlimax to travel no more than fifteen miles over the crest of the Siwalik Hills to Mohand, on the southern slopes.

For we were posted to the 38th Gurkha Rifles, a composite battalion set up by the 3rd and 8th Gurkhas for the purpose of post-basic training, especially in jungle warfare. From here, sooner or later, according to the needs of battle, most of us could expect to be sent to an active battalion on the Burma front (though some still went to Italy and the Middle East). In this same area were joint training battalions of all ten regiments of the Gurkha Brigade, and of other Indian Army regiments.

The 38th Gurkha Rifles had begun to operate late in 1943 and was still in its formative stage when I came. With a break for a 'small-arms' course at Saugor, I stayed with it through the hot weather and into the monsoon, until early July. If our distance from the 3rd Centre was not great in mileage, it was so in spirit. Though we were not comfortable—I think every building was made of canvas or materials from the jungle—I enjoyed those months.

In jungle warfare the infantryman is paramount, and must be trained to high standards. He cannot be churned out in

short order, as happened in the First World War, without
inviting disaster. There had been enough disasters in Burma
during 1942 and 1943. Here is a list of what one training
authority considered were the elements most necessary:*

Confidence in himself and his weapons.
Initiative and ability to operate alone by day or night.
A very high standard of observation and a suspicious mind.
Ability to move and carry out all functions in absolute silence.
Ability to react instinctively and immediately to surprise.
Quickness on the draw.
Ability to freeze and fade to a recognisable rendezvous.
Ability to find his way in the jungle.
Familiarity with the jungle, and especially jungle noises by
    night.
Knowledge of how to live on the jungle in emergency.
The use of materials indigenous to jungles for water-crossing,
    for obstacles, for shelter and for cooking.
The habit of leaving no trace for the enemy.
Ability to climb trees, scale cliffs, cut his way through dense
    growth and cross water obstacles.
Team work.
Ambushes, how to avoid them and how to lay them.
A very high standard of fieldcraft and patrolling.
Cunning.

In our reach towards perfection we performed a variety of
exercises designed to develop such skills. I remember a four-day
patrol at the beginning of June. A number of platoons set off,
each on separate routes so designed that at intervals (of which
we were ignorant) they were likely to cross. These other patrols
were to be treated as hostile, could be ambushed if possible, or
at least avoided. We had to pass certain specific points on the
ground, but could choose our own routes between them. We
had to spend the night in a designated area.

I set off with a platoon whose commander was a young
Jemadar. I was not the commander of the platoon. Yet I was
more than an observer, for I too was supposed to be learning.
We did the job together, a combined effort. Gurkhas are good

* Major-General J. G. Elliot, *A Roll of Honour*, p. 181, Cassell, 1965.

at this kind of relationship. The Jemadar knew about bivouacking and minor tactics and his men. I was good at map-reading and use of country. The men knew about living off the country and making us and themselves comfortable at night. We enjoyed ourselves.

The first lesson I learned, and the only one I now remember, was that I could not carry a pack that must have weighed about seventy pounds, plus rifle and ammunition. We had accepted all the rations issued to us by the Quartermaster, and also carried what clothing and bedding we considered appropriate. I could scarcely swing my pack on to my back. Once it was there I plodded across the dry, rustling jungle floor, bent at an acute angle, and raising my eyes to view the way ahead as seldom as possible. Fortunately we did not move too far that first afternoon and evening. I was exhausted.

Fortunately, too, even these sturdy Gurkhas, short, squat and accustomed to carrying from birth, found the weight and the heat a trying combination. By mutual consent we had a vast feast evening and morning, consuming between us a high proportion of those heavy tins of fruit, those bulky vegetables, those weighty bags of rice that had been generously showered at us. From the map we could see that our route next day took us out of the Siwalik forests on to the cultivated plains. There, said the men, we would buy eggs and fruit in a village. So we saved some rice, biscuits, dried fruit and chocolate, and set off next morning with distended stomachs and light packs. Never again did I let a pack get so heavy.

A week later I did a similar patrol. I remember this one because I missed the dawn start. I had relied for being woken upon my orderly, Sherbahadur, a simple Gurkha soul too old and dim-witted for active service. He overslept. I overslept. The Training Major, who was fond of riding in the early morning, had arrived on his horse to watch the patrols set out. My patrol was dispatched without me. I was hauled up in front of the Second-in-Command almost as I emerged from my hut, perturbed, anxious to be after them. No reasonable excuse. I was made duty officer for three weeks running, which meant that for three weekends I should not be able to join the evening truck that took officers to the high life of Dehra

Dun. A pity, but not disastrous. I swung pack and rifle on to my shoulders and was off, about three hours late, to catch the patrol.

That Sherbahadur was an unusual man to find in a Gurkha unit, even in wartime. He moved with a bent back, inside a permanently scruffy battledress and behind a drooping moustache. He was a Newar, a tribe from which the regulars of peacetime were never recruited, and he was quite exceptionally stupid. I came to believe that he had been recruited for the army by Japanese agents, or that his relations, hearing of the British King's great need for men, and desperate to be rid of a fellow who kept on sowing the wrong seed and driving goats over precipices, bundled Sherbahadur down through the hills to the recruiting depot and armed with massive bribes, or effective magic, got him accepted. He was notorious in our Company. The men treated him as a child and were kind save for the occasional friendly taunts. Mentally he was a child; when he was happy his face wore a fixed childlike smile.

I suffered from his forgetfulness. He was apt to mislay my possessions. Most of them turned up within a week or two; but my kit was not extensive and much of it essential to me every day. It was irritating to return from a long day in the forest, sticky with sweat and swallowing dust, to find no water for my bath and the nailbrush missing.

Sherbahadur did not remember my anger for long; ten minutes later he would be smiling to himself, arranging and rearranging my comb and my shaving kit on top of an old packing case, wanting to help but unable to think of anything else to do. I became quite fond of him, as one grows accustomed and attached to a leg in plaster, or a decaying tooth.

But to return to that second long patrol: it was good to be alone in these jungles, in spite of the rain that fell at intervals. I chewed dried fruit and chocolate for lunch, and watched the dung beetles pushing and pulling at their curious cargo, and a corridor of ants moving up and down the trunk of a tree. There was little chance of meeting animals in an area so regularly thrashed by troops; but insect life continued undiminished, indeed was at its most frenzied at the beginning of the rains.

An hour before dusk I abandoned the chase until morning and settled down to make a fire and cook some rice. Although in an unanalytical way I must have seen rice cooking dozens of times, I had not cooked it myself. I got a fire going between two stones, balanced my mess-tin of water on top, and chucked in a couple of handfuls of grain. The water took a long time to heat. Before anything at all like cooking had begun a twenty-minute downpour put out the fire, topped up the mess-tin with fresh cool water, and set me cowering under cape and hat. I tried again, but now everything was soaked and the relit fire merely smoked. Evidently I did not share the Gurkha genius for producing flames. For the only time in my life I wished that I had been a boy scout. I chewed more dried fruit and chocolate, and rather miserably settled down for the night under a large bush. Rain and mosquitoes made it an uneasy time. I was off very early next morning.

I reached the open country, and here it was simple to spot movement when I knew roughly where to look. I caught up with the platoon about ten o'clock, embarrassed and crest-fallen at being so inefficient at looking after myself. But the men only grinned, enjoying the story of my failure, and promised me a banquet that evening.

This highly cultivated area south of the Siwaliks was interesting. For the only time I was at close quarters with peasant India. India is a land of villages: 80 per cent of the population lives in communities of under five thousand souls. The land was dotted with groves of trees, generally mango trees. They were half a mile to a mile apart, and our problem was to remain unseen while crossing from one to another. The groves could provide perfect cover (and shade) for a battalion, but of course another patrol might be already ensconced. In between them the countryside was open, often just ploughed stubble. At this period, transitional from hot weather to monsoon, few crops were showing. There were occasional fields of half-matured sugar cane. The water-courses, of varying sizes, being sunk, could be used when they led in the right direction. There were no hedges, few ditches, and very little of that undulation of ground that gives concealment in the English countryside.

We avoided most of the villages. But perhaps once a day we scuttled into one as the inevitable pi dogs barked about us. While someone bargained for eggs, vegetables or fruit, and sentries were posted in case another patrol was drawn to our nest, we released our packs and relaxed in the shade, filling water-bottles from the well, chewing dried currants or sweets. The mud houses were clustered close, often joined one to another. They reflected the general poverty of the inhabitants. The children stared with large round eyes, pot-bellied and thin. The youngest were shy, ready to run; the older ones were sufficiently sophisticated to try a 'Bakshish, Sahib'. Women kept away; the men who were not in the fields gathered round—older men predominantly, with lined faces, full of character. In their prime some had themselves been soldiers.

There were no metalled roads between these villages, only broad earth tracks, in dry weather navigable by bullock carts. Nor in this district was there a railway line nearby, nor electricity. India is a land of self-contained units. Electricity, oil, gas, petrol, were still mostly absent. There was no running water, no drainage. This was brought home to me one day after we had reshouldered our packs, made our farewells, and were again trudging into the blinding sun. We left the environs of the village and shook out into open formation. And we passed across the field which was the village latrine, a dry stony expanse dotted with fly-covered heaps of excreta, and stinking. Our young Gurkhas, who had learned to use water and earth closets, murmured in disgust, but they themselves would follow the pattern back in their mountain villages. They had no choice.

I did not mind. I never felt a stranger in India and for the most part accepted what I saw uncritically. I did not understand all I saw, and did not always like what I saw, but I accepted it as, when very young, one accepts relations and houses, hardly noticing the warts and the draughts. For I was at home in the land, was not afraid of what I did not understand and was without compulsion to change it. I cannot explain this feeling of belonging; perhaps it came from those first five years lived in India. This is not the place for an account of those years, nor of my civilian connections with the country while on leave with my parents, but the reader should be reminded occasionally of this extra dimension to the military life here chronicled, for it formed an antiphonal background that was seldom far from my thoughts, though it took little of my time.

Forays to the plains were rare. Most of our time was spent among the forested slopes of the Siwaliks, learning how to move through jungle and how to use it. Jungles in the tropics contain many useful plants: plants that a man can eat (rare), plants that contain drinkable liquid (quite common), and plants that can be used for a hundred practical purposes—for ropes, rafts, beds, roofs, stakes, stretchers, smokeless fires, booby traps, for curing fevers and healing wounds. There are a few dangerous plants. The jungle will tell a man who or what has passed through it, if he knows the signs and where to look for them. When he knows these signs he can take precautions to remove at least some of them as he himself moves through the jungle.

A soldier in the jungle needs to acquire for his surroundings a positive partiality, almost an appetite—an appetite for enquiry and minute observation—and a frame of mind that denies the need for fear. The jungle is to be used. It is not an enemy. The enemy use the jungle. Like us, they have to; but, so we learned, they are not so very good at it. They too come from an industrialised country with little forest. They often make a lot of noise and leave obvious trails. An intelligent soldier can do better. An intelligent soldier will make the jungle work for him and against the enemy.

For myself I preferred the thought of the jungle and the Japanese to Italy or France and the Germans. The jungle gave to the individual infantryman the possibility of using brains, judgement and trained common sense; and the old skills of the hunter and the hunted. The element of luck was less, of design more. I had read of campaigns in other places, and knew how often the larger impersonal weapons of war dominate the battlefield. Hundreds of guns fire thousands of shells, multiple mortars throw down curtains of steel, belts of mines, barbed wire and booby traps block the way ahead, dozens and scores of tanks swarm over everything, fleets of bombers saturate a small area with high explosive; all this is beyond the infantryman's control. He can only cringe and suffer and die.

In Assam, in Burma, in the jungle campaigns, three tanks together were exceptional. The Japanese had few aeroplanes at any time and by now almost none. Our troops were seldom fired on by more than half a dozen heavy guns simultaneously. The extraordinarily difficult country and the vast distances of both armies from their sources of supply meant that heavy arms were few and generally short of ammunition, and that war was often restricted to men and animals and what they could carry. The individual mattered.

One evening before the rains a hundred men and a bundle of us officers stepped out on a night march to Hardwar, to emerge once more from our jungles in order to practise in the Ganges what was called watermanship. The distance was about thirty miles, not excessive for trained men; but we carried arms, ammunition and full pack, and the route was wholly on a rough and rutted forest track that skirts the lower Siwalik slopes. In the dark it was difficult to pick the smoothest path, and impossible to maintain the marching rhythm that covers the miles without too much effort. During the black early morning we halted for an hour, which was probably a mistake. At any rate it was a mistake to lie on the cold earth to doze, as I did. I cooled off rapidly, stiffened up, and developed a fever, so that on arrival at the river bank I was useless for twenty-four hours. Most lessons are learned the hard way.

Watermanship consisted of teaching as many Gurkhas as possible to swim (few can), and of teaching all Gurkhas to cross water whether they could swim or not. We had a lagoon-like backwater of the Ganges to play in, with wide safe shallows and a minimal current. It was fun. And for once we were dealing with an element in which I was more at home than the men. They were taught to lie astride bamboo poles (the female bamboo is hollow and floats well) and to paddle across the water. They were taught to construct rafts from bamboo and groundsheets on which equipment could be piled for dry transportation. There was method in the work but it was also a kind of play: to be mucking about with rafts and water after the claustrophobic heat of our jungle camp was a true holiday.

Hardwar is at the lower end of the gorge by which the Ganges breaks the Siwaliks and debouches on to its own great plain. Hardwar is a place of antiquity, and of sanctity for Hindus. Thus our men, light-heartedly Hindu though most of them were, found a double merit in this training. Hardwar is always a place of pilgrimage. You must bathe in the holy Ganges at the *ghat* where the footprint of Vishnu is impressed on a stone in the upper wall. And once every twelve years there is a special festival for which half a million pilgrims may come.

Hardwar railway station, where every train to and from Dehra Dun halts, is a picturesque spot, sandwiched between cliffs and a broad arm of the Ganges. There is a temple on the steeply descending ground below the track, and on the temple roofs, near eye level, and on the track and sometimes all over the station too, swarm long-tailed villainous-looking brown monkeys. The monkeys have a reputation for begging over-boldly—robbery with violence, as it were. I used to stare at them from the carriage window, ready to close myself in at short notice. They were holy monkeys, protected, and would have won any court case in respect of injury from train passengers. Nothing ever happened. The monkeys gambolled innocently enough, sat picking fleas from one another's fur. Soon the train steamed slowly off into a tunnel, and lost the river, and sanctity, and the mendicant monkeys.

The small-arms course at Saugor made a welcome break from Mohand and the jungle. By small arms are meant the weapons used by a platoon of infantry. At that time these were rifle, bayonet, grenade, bren-gun, sten-gun, tommy-gun and 2 in. mortar. It was a good course. It gave the kind of intensive instruction I had expected and missed at Mhow. The instructors were expert fanatics, mostly sergeants from British regiments. If we thought we knew how to handle any of these weapons, half a minute watching the sergeant kept us quiet.

Saugor in April was exceedingly hot. The journey too and

from the place was hotter. Our first-class compartments had fans, and I suppose that revolving the air in an oven is preferale to not doing so. But we baked.

The heat at the 38th Gurkhas also grew oppressive, and rose well above the 100-degree mark. The year 1944 provided a particularly hot hot weather. We had shade enough. But thin grass roofs and walls do not provide a high degree of insulation. And the trees kept from us the lighter breezes. At Mhow and at Dehra (both higher than Mohand) the old stone buildings were always cooler than the outer air, and gave relief off parade. Here there was no such relief. Inside or outside it was hot. Our weekend jaunts to Dehra were for more than a change of scene: we were able to have a cool drink in a cool room.

The rains were preceded by days during which sudden strong winds blew up from the south, laden with dust. Everything became coated with dust, impregnated with the stuff, and dust was gritty between the teeth, in the hair, in one's bed; it blew slap through the walls of our huts.

These days before the arrival of the first heavy rain are an odd experience. The air is charged with tension. The long hot weeks have frayed at nerves: people are irritable, restless, unable to sleep; they drink more and eat less; sometimes they shoot themselves. That great turbulent front of saturated air advances across the plains like some Nordic god. The world is waiting for it. One day, suddenly, it is there; the clouds are visible, piled up against the southern horizon. But they take their time and it may be a week before the first drops of rain. The dust storms grow to cyclonic intensity, and become malevolent, striking at mealtimes, or when papers are spread over bed and table, or the men are being paid and the table under the tree is covered with neat stacks of rupee notes.

When the rains did come we swopped one discomfort for another. Grass roofs and walls do not keep out water, not monsoon storms. According to the wind and other undiscoverable pressures, the leaks kept changing, so that, for instance, in the Mess we could not leave our dining-table for long in the same position.

But I was an officer of the Gurkhas. It would not do to be

depressed by a little physical discomfort. In Assam, I told myself, the war's bitterest fighting was in progress. I at least was not in danger, was not hungry, was not wet all the time. I ought to be happy. And on the whole so I was. I had learned much at the 38th. I had learned to adapt to the jungle the training in fieldcraft I had imbibed with the Junior Training Corps at school, and later with the Home Guard. I had learned to live with Gurkhas and could now speak Gurkhali, of a simple sort, fluently. I had learned much about how to administer a body of Gurkha soldiers: what they required of food, clothing, equipment, ammunition and amenities to keep them in good condition. I had had confirmed what I already knew: that I preferred a rough simple life to the often inane boredom and formal disciplines of the military cantonment. I was ready now for my battalion, any battalion. The 38th had taught me all it could. But a posting to a battalion depended upon the needs of the battalions, and not upon my readiness. I might have had to wait for many weeks, for months. I did not.

'Lieut. P. D. C. Davis is authorised to go on 10 days casual leave commencing 5 July 44. Subject to immediate recall by wire.'

This was it. This was 'embarkation leave'. I had been posted to the fourth battalion of the 8th Gurkhas, a cross-posting. Bill Blenkin and I are thought to be ripe for infliction on an active battalion. The 4/8th need officers, and the battalions of the 3rd Gurkhas do not. Do I mind? asks the Colonel. I am glad, though I do not say so. My association with the 3rd Gurkhas has not been happy whereas I have nothing against the 8th Gurkhas. I am delighted with a posting to any active battalion of a Gurkha regiment.

Quick. Pack a bedding-roll and suitcase and off with Bill in a truck for Dehra Dun station. No time for letters. We send a telegram, catch a night train and a morning bus from Khatgodam up the vertiginous road to Naini Tal, and arrive before the telegram. I inflict Bill upon my parents, who are delighted to see me (and him), but disturbed that this heralds the probability of fighting.

For some reason I have not mentioned Bill. Lieutenant William Blenkin was one of that group of older cadets who came to India and Mhow with us. He was commissioned into the 3rd Gurkhas two months earlier than I was, and therefore was my senior. Lieutenant Bill Blenkin was a knock-out, a gin and tonic, a wag, a mimic, a raconteur *premier classe*. I would wager that he was the most fluent, least-likely-to-dry-up and funniest teller of dirty stories in the Indian Army. He not only remembered every story he heard and improved on it; he invented new ones. He could be just as funny about the everyday occasions of our humdrum lives, and in company that did not appreciate obscenity in wit. Bill had yet to accumulate his full repertoire, and had not achieved quite that peak of skill that later came with much practice, but he was pretty good. One of the frustrations of writing this account is the impossibility of reproducing the occasion, accent and matter of Bill's daily table talk.

Naini was damp and cloud-ridden. The great Himalayan summits which had seemed so close in the clear air of October when I first gazed at them were now seldom to be seen, and even the seven peaks surrounding the lake were often blanketed. But social life had not diminished: sailing on the lake, drinks in the boathouse at the edge of the water, roller-skating with my sisters, tea at Valerios, meals at the Chinese restaurant, dinners given, dinners received, drinks and dances in the club, bridge parties, amateur dramatics, visits to the Roxy or Capitol cinemas, invitations flying through crowded rooms like blown leaves.

I found some of this social round uncomfortable. I knew few of the people, was unlikely to meet many of them again, and am a rotten performer at small talk. Shaggy from jungle training, and about to go to war, I felt like a pit pony in a stable of thoroughbred racers. I was often drinking or dining with senior officers. These men were contemporaries of my parents. They were Jim, John and Harry. War had brought them accelerated promotion. Brigadiers, lieutenant-generals and major-generals were apt to appear through the front door at any time. I vanished when I could for long walks among the mist-shrouded hills. The generals and I were not at ease together.

But if uncomfortable in the clubs and with the generals, I enjoyed myself elsewhere. No one could dislike Naini. It was beautiful, even in the monsoon, as well as gay. After the damp grass-hut life at Mohand, I relished the comforts of Fern Cottage, my parents' house. I relished the absence of responsibility, the release from the tyranny of the timetable. Out of uniform I did not have to salute or be saluted. The double burden of being an officer, and of being an officer in India where, like it or not, an Englishman could seldom cease to act an imperial part, was eased. I could be myself, unimperial, anonymity-loving, non-responsible.

Naini Tal, tucked away in a cleft over six thousand feet above the sea, high on the edge of a great mountain chain, was a kind of 'Shangri-la', a real never-never land, a creation of the British that was cut off from the heat and struggle and disturbing fascination of the bulk of India. In Naini an Englishman could forget a good deal of what he disliked of India, and by the trees and temperate flowers and the cool resin-scented air be reminded of his own country. I liked India. But, at the simplest level, it was certainly good to be cool as well as irresponsible.

The ten days passed too quickly. And then with Bill back to the 38th Gurkhas; down the twenty-two miles of hill to Kathgodam, wondering if I should see this exciting and beautiful road again, on to the train and out into the plains, change at Bareilly, westwards past the monkeys at Hardwar, along the *dun* with its now familiar succession of culverts, streams, stretches of tall green forest, and its occasional views of the foothills. I stored most of my kit at the 3rd Gurkha Centre. And on the 18th of July we left, Bill and I and Mike Tidswell, a quiet and engaging lieutenant of the 8th Gurkhas, who was much our senior and so in charge. We were off to the war.

V

TOWARDS A WAR

It is a long way from Dehra Dun to Manipur. For an easy first leg there was the train journey to Calcutta; nine hundred miles measured across the map, more on the ground, past Lucknow, past Allahabad, past Benares, names that recalled half-remembered and romantic tales of the earlier days of the British in India. For a boy those stories were exciting: forced marches through the heat and heart of India, sudden fierce battles, sieges, jewelled rajahs on canopied and caparisoned elephants, who went down gracefully in defeat and then gave to their conqueror unswerving alliance; stories of small numbers of my countrymen who came to trade and remained to conquer; stories in which, on both sides, courage and daring, cupidity and cruelty were mixed in gripping proportions.

The tone behind such stories was feudal. The Empire was still a proud and glittering structure, and Englishmen still knew what was best for the natives. I absorbed this tone. And now that I was a young man and walked through the real India, I was a little bewildered, unsure. Times had changed since my history books were written. And I had changed. I discovered that I had a liberal superstructure upon an imperialist hull. Many of the 'natives' might still be the simple children of the benevolent legend; they did still fall to the greed and the corruption of their own countrymen, who might still produce too few who could mimic the English passion for justice and efficiency. Yet there were cultured Indians and there were efficient Indians; and the humour of the times, which I shared instinctively, suggested that Indians might prefer to risk inefficiency with self-rule to efficiency and foreign

dominion, that nationalism was no longer a conspiracy of the
few but might be a hunger of the many.

There was time to think of these things on a train journey
such as this, three days and two nights of time in a small moving
box, like an oven in that sultry heat, a time that was divorced
from the preoccupations of yesterday. The train pushed on
and on across the plains of Oudh, Behar and Bengal that
stretched on either side without visible end. Though these
plains were dull to the heat-laden eye, they were not easy to
ignore, for they were home to millions. Those patient and
abused people, absorbed without remission in a struggle to
eat, did they hate me, the Englishman? Bengalis were not
recruited into the army. We had been taught that they were
not the martial type, yet they had the courage to be terrorists.
I was not keen to believe that I was hated. An Englishman
likes to be liked and does not thrive upon hate. It was dis-
concerting, but perhaps salutary, to suspect that these people
of the great plains might care less for the English than for the
Japanese towards whom I moved steadily nearer, a revolver
in a holster on my hip, and in my middle a fear of being found
to be afraid. At every station there were surging crowds, and
at every station a gathering of those who were even more
unfortunate than the majority—the starving, the maimed, the
diseased.

People from lands where climate and fortune give them full
stomachs and good health should spend a day on an Indian
railway station. They will see human beings reduced to such
final degradation—and see them as routine sights, commonplace, thus ignored—that they can never again take for granted
their own untorn clothes, their barbered hair, their wallets,
their indigestion. If I believed in Christ up there in his Christian
heaven, I'd ask him why he was not born in India, where there
was so much love yet such indifference to misfortune, so much
tolerance alongside such fanaticism, where each year uninsured
thousands, sometimes millions, died of earthquake, flood, riot,
famine and disease, the acts of God.

Yet I hated to see these wretched people at the stations,
hated to be pestered by them for a coin from my pocket, could
not get accustomed to them. There was here none of the

dignity of the afflicted in Arab lands. There was only cringing, and servility, and misery. I was not large enough for it. I wanted to help them, but could not do so fruitfully and permanently. Therefore I was angry and wished to escape; angry at myself and at a universe that allowed this, angry with them for bringing their bodies to my notice, ashamed that I was caught in my clean uniform, sustained by a social and political system in which I was unassailably safe, member of a ruling élite, while they had lived only to rot. Good fortune is a hard burden in India, yet not so hard that one throws it off. I gave the customary coin and greeting as we passed along the platform to eat in the station restaurant a dinner that probably contained more calories than these beggars found in a week. I walked along the platform to eat and to forget the beggars. The problem was too gross. Pity is fugitive. And where does one go after pity? I had no answer.

Once we nearly lost our train. Emerging from the restaurant after a lunch, unhurried, for there was always ample time, our eyes grasped the moving train in disbelief. 'Hell! Run!' We sprinted wildly between the beggars, the food vendors, the piled-up goods, and each wrenched open the door nearest to him. Mine plunged me into the middle of an extensive family of Indians who occupied the whole of a second-class compartment. If they felt surprise or annoyance, they controlled themselves. My breathless apologies were accepted charmingly, and together we racked our brains for small talk until the next halt, an hour later.

Then at last we were steaming slowly into Calcutta's Howrah station, a vast Victorian container of sleeping bundles. The Movement Control Officer sent us over the Hooghly river on the new bridge to the Grand Hotel, Chowringhee. Every junior officer of the Burma armies must have stayed there. Once was enough. At this season Calcutta was a Turkish bath, impossibly humid. Night and day we ran with sweat, porous envelopes into which we poured liquid almost continuously. Patches of prickly heat developed within hours, fans and punkahs seemed unable to stir the warm heavy air, appetites were minimal. There were iced drinks in the hotel bar. In the dining-room a few large fans revolved slowly from the ceiling to give the air around the tables immediately beneath a pretence of freshness. At these tables you could wait for the indifferent food with no more than mild discomfort. Elsewhere the delays often seemed insupportable. People gave up and returned to the bar for another gimlet. Probably we drank too much. There was an air-conditioned cinema, the only such one I met in India. But when you left this cool haven for the street, the heat corralled you; in three minutes there was lost the dry comfort of the past hours.

Now I could understand why the central Government of India, lodged in Calcutta for so long (from 1773 until 1912), should have started in 1864 its summer migration to Simla, a thousand miles away in the hills. Calcutta, the fulcrum of British power in India, had a pernicious climate from April to October: it was not surprising that Europeans committed suicide or drank, and that the Bengalis ran riot. Unlike Madras and Bombay, those other historic centres of British influence, Calcutta is 120 miles from the sea up a shoaling estuary. It is surrounded by a vast delta. Calcutta was founded by the British for trade, and through trade it has grown and flourished despite climate and swamp. And if Calcutta was no longer dangerously unhealthy, if the European gentlemen there no longer met every year at a reception in November to congratulate one another on having survived, it was still an unpleasant city to a man from the hills like myself.

Calcutta was roaring trams bulging with brown men in white; it was rickshaws and bullock carts and tongas and taxis, and cows athwart the pavements; it was flat white roofs, round white arches and miasmic hordes of people; it was Fort William and the Victoria Memorial in the Maidan; it was cane chairs and turbans and gin. Calcutta was the only city of India near to the fighting. Calcutta was dumps of refuse. Calcutta was the second city of the Empire. Calcutta was sweat.

The Grand Hotel was packed with officers travelling to and from Assam. We heard stories of the current fighting, none of them pleasant. The only place to be during prolonged and heavy rain is inside some stout building. Among the Naga Hills there were no houses except for those of the hill-top

villages, infrequent and full of Nagas and their pigs. The rain
was constant; fighting went on regardless. The Japanese still
shot to hurt. No one knew where the 4/8th Gurkhas might be.
Or if they did, they were being good boys and not telling.
We gathered that we were really winning—the newspaper
reports were not just morale-boosting—but that half the troops
had suppressed malaria, active dysentery, rotted clothing and
diminishing morale. They had been asked to go on for too
long.

I wish that I could remember more of how our journey
continued from Calcutta. I cannot remember where we slept,
or how we ate, or even what clothes we wore or the kit we
carried. But after two days of uncomfortable waiting in the
city, we boarded another train from another station, and this
took us north-east to the banks of the unbridged Brahmaputra.
Looking at the map now, we must have been at Sirajganj,
about 180 miles up. The river was broad (a mile?) and slug-
gish, with low banks that were often invisible. A steamer bore
us slowly upstream for several hours through the late afternoon
and into the night. This was a good way to journey to war,
in a deck-chair on deck, drinks to hand, the lazy river scene
changing minutely, and then the setting sun turning our
watery world to pink and red.

The landing place and railhead was probably Jagannathganj, some twenty-five miles upstream. The new train did not
maintain the standards set by the steamer. Abandoned were
comfort and distinction. The narrow-gauge third-class trucks
were crowded, dirty and without lights. This was accepted
philosophically, for the lines of communication to the Assam
front were fantastically long and obviously strained. No one
had supposed that an invasion of India would come from the
east. It was even a relief to feel that in some places behind the
fighting a few guts were being stretched; there had not been
much evidence of this so far.

From Jagannathganj we must have been carried by this
train south-east to one of the airfields near Comilla, another
150 miles or more. Comilla airfield was being used for reinforcements at this time, and certainly the next stage was my
first aeroplane flight from somewhere hereabouts across the

wild Lushai Hills to Imphal. We must have been the only
officers on the plane, perhaps the only live cargo. At any rate
we had a comfortable and interesting journey, all three of us
in the pilot's cabin.

These R.A.F. and American transport pilots had been
working flat out for weeks through treacherous monsoon
weather to keep flowing the supplies of food, ammunition and
reinforcements to the divisions at Imphal. The land supply
route, a single road across the mountains via Kohima down to
Dimapur and the railhead, had been cut on 29 March. Although reopened on 22 June, much still had to come in by
air. The airfields on the Imphal plain had been bombed, only
one strip was all-weather. The surrounding hills were close
and often cloud-covered. Planes were in short supply and
overworked; pilots had flown to the point of exhaustion.
Nevertheless, they were anxious to help. Perhaps they both
pitied and admired the troops on the ground, whose life,
compared with theirs, was really much more likely to be
nasty, brutish and short.

I sat in the wireless operator's seat, cramped but enthralled.
To be in flight for the first time would have been sufficient.
To be forward among the maze of controls, able to see ahead
through the nose, able to watch the pilot manœuvring, to
relate the changing thunder of the engines and the banking
of the wings to movements of his wrists and fingers, was bliss.
The flight was doubly memorable for the tension caused by the
knowledge that on our arrival at Imphal the enemy would be
only a few miles away. Hitherto we had counted the distance
in hundreds of miles. Now with one short flight we were on
the edge of battle. Anything might be asked of us.

'Men, draw your pistols,' said Bill, sucking a sweet and
peering at the unpromising jungle-covered hills below. And
he was only three-quarters joking.

We banked and dropped alarmingly. The hills swept up at
us until individual tree-tops were easily distinguished. Then
the Imphal Plain spread before us, hills on either side higher
than ourselves, the runway ahead. We roared over a convoy
of lorries on a road that skirted the near end of the runway,
then were bouncing along the uneven surface, stopping near

some huts. Stiffly we climbed out. Everything was quiet and
reassuringly casual. No sound of guns. No bombs. R.A.F.
ground staff and army personnel got to work on the plane
and its stores. We thanked the pilot and moved off.

'Relax, men.'

We found the Movement Control Officer, that ubiquitous,
essential but unglamorous person who always knew the
answers.

'4/8th Gurkhas?' He looked at his lists. '7th Division,
89 Brigade, Kohima. Let me see. There's a truck leaving at
six o'clock this evening. You could squeeze in. I'd get that if
I were you. Meanwhile, you'll find something to eat over
there. What? No, 7 Div. is in reserve now. Resting, I think,
refitting. They probably deserve it. You're in luck.' He waved
us off. We relaxed.

So this was the recently encircled Imphal Plain. And we
were directed to Kohima, up the road along and around
which there had been so much fighting since April. There
were no signs of it here. The low surrounding hills, sharp
against the rain-washed afternoon sky, looked peacefully
innocuous, and luxuriantly green. The plain stretched between
them, flat and featureless to a casual glance. Mud and puddles
surrounded the huts; for the worst enemy of both sides was
the weather. To us the weather suddenly mattered very little.
We were not to meet the Japanese tomorrow. We were not
yet gladiators in the arena. We had been reprieved. Our
Division was resting.

'Ah sure am disappointed to hell,' said Bill, looking
particularly at ease. 'Let's go eat.'

I felt gay. I thought that I too could just about put up with
some more weeks of preparation for war. Battle was the price
I would have to pay to join an active unit, where the proportions of life were closer to my own feelings for what was good
and satisfying. Now that I was joining such a unit, there was
no hurry for the battle.

Bill was mimicking the Movement Control Officer. ' "I'd
get that if I were you." Did you hear the dozy bastard?
Orders!' He adopted an extreme Oxford drawl. 'I say,
Derrick, do you think you could attack that knife-edge ridge

defended by six hundred Japs and half a dozen medium
machine-guns in deep shell-proof bunkers? Take a platoon if
you like. Best of luck, old boy.'

By the time we set off in the back of a three-ton truck, which
was packed with stores and other bodies, it was dark. We saw
nothing of the infamous road save what was revealed of chasms
and cliffs in the headlights of following and passing traffic.
On either side, probably along every mile, men had recently
lost their lives; individuals not much different from myself,
with the same kind of fears, the same hopes. On ancient
battlefields the passage of time seems to reduce sensitivity to
the suffering of the human beings who fought. An abstract
consideration of tactics and strategy in historical perspective
fills the curious mind. Perhaps the view is pleasant and the
summer air lethargic with bees and grass scents. Arrows too
grow abstract, and never brought sweated agony to youthful
bodies, or thirst and unwanted death, nor hungry bereavement
to women and children. But the fighting along the Imphal
road was recent, so recent that I might easily have taken part
myself. It was men of my age and my world who had died.
Darkness hid the rack of battle, and perhaps this made the
imagination more vivid.

VI

AT KOHIMA

1. *Arrival*

The track running north from Kohima village was unsafe, or
so it seemed to me. The Gurkha driver appeared unmoved,
but I did not know whether this was due to confidence or
lack of imagination: one seldom did with Gurkhas. The track
was traversing a ridge, with a steep drop on one side or the
other to valleys some two thousand feet below. The surface
of the track was mostly thick rutted mud, hidden here and
there by lakes of standing water that glittered with reflected
light as we ground towards them. The jeep was sliding from
side to side, towards a vertical bank or towards a forested
chasm. It would have been reassuring to believe that every
journey continued happily into the dawn. . . .

Along the track at intervals were those cryptic signboards
that burgeon wherever the army squats for a few hours.
These signs and letters, which meant little to me that day,
later grew into my vocabulary. Without knowledge of them
conversations and journeys were half meaningless. 'You tell
the Q.M., Bill, and I'll confess to the C.O. The M.T.O. had
better lay on a truck for 0700 hours, with a driver who knows
how to reach the M.D.S. and that I.E.M.E. camp. The
Adjutant can draft something for tomorrow's B.R.O.s.'

An infantry division had many units within its fold besides
the three brigades (nine battalions) of infantry. In our area
there were probably several regiments of artillery of varying
calibre, half a dozen or so field companies of Engineers, at
least three Field Ambulance units, the Divisional and Brigade
Signals, and a miscellany of Divisional Headquarter troops.
There might well be a regiment or several squadrons of tanks.
All these units must have sleeping, eating and defecating space.
All of them need vehicle parks. Most of them in our 7th

E

Division had or soon acquired mule lines. While out of action and retraining, known so beguilingly and inaccurately as 'resting', they also needed parade grounds, rifle ranges, some minimal space for sport and plenty of country over which to hold exercises. There was no shortage of country around Kohima. The stuff stretched for hundreds of mountainous miles in all directions. But there was a shortage of flat country. The units and sub-units of the Division had to scatter widely to find it. Along the ridge where we now jeeped 89 Brigade alone was forced to stretch itself for several miles.

Sometimes the signboards pointed down or up a narrow track that was lost immediately among the trees. Sometimes groups of tents were visible, with jeeps and trucks parked, and figures moving each on his own mysterious business. Then for half a mile the track might wind in and out of minor spurs and re-entrants, following the contour, while there was no sign of man, and there would be superb views suddenly released by an absence of trees, views across the valley and along the valley to the far ridges and beyond.

The jeep slipped, slithered and sloshed its way on, water spraying from the wheels, seldom out of a low gear in four-wheel drive, until it came to where a bare easterly spur of some size took off below the track on the right and dropped rather less steeply for the first few hundred yards. The spur was dotted with tents, and with men who were obviously Gurkhas. We had arrived. We had reached the lines of the fourth battalion of the 8th Gurkha Rifles, of 89 Brigade, of the 7th Indian Division, of the 14th Army. It had taken us eight days and perhaps one and three-quarter thousand miles.

Our arrival was undramatic. We reported to the tent which was the Adjutant's office, as is customary. The Adjutant was Peter Wickham, tall and thin, with a charming smile, penned behind a makeshift table like a giraffe in a rabbit hutch. I was in automatic awe of adjutants and did not appreciate the smile. Mike Tidswell did the talking. I have forgotten what then happened.

When I joined the 4/8th Gurkhas the men were thin, wasted, close to the basic structure of the human frame, cheekbones, shoulder-blades and ribs prominently outlined beneath receded flesh; and for the most part they wore uniform that asked for instant renewal. The few present who had not been on the campaigns of the last ten months stood out like stockbrokers in a crowd of beggars. The recent defeat of the Japanese invasion of India, whose most notable action had been here at Kohima, had not come cheaply. The 7th Division had fought for about as long as troops can fight and remain a recoverable unit. When I joined there was still circulating the unpleasant rumour that the Division was to be sent back to India; unpleasant because once there, return was problematical, and endless months of tiresome and unrewarding duty on internal security was likely to be its fate. I never met a soldier who preferred internal security in India to the chances of the Japanese campaigns.

What had these wasted men been doing ? What was their recent history ? I wanted very much to know but was usually too shy to ask direct questions. Thus much of the Arakan and Imphal fighting remained for me a matter of unco-ordinated personal reminiscence, listened to in the Mess of an evening. Neither I, nor probably the men involved, had any kind of historical picture until the books began to be published years later.

Down in the dense bamboo forests of the Arakan our 7th Division, newly raised and trained for jungle fighting, had been in action since September 1943. Under General Frank Messervy it had fought triumphantly back when surrounded in a major Japanese offensive during February, the battle of Ngakyedauk Pass. During March it had gone over to the attack. By April it was back in Corps reserve. It had earned this partial rest after six months of battle, some of it among the fiercest of the war; six months with no front line, no absolute safety anywhere, no escape from the climate and the often inadequate food. The wear on nerves and health was heavy.

In early May the Division was flown to Imphal, hundreds of miles to the north, where a more serious Japanese invasion was at full tide. The men were in action at once, on reduced rations and beneath the monsoon rains. Through May and June the fighting continued, climaxed by an exhausting trek

from Imphal to Ukhrul, part of the effort to cut off the retreat
of the defeated Japanese. Of this march the official *History of
the Second World War*, an unemotional piece of work not
frequently caught painting in 'local colour' says:

> The main obstacle to the advance was the climate and
> country. The columns, struggling through blinding rain,
> swollen torrents, deep cloying mud and along treacherous
> slippery paths on the mountain sides, were often hungry,
> for there were periods when air supply was impossible. The
> physical effort of ascending and descending as much as
> 4,000 feet in a single march, with the temperature varying
> from the sub-tropical heat of the valley bottoms to the cold
> mists of the mountain tops, imposed a fearful strain on the
> fortitude of troops already beginning to suffer from under-
> nourishment, exposure and fatigue. Dysentery, scrub typhus
> and skin diseases became rife and there was no comfort or
> shelter for the sick and wounded.
> (*The War Against Japan*, III, p. 363, H.M.S.O., 1962.)

And in *The Marauders*, one of the few good books on the
Burma War that I have read, Charlton Ogburn said:

> Modern armies had never fought under such conditions as
> those that prevail in Burma during late spring and summer,
> when an inch of rain is falling daily and rising rivers inundate
> the lowlands. But in April, 1944, as downpours grew more
> frequent, the tapering off of operations that could have been
> expected did not take place. Instead, both sides summoned
> up their reserves of strength to win what each hoped would
> be a crucial decision. Before the climax was reached in mid-
> summer, the combatants would have been tried to their
> limit, and the example of troops dragging themselves over
> rain-beaten mountain trails and gutted roads knee-deep in
> mud, never knowing from what quarter to expect attack,
> cut down by machine-gun fire from an ambush, blasted by
> artillery, but more often overcome by fever and exhaustion,
> was common to all. In the similarity of their ordeal and the
> pitiful sense of duty or—equally pitiful—acceptance of the
> lack of an alternative that drove them on, there was little

to distinguish among the nationalities assembled in that
unlikely theatre, Japanese, Indians, Gurkhas, British, East
and West Africans, Chinese and Americans.'
(p. 232, Hodder and Stoughton, 1960.)

I sketch in this brief history because it was of importance
during my first months with the Battalion. The way men
talked, their health, their looks, the work I and they were
given to do, was conditioned by this recent ordeal in which I
had not shared. Those curious Arakan place-names punctuated
conversation: Buithidaung, Razabil, Ngakyedauk, Sinzweya,
Waybin, Taung Bazaar, Kalapanzin river, Maungadaw, the
Kaladan valley, and many others. To the actors these places
held individual memories tied to the reality of trees and track
and dust and mud and ridge and valley, of fear and hope and
hunger, of safety and danger, of wounds, death, and miraculous
escape. To the casual reader of these pages the names can mean
nothing. To me they still bear a charmed, fairy-tale quality.
Around them my new companions had faced death and survived, the ultimate experience that still awaited me. They were
knights, however reluctant, however tarnished with frailty. I
was the new squire. Their anecdotes, their occasional explora-
tions of what had happened to them, held me in thrall. Names
of places and names of people—those who had been killed,
like Rex Perkins, 'Billy' Twiss the Colonel, Stanley Ball, Hugh
Harrington, who had been wounded, and was shot two days
later by Japanese who overran the field hospital where he lay;
those who had been wounded or stricken by disease and did
not return—I knew them in the richness of imagination,
uncluttered by facts. Such knowledge is vivid.

The British officers were a small group, inevitably close,
spliced to one another by language and nationality within a
sea of Gurkha. The full complement of officers was, I think,
nineteen. We rarely had fourteen, usually not so many. (The
abbreviation for British officer, I am delighted to record, was
B.O.) Within this small group there was not freeway for clans
or factions and if such crept in, as they did in some battalions,

morale suffered. The British officers needed to be brothers, able to work in harmony, and with trust. There must not be the anarchist, the idler, the self-indulgent, the old soldier.

When a new officer joins he is welcomed as a body who can be given work to relieve the burden on others. At the same time he is a foreign body in a complex and intimate community. Perhaps in this community they do not all like all, but they have adjusted to one another, know each other's weaknesses, avoid matters that create disharmony, and, in my battalion, had the strength of shared suffering. A newcomer disturbs the balance. There has to be a period for readjustment while suspicion becomes acceptance. The new part has to wear itself in. Mike, Bill and I had the advantage of numbers. We could help one another until time had produced a natural integration. Nevertheless we must have made our mistakes, ruffled one person here, another there.

As for me, I had a natural inclination to pessimism, a feeling of inferiority, which time has much diminished but not obliterated. A report on Lieutenant Davis might have read thus: He expects rebuff and indifference from others, and is therefore delighted with a quite nominal kindness. He over-estimates what may be required from him to reach a particular objective. When he completes an assignment successfully, as generally he can, he displays symptoms of uneasy surprise. Later this may turn to a sudden brash superiority. At first he does not trust his judgement; then trusts it too much. At first he believes that men are paragons, then that they are fools. He is simultaneously aware of inadequacy and of talent. He is good with his subordinates but could use more tact with his superiors. No doubt he and they will survive.

VII

AT KOHIMA

2. *Preparing to Kill*

Motto of the 4/8th Gurkha Rifles:
Live Hard, Fight Hard, and when necessary Die Hard

In early September I was made Intelligence Officer. I liked
this. I was saved from much of what seemed to me the dreary
mechanics of infantry soldiering. I had independence, a small
command of my own, yet was close to the heart of the Battalion,
responsible direct to the Colonel. I had a vast patriarchy: an
Intelligence havildar, six men of the Intelligence Section, eight
snipers and my batman—or as many of them as were present.
There were always unfilled vacancies, and men on leave, on
courses, or sick.

Bill Blenkin, who was made Motor Transport Officer (after
attending a course), held a more exposed outpost. Jeeps and
trucks break down. Bill was responsible. They have accidents.
Bill was to blame. These events tend to happen in full view.
They inconvenience someone of substance and short temper.
The truck that shot smartly over the precipice at one end of
the transport park because the driver hit the accelerator in
mistake for the brake was a battalion sensation, and it was
Bill's fault. The driver was found lodged in a tree halfway
down, unharmed by his fall but dazed from the impact of the
spare tyre which had followed him too faithfully.

Mike Tidswell was sent as second British officer to a rifle
company. Platoons were commanded by Gurkhas, so his
position tended to be the Company Commander's dogsbody.
Later Mike did a spell as acting Adjutant, the Colonel's dogsbody, his staff officer, the administrative hub of a battalion.
This is an important, arduous and uneasy post, in which the

weak get squeezed between the Colonel and his senior officers, and the strong may get heartily disliked.

I was happy that such positions were not mine. I had my own corner, and could often operate free of direct supervision.

For a time at this period, while someone was on leave, I was Officiating Commander of H.Q. Company. With so few officers, everyone found themselves doubling up, trebling up, for periods short and long. Headquarter Company contained most of the Battalion's specialists: the Signals Platoon, the Mortar Platoon, the Pioneer Platoon, and the Battalion Headquarters Platoon, which was a platoon of infantry for the defence of the Headquarters. Total strength all ranks 144; strength while I was in charge probably nearer a hundred. I was not responsible for their specialist training, but for their administration, health and discipline. The only two letters to survive from this period, both written to my parents, illustrate the change in tempo that took place between the end of July, when I arrived and the Division had just been withdrawn from battle, and eight weeks later, when the retraining programme was gaining momentum and I had these responsibilities.

The first, dated 6 August 1944, admits this passage:

> We go about shirtless most of the day and I'm getting browner than I've ever been before. I can't say we're working horribly hard. . . .

The second, dated 8 October, says:

> I'm afraid I haven't written to anyone for ages. I've been very busy, often working up to twelve o'clock. And as we get up at 6.15 every morning there's not much urge to write letters in the interval. But today being Sunday, things have slackened off a bit. In fact I've been having a thorough turn-out of the dreadful mess of circulars, orders, letters, pamphlets, etc., on my desk. It all mounts up with incredible rapidity. I've been commanding a company as well as doing intelligence officer for the past month and a half, and the number of things that have to be seen to nearly drives one scatty. All divisional signs must be sewn on 1 in. below the shoulder and at an angle of 45°. Please fit your men out with

the second suit of green battledress at once. Why is Rifleman
So and so's Gurkha hat in the state it is? Speak immediately.
There are too many flies round your company refuse pit:
why? Men recently returned from leave will parade separ-
ately for P.T. and will see the Doctor three times a day for
the taking of mepacrine tablets. Etcetera, etcetera. It's a
queer life. It's also the first time I've been of the slightest
use to anyone in the army, and the first time I've really run
anything. I must say I enjoy it, though it leaves no time for
letters and reading.

From 10 to 14 October I attended an Intelligence course at
Divisional Headquarters, mornings only. I made a lot of
notes, for this was my first specialist training in intelligence,
but the notes are gone and memory recalls little except chino-
graph pencils and map cases.

Intelligence at Battalion level was not complicated, and
required common sense rather than intellect. It was two-way
traffic. I gathered from Brigade Headquarters and from the
Colonel all they would tell me about the course of the war
elsewhere, and once a week had to spend ten minutes imparting
these scraps to the other officers. Most of them knew most of
it already.

I learned too what I could about the Japanese Army, its
organisation, weapons, badges of rank. The 14th Army captured
very few Japanese, and till now the 4/8th had captured none.
If we did capture some in the future we should not be able
to talk with them. Even so, it was useful to know the rank of
any officer killed, to be able to identify units, to have a rough
idea whether documents found might be valuable. The
Japanese were often indiscreet in the papers they carried.

We could learn so little from dead or captured Japanese
that the major task for me was to collect information from or
about the enemy by patrolling. The Intelligence Section was
expected to provide special reconnaissance patrols capable of
travelling far by day and night. The Burma fighting was
characterised at all times by the vast scale of the country
through which comparatively small bodies of troops operated.
Whether advancing, retreating, defending or attacking, both

sides found themselves surrounded by miles and miles of
mountain or plain which could not be physically occupied by
men. There were no conventional front lines, and no-man's-
land began outside your own small perimeter. Both sides dealt
with this problem by means of patrols. Air reconnaissance
was never of more than marginal help to us. The Japanese
kept first-class camouflage discipline and moved whole divisions through the jungle undetected from the air.

Successful reconnaissance patrolling needs a mixture of
boldness, patience and steady nerve. On patrol a man will be
miles from his friends, and the enemy perhaps around the
next bush. Though he may know most of the enemy's positions,
he will never know them all; the enemy too will have patrols
out, and may set ambushes on the few tracks. The patrol
leader needs to be expert with compass and map. And he has
to ask himself the right questions. He is not likely to get answers
to questions he does not ask.

As for the snipers, I cannot remember why they were put
under the Intelligence Officer. In battle their role is very
different. They are not collectors of information. They are
selective killers. They must be fine shots. They must be expert
at camouflage and deception. They must have the patience
of a cat at a mouse-hole. But they are never likely to be used
far from the main positions of our troops, and in practice in
battle I had nothing to do with them.

He who sees first, shoots first
Rifleman's Creed of the 8th Gurkha Rifles

Kohima and its surroundings were beautiful. Perhaps this is
why those months from July to the end of December have in
memory a halcyon quality. The monsoon rain was an irritation
while it lasted. Tents developed leaks, the hillsides of our
camp were slippery, much time was spent over constructing
paths and steps of small branches laid crossways in close
succession, which were better than mud, but were not notably
secure. In August the rains eased and seemed always to come
in the late afternoon. Then they ceased and our camp became

a joy. The hills stretched to a very distant horizon, the sun sparkled, and the most wonderful cloud formations piled up and rolled past day after day.

Soon after my arrival I had noted that the men were arranging stones around the quarter-guard tent and were white-washing them, and that low railings were beginning to border the main paths. When a military unit does this, you know that it believes itself to be safe from imminent removal. Returning back to the Battalion after some venture abroad, rounding that final corner of our giddy track, I looked down on the tents encircling the parade ground on the first spur, on others disappearing down the slopes, and on the activity of all those squat brown men, my brothers, and felt intense affection. This was home, my home, and for the present I wanted no other.

I had a small one-man tent on that first plateau, close to the Officers' Mess and the Headquarter personnel. The dawn was imperceptibly lightening the sky when one of the pipers walked the lines blowing reveille on bagpipes. It was a good way to be woken. My orderly, Nandalal, would bring in a mug of hot tea; then one of hot water for a shave, and some cold in a canvas bucket for a wash. As the winter months drew on, the cold water grew very cold. At five thousand feet the mornings became brisk.

Usually the first parade was P.T. I enjoyed P.T. I was fit and unworried by the mere exercise of muscle. Anywhere in the tropics it is a pleasure to be abroad in the very early morning, perhaps before the rain starts, or the sun has sucked all life from the air. We might run along the winding contour-clinging track, with the sun not yet risen above the great north–south ridge on the other side of the valley, in whose depths the morning mist rested like a vast white lake. Yet the sky above was already blue with the promise of a fine day. To the north stretched more ridge and peak of this mountainous land, etched against the far horizon with extreme clarity. It was land on a grand scale. Somewhere up there were Tibet and China, and untamed hill tribes in unsurveyed valleys. Nearer and around us were the Nagas, partially 'tamed', headhunters still when they could be, independent, proud.

Sometimes the Colonel would order the whole Battalion into the mist-shrouded valley two thousand feet below in a helter-skelter pell-mell rush of six hundred bodies sliding, leaping, whooping down a precipitous jungle-bordered track; then the grinding, panting upward slog. The British officers could never lead the men at this, but pride demanded maximum effort so as not to be found too far back in the order of re-arrival.

Not all of us were able to avoid the rearguard. Bill, for instance, hated exercise, and normally his job as transport officer pandered to his inclinations. It came all the harder when the Colonel ordered everybody out. For so long as Bill had the breath to spare there would be mutinous mutterings.

It is difficult now to recall that phase of intense application to training for war, difficult to break back into that younger skin. Until Kohima I had been at school, the army's school, learning along with other men who were learning, a pupil, an apprentice. We absorbed our lethal skills as much to please instructors as ourselves. We had been often serious over what we learned; yet there was that unavoidable air of make-believe because the enemy was a thousand miles or more away, our preoccupations could not be with that distant dragon, and sooner or later we should all disperse.

There was no feel of the schoolroom in what I practised at Kohima. This was no novitiate sail in sheltered waters. This was preparation for a deep-sea voyage; there would be real typhoons ahead, and the ship that sank with all hands might be mine. Mine might be the hand whose failure brought disaster if I did not train myself and my crew effectively.

Our 'now' was all-important, engrossing the whole self, excluding the future, which was so uncertain, and the past, a completed chapter. I had no career to be redeemed, no waiting wife, no children, nor even, by this time, a particular wish to return to my own country.

Training began at the beginning, in the traditional cycle of the army's year. First men practised their personal weapons, their individual skills. Then they worked in section groups (a section consisted of ten men, and included a light machine-gun), threading the forest-clad mountains on minor tactical exercises, attempting always, whatever else they were about, to remain silent, invisible, quick to react, quick to shoot. Then platoons (three sections), then companies (three platoons) practised together and against one another. Then the Battalion performed and finally there was just time to have one Brigade exercise. For all this we had some three months instead of a year.

The Battalion's recent fighting had provided practical experience in jungle warfare. Most of the men knew much of what was needed to survive. They did not have to be bullied to dig their slit trenches quickly, to clear fields of fire, to keep their weapons clean and ready, to be silent, to use dead ground and cover. These lessons were no longer the academic orders of superior officers. The first bullets, the first shells, the first wounded and dead, are wonderful spurs to the educational process. Yet as a football team that does not train between matches would soon degenerate, so in a battalion the lessons of battle require analysis and practice to yield full value. Casualties and leave mean promotion for many, with new responsibilities. Reserve leaders must be selected and trained. Reinforcements have to be absorbed into teams with the veterans. Lessons that are known need repetition till they grow instinctive. A battalion is a living organism that never remains static; if a technique was perfect last week, it will not be so next week unless somebody sees to it.

The difficult can be done at once, the impossible takes a little longer
Junior Leaders' Creed of the 8th Gurkha Rifles

This is not a training manual, and I will not bore anybody with the details of what we were engaged upon for so many weeks. One of our pamphlets quoted Napoleon:

If I always appear prepared, it is because, before entering on an undertaking, I have thought about it for a long time and have foreseen what may occur. It is not genius which reveals to me suddenly and secretly what I should do in a crisis. It is deliberation and forethought.

The situations for which we had to forethink were complex and varied, and the increased tempo of modern war demanded quick reactions. Most of our training was designed not merely to instill knowledge and skills, but to make us use that knowledge and those skills with speed. This could involve hours of explanation, demonstration and practice by day and by night, and in as many types of country as could be found in our neighbourhood. It involved repeated practice of our battle-drills, which are simply aids to the use of intelligence in battle, a kind of shorthand that everyone has learned, and on which all can rely.

It grew very clear to me why an infantry battalion needs months rather than weeks to retrain itself, and I was grateful to fate for giving me to the Battalion for the whole of this long interval between its last campaign and the next.

Yet from this distance, as I write, there are elements of unreality about those days, like memories of a bad film or a poor novelette. Or maybe even then it was not easy to believe that one might eventually kill another human being, skilfully, cunningly, with deliberate and much practised artifice. It was easier to imagine being killed, blown up by a shell or hit by an impersonal bullet.

I have been inserting at intervals items from the Rifleman's and Junior Leaders' Creeds, compiled by Walter Walker. Every day at the head of battalion orders, which were read out to the men, was printed one of these aphorisms. Each man was to understand their full implications. At any time and by anybody he might be asked questions about them:

Destroy the enemy, do not allow him to retire
Move quickly, fight fiercely, shoot low
The only good Jap is a dead one
Shoot to kill—kill to live
It is the last ounce of toughness that wins the battle so I
    must be tough, look tough and act tough
The answer to noise is silence
Dig or die
Dead ground, live men
If not cover from fire, then cover by fire

In any situation the one unforgivable crime is INACTION
I prefer life to death, therefore I must never surrender
It should be the ambition of every man of the 8th Gurkhas
to redden his kukri or bayonet in the enemy's blood

Most of these are instructional maxims. But some are exhorta-
tory, undisguised stimuli to kill, which seem unreal now,
perhaps did so then. It was never my ambition to redden my
bayonet in the enemy's blood, though I cannot answer for our
Gurkhas on this point. I hoped that I would not get so close
as to make the reddening possible, for then it might be my
blood that sheathed his bayonet.

'The only good Jap is a dead one.' Did I believe that? I am
not sure. Some did, for Englishmen still tend to think poorly
of other peoples, and were encouraged so to do in wartime.
To us the Japanese were a strange and distant people. We had
not learned much about them at our schools, and wartime
stories of their behaviour, enriched by propaganda, did not
endear them to us. We admired their courage and their endurance, but it was easy to think of them as dangerous animals
rather than human beings, and in that context the only good
Jap *was* a dead one.

Our Gurkhas, of course, would kill anyone—Germans,
Japanese, Italians, Burmese, French, anyone. They did not
share our civilised scruples and did not need a pseudo-moral
commitment. They were paid to be soldiers, not to believe in
a cause. They believed in loyalty to the Regiment and to
friends, and in courage, and in giving the best of themselves,
but not much in King and Empire, and not at all in Western
civilisation, freedom, democracy.

Another obstacle to recalling the mood of those months is
that for twenty-five years now I have reacted against the idea
of war. I have to work back through this to a time when,
perhaps, I accepted the situation philosophically enough, and
was concerned principally with my own ability to perform a
part. At that time war for me was both a dread and an excitement. War was difficult. It was dangerous. Could I do everything that might be required of me? There was no way of

telling. War is a lottery. Some men are selected to face extremes
of danger and hardship; rather more men have to face a nasty
but bearable dose, and most do not have to face anything
much beyond boredom, perhaps discomfort, and a break
in the routine of their lives. No man can tell in advance
what his enlistment will bring, nor can he know how he will
react.

Along with training went administration, a never-ceasing
chore. If any reader has assumed that officers of the Indian
Army sat back and left administrative detail to their Indian
and Gurkha subordinates, the following typical item from
Battalion Daily Orders of 9 September will enlighten them:

> All Battle Dress will be fitted under the personal supervision
> of Company Commanders. There will be three fitting
> parades:
> (a) Firstly when the battle dress is issued from the QM's
> store. The QM will attend this parade not only to assist the
> Coy Cmnds but also to ensure that as far as possible the
> correct sizes are issued; when issuing the various sizes both
> the Coy Cmnd and QM will take into consideration the
> fact that the material shrinks by one size, and that the
> length of the trousers after shrinking must be approx 1 in.
> longer than slacks, so as to ensure that they can be turned
> down over the anklets.
> (b) The second fitting parade will be held after the blouse
> and trousers have been properly shrunk by the Darzi. At
> this parade the Coy Cmnd, accompanied by the Tailor,
> will personally fit each man and ensure that the Pl Cmnd
> makes a note of the alterations required.
> (c) At the third fitting parade the Coy Cmnd himself will
> ensure that the alterations have been satisfactorily carried
> out.

This is just one example of how a junior officer was taken
into a most detailed concern with a soldier's daily life. We were
no figureheads to appear on ceremonial parades only, or at
moments of battle crisis. The condition of a pair of socks

occupied us as closely as accuracy of marksmanship. A unit must not only be efficient, it must look efficient.

And along with administration, a vital part of it, went health discipline. At dusk each soldier was on parade in his company lines to swallow his mepacrine tablet. Sleeves were rolled down and buttoned, whatever the heat, in tents or out; trouser-bottoms were tucked inside gaiters or socks, anti-mosquito oil rubbed over face and hands, mosquito nets hung and tucked under bedding. There was no excuse for failure. 'British and Gurkha officers are reminded that they must pay surprise visits during the night to see that orders are being complied with', said a paragraph in another of our Daily Battalion Orders. Unfortunate the man in whose net a hole was found, or whose net was not set out square and tight (the sleeping body should not be in contact with the material); more unfortunate his section commander, his platoon commander. The mepacrine turned our skins yellow, the mosquito oil was sticky, we sweated under the long sleeves; but it was declared a crime to be in hospital with malaria. 'If I meet a mosquito, a Jap and a cobra at the same time,' said the Junior Leaders' Creed, 'kill the mosquito first and the cobra last.'

In 1943 for every man evacuated with wounds there were 120 sent back sick. By the end of 1944 the ratio of sick to wounded had dropped to 10 : 1. In the 1945 campaign this ratio fell to 6 : 1. This was because we junior officers staggered out in the middle of the night to wander up and down the stepped paths between the tents, shining a torch inside over the nets and the sleeping lumps they enclosed; because in a score of detailed and time-consuming ways the health regulations devised by senior doctors were translated into actions carried out by thousands of soldiers of all nationalities. To this day I cannot be indifferent to the whine of a mosquito. I have to have its blood.

The Battalion then settled down to regenerate itself and I settled down to membership of the Battalion. Men went on leave. Fresh drafts arrived, fat and eager. Men who had been wounded or sick returned. The once thin, worn and ragged grew indistinguishable from the latest reinforcement, moved

F

briskly, laughed gaily. And the person under whom all this activity flourished, who fed it with his spirit, steered it with his knowledge, gave to its shaping his own high standards of excellence and eighteen or twenty hours out of twenty-four of every day of his life for months on end, was Walter Walker, the Colonel.

I served under four colonels during three years with the Battalion; one only is properly concerned with this story. The first left soon after I joined. He had come five months earlier to fill the gap left when Colonel Twiss and the Adjutant, Stanley Ball, had been blown up with their carrier on a mine. He was not popular with the junior officers, and since the reasons for his unpopularity came to me second-hand, I will say no more. He was succeeded by Walter Walker and it was W.W. who was in command until near the end of the war.

Lieutenant-Colonel W. C. Walker was (and is) a remarkable man. In five months he transformed his battalion from one which, I suspect, had been low in the order of merit of the Division to one which, if not at the top, was jostling a couple of others on equal terms for first place. The reader who has not experienced the effect that one man can have on a unit, military or civil, may think I exaggerate. But I watched too the reverse process, when Walter Walker was promoted and his place was taken by someone who was not his equal. A military unit is as good as its leader, and a fine leader will extract from his subordinates great actions which the lesser leader would deny them to be capable of. As for the led, they stretch to full potentiality; it is exciting; and a slackening of the tension later under a lesser man, though welcome to part of oneself, is an abasement. With leadership so personal, so charismatic, there can be a disastrous falling apart.

Walter Walker drove us hard. During this long period of recuperation and re-training he caused much heart-ache, much grumbling, sometimes feelings for which grumbling is a polite euphemism. He was strict. He insisted on high standards. He was not afraid to punish. He was not afraid to winnow: a few left, other ranks and officers, but not many. Occasionally we thought him unjust, but only occasionally. For myself, I was in awe of him, but committed to his way of running things. I thought it right that he was tough and hard on us. We were not playing a game. There would be no umpire to rule the enemy offside. No one would bring back to life our dead.

In his early thirties, medium height, lithe, dapper, dark hair and trim dark moustache, at Kohima I seem to remember the Colonel always with an officer's swagger stick under one arm, upright, alert eyes watching, ready to praise as well as to criticise, often smiling, by no means unapproachable. At Kohima he was the only pre-war 'regular' officer among us heterogeneous war-collected emergency-commissioned civilians. He knew what he wanted and how to get it. If he had his doubts, they were hidden. He dominated events and was never, in my experience, caught by surprise. What more could a soldier ask of a commander? Probably those who were nearer to him in age and service would give a different picture. For me, very junior, rather diffident, inexperienced, but reasonably intelligent and potentially most willing, he was a beneficial dragon. I gained confidence. I was given five months in which to learn more about this lethal trade under a man who was an expert.

War focuses interest on the mystery of leadership. Like every other officer in the army I read the manuals and the training notes, and I knew well enough that I was not a first-class leader, though I hoped I might become a reasonable one with more experience. I gave the orders I had to give and the men, bless them, obeyed. Gurkhas obey readily, yet retain a refreshing independence of spirit. They have no servility, and none of the legal insubordination of the 'old soldier'. We were spoilt. Indeed, our Gurkha officers and N.C.O.s were adept at correcting our faults without destroying our confidence. I learned to respect their knowledge, their experience, without feeling loss of authority. It was a curious relationship, feudal, delicate, easily strained you might suppose; yet most of us slipped into it without difficulty.

I am an individualist, and work most happily with people as an equal—a matter of mutual co-operation for agreed ends.

This was well enough for a small command on active service; persuasion and example were sufficient. But a successful leader needs a streak of ruthlessness, and ambition. He must not make too many excuses for the natural lapses of human nature. He must not tolerate a poor performance. Often he must work against the grain of a man's temperament. 'Discipline'—I quote our General Slim—'isn't natural. It is acquired. . . . A soldier's discipline, for his own sake, to give him a chance not only of success in battle but of survival, must be unshakeable and unhesitating—strict, if you like. Any subordination of oneself to something greater than ourselves must at times be irksome.' (*Courage and Other Broadcasts*, p. 27 and p. 82, Cassell, 1957.) I could accept this for myself, but disliked pushing it on others. This became clear to me after the war, when the cohesive tensions of battle that claimed the highest self-discipline were relaxed, and had to be replaced by discipline imposed from above by officers and N.C.O.s.

The army takes to extremes attributes which most people would agree to be important in moderation: cleanliness, punctuality, smartness, obedience, and so on. But then the army has to train men to face extremes. It assumes that the basic common denominator of its devotees is low, and that only constant repetition and relentless attention to detail will turn this poor, weak stuff into skilful heroes. Probably the army is right.

As for me, I discovered what others had discovered before me: that opportunity creates the man; and that a man has the facility of the chameleon for changing his colour. We gradually become what other people expect us to be. If the world believes us to be responsible, efficient and brave officers of the Gurkha Brigade, then that is what we are. It is a constructed identity, a better fit for some than others. But if it continues for long enough, the doubts diminish. Experience in the part breeds confidence, and confidence is at the heart of successful leadership.

At Kohima I grew accustomed to being somebody, to setting an example, to being looked at, saluted, a body whose existence could not be ignored by the soldiers among whom I spent most of my time. I not merely grew accustomed to this, I

began to take it for granted. I not merely took it for granted,
I enjoyed it and perhaps began to believe in it.

The Colonel was the head and heart of the Battalion, could
make or break it, but every officer was important. Alas, I find
it no longer possible twenty-five years later to sort out the
comings and goings of my companions, and to give convincing
portraits of them. Mike Tidswell and Peter Wickham I have
mentioned. Peter's height, his social skills (he seemed to know
every officer in the Division and was able to remember at
will everything he had ever heard them say or seen them do)
and his faintly avuncular air fitted him rather well for the
job of Adjutant. In the evenings in the Mess he could be relied
on to provide some new piece of military gossip, told with
kindly (but sometimes barbed) humour.

Denis Sheil-Small, a lieutenant when I joined, became
Commander of B Company, and a major. Denis was short and
neat and soft-spoken, almost diffident. Geoffrey Bull arrived
as a major, an ex-cavalry officer from the Western Desert,
and took D Company. Geoffrey was the opposite of Denis: tall,
confident, smooth, with a touch of the pirate's bravado.
Frank Crouchman commanded A Company.

Of all us emergency officers it was Peter Myers, the Commander of C Company, who fitted most naturally the officer
image. He was handsome, tough, had proved his courage (his
Military Cross for the fighting around Ukhrul came through
that autumn), and seemed to be at home with military matters
in a way that I never did match. He was only two years my
elder, but those two years held a world of experience that set
us as far apart as egg-boiler from chef, lock-picker from safe
cracksman.

When Jimmy Henderson with his monocle arrived he was
given the 3 in. Mortar Platoon. I too had been on a 3 in.
mortar course, but as was often the way of things in the army
I never used my intensely acquired knowledge. Jimmy was
my age. He was extrovertly enthusiastic about his mortars,
jealous of their performance and welfare. Bob Findlay joined,
a young Scotsman, serious, dependable and keen who, some

months earlier than I, had come out on the same trail of troopship, Mhow, and posting to a regimental centre (8th), where he had stuck for longer. Others who were there included Toby Willcox, Jock Purdon, Peter McQueen, Frank Seaman and Tony Brand-Crombie, our Quartermaster; but many left on leave or transfer before the end of the year or soon after. And who is there whom I may have completely forgotten? Such a catalogue of names can mean nothing to the reader, yet I must put it down. It would be a kind of treachery to ignore those with whom I shared this quality of experience, though they may repudiate my version of it.

Two gentlemen I have deliberately kept in reserve. The first is Lieutenant Scott Gilmore. Scotty was an American, one of the very few ever to be commissioned into the Gurkhas. He had begun his military career with the American Field Service, a volunteer ambulance unit attached to the British Army in North Africa before the United States entered the war. Somehow he had transferred and here he was, large, casual, crop-haired, extrovert and humorous. His understanding of military matters was patchy—he could not, for instance, read a map. His appearance never, to the last day of his service, conformed to the Englishman's notion of a soldier: at the most tense ceremonial moments there was an unmistakable trace of a round-shouldered slouch. His Gurkhali was delivered with a fine American intonation. We noticed that Nebilal, his orderly, also spoke American Gurkhali, and later, so some maintained, the whole of A Company. But if Scotty was not the smartest soldier of the 14th Army, he was one of much value. Above those personal qualities which endeared him to us, he was an American, a little exotic, a visible reminder of our most powerful ally, an irrefutable living counter to the nasty cracks one heard against the Yanks. How could we believe that all Americans were loud-mouthed, over-paid, ignorant bastards when we had Scotty?

Then there was our doctor, the 'Doc', Captain I. S. Dalton, of the Indian Army Medical Corps. A battalion doctor has a solitary, privileged and responsible position. He is the only officer dedicated to the saving of life in a band of killers; the only man who has not received military indoctrination, who is not of necessity in some awe of the Colonel. Not only does he treat the sick and the wounded, making those first decisions that can mean life or death; he has a more difficult and general responsibility for the health of seven hundred men. He has to prevent sickness, watch for malnutrition and battle fatigue, and advise the Colonel and his own medical head-quarters on the overall situation in a part of the world where casualties from disease and mental fracture always out-numbered those from battle. The Doc's enemies were dysen-tery, scrub typhus, malaria, typhoid, dengue fever, poisoned cuts and jungle sores, leeches, sunstroke, heat exhaustion and the less obvious but insidious effects of prolonged mental strain. As the one man outside strict military hierarchy, he found himself counsellor as well as healer. The reader should remember too that there were no hospitals in the hills of Nepal then, and very few now. The whole of Western medicine was a fresh experience to our Gurkhas, and sometimes they needed to be led towards it tactfully.

Doc Dalton was small, quiet, with glasses and a black moustache, and a matter-of-fact approach to his task that covered a spirit of considerable sensitivity. I doubt that he was close friends with any of us. He did not release his feelings at the sinking of a gin. But he was trusted. When a man is dead he's dead and that's an end to it. If he is wounded he wants to trust his Medical Officer; he is then more likely to live.

VIII

AT KOHIMA

3. *Snapshots*

Parties

There were several of these. Drink was rationed, and at first
the ration was small. As supplies improved I learned more
about hangovers. There are three answers to a severe hangover:
stay on your bed for enough hours to let the alcohol peacefully
work its way out of the blood (mildly unpleasant, boring and
only possible on dutiless Sunday mornings); sweat out the
alcohol by fierce exercise (agonising, but quick); kill yourself.
Some men do not suffer much from hangovers. Probably they
are identical with those who look superior at seasick sufferers.
I am of the group that wallows in both.

My companions at Kohima could be wild compared with
those of Mhow (where we had little money and no example to
follow), and of Dehra Dun (where we had little money,
copy-books we wished not to blot and an inhibiting layer of
senior sobriety sitting upon our heads). There were few
inhibitions here, and no stuffy seniors. Ability to work next
morning was the sole restraint.

Our large Mess tent was pitched broadside on at the extreme
edge of a considerable slope. More than once an upright,
proud but unsteady British officer disappeared unexpectedly
through the loose bottom flaps into the darkness of the lower
night. He would reappear two or twenty minutes later, muddy,
crawling, determined. Once Jimmy Henderson was lost for
nearly half an hour, and was much cheered when his red face
poked through the flaps, monocle still in position.

Most of our parties were male only. There was little we
could do to change this. Kohima was still a war area, scene
of ferocious fighting from April to May. It had been an
isolated outpost even in peacetime. Walter Walker was the

only married officer, and though his wife was in India, she was not allowed up to Kohima. We amused ourselves with drink, song and story, and only the whisky was clean. We exchanged parties with the 4/1st Gurkhas of 33 Brigade, with whom there was a close friendship (their Colonel, Derek Horsford, was an 8th Gurkha), and with the 1/11th Sikhs of our Brigade. Bill Blenkin and Peter Wickham could be relied upon at these guest-night parties to uphold the Battalion's reputation. Between them there was always another story, humorous, obscene, perhaps wildly farcical. Bill was the improvisor, the inventor, the embroider-as-you-talk teller of tales, so that you never heard the same story twice in the same way, and anticipation kept the listener alert. Peter preferred the Homeric tradition, the set piece, with long involved plots whose twists and turns we knew well, and whose language scarcely varied. And the songs, they seemed to be universal. Everyone knew them, though some could remember more verses. 'Mobile', 'Star of the Evening', 'Balls to Mr. Banglestein', 'Barnacle Bill', 'O'Reilly's Daughter', 'Red Plush Breeches', 'Morphine Kate and Cocaine Sue', 'If I Were a Marrying Man', 'She was Poor but she was Honest', 'The Good Ship Venus', 'The Ball of Kirriemuir', 'Cathusalem' who was the harlot of Jerusalem, and scores more. How far back do these scabrous ditties go? Some of them, in one version or another, like nursery and street rhymes, must be very old.

As for the latest hit tunes from film and stage, this was a period of famine. Though in India we had been out of date, perhaps a year behind America and England, eventually the songs came to us. Now we heard nothing. We had no cinema, no gramophone, and so far as I remember, no wireless. I suppose that from July 1944 until long after the end of the war in August 1945, I heard nothing new. Our Gurkhas did not whistle the latest Irving Berlin.

We did have at least one party with women. The hospital at Kohima had been restored and staffed, and from it one evening half a dozen nurses came to us. I found the evening slow. The older officers monopolised the guests, we could not sing our songs, and I was shy and bored. If you wish to be at ease with women when young, to enjoy mixed company, it is

best not to spend ten years at English boarding schools, and
then to move straight into the wartime army and sail for India.
Some men, naturally gregarious and extrovert, survived this
anchoretic treatment unimpaired—indeed, like hard-pruned
shrubs, they shot forward the more ardently for the initial
deprivation. It was not so for me. At nineteen I was introvert,
inexperienced, unwilling to compete against the twelve more
adept performers who battled for favours (with reasonable
decorum) in the one not over-large tent.

Bill was more adventurous, and taking a nurse back to the
hospital on this or some other evening had his face slapped.
Denis Sheil-Small, soon after the war ended, married Sally,
one of those Kohima nurses, which for years surprised me, for
I had thought that none of us could have got to know them so
well. But then he told me how he had already met her down at
Army Base in Dimapur, where he had spent several weeks
dispatching leave parties to Nepal, and she, a refugee from the
overrun hospital at Kohima, was helping at the Base hospital.

It was Denis, I suspect, courteous and unferocious-looking,
who must have charmed the matron of the Kohima hospital
into releasing her nurses to us, for matrons of army hospitals
are as a rule implacably reluctant to risk their charges within
a mile of able-bodied males.

Slim

General Bill Slim (now Field-Marshal Sir William Slim) was
a man known by repute to everyone. His rise had been rapid
since 1939: a brigade in Abyssinia in 1940–1 (wounded), a
division in Iraq and Syria in 1941, a corps in the Burma retreat
of 1942 and later; and now, since 1943, Commander of the
14th Army. This did not worry us. He had earned his promotion
in the only way an infantryman respects: he won battles. We
trusted him not to embroil us in a major botchery. We accepted
the possibility of death, and the certainty of danger, discomfort,
fatigue and hunger, provided that our fighting was constructive
and with a reasonable chance of success. Moreover Slim had
been weaned with the 6th Gurkhas, so we had an extra reason
for liking him.

I saw him only once. He came to Kohima and addressed a gathering of all the officers in the Division. This was in itself, for me, a unique occasion, the only time that I can recall when the Division's officers were so gathered. I was aware of the other infantry battalions in our Brigade: the 2nd King's Own Scottish Borderers and the 1/11th Sikh Regiment. I knew of but did not know the many other units in the Division (except for our friends the 4/1st Gurkhas). The Brigade was our larger home, and beyond the Brigade, somewhat dimly, the Division, the 7th Indian Division. Beyond the Division I doubt that many of us looked except to that largest formation of all in our area, the 14th Army and its General.

I do not remember what Slim said on this occasion, which did not matter, for his character was impressed upon me by a farcical incident that took place just as he had stepped forward to the front of the platform to speak. We were sitting on benches tightly packed in a long, low shed or hut, and had just resettled after standing for the General's entrance. Suddenly, into the expectant hush, came a fizzling crackle, just loud enough to be distinctly heard by everyone. It was very like the small pop and fizz made when the lever is released on a hand-grenade and the four or seven second fuse begins to burn. Those officers with the quickest reactions tried to lie on the floor, but were unable to do more than bend or crouch because we were too close to one another. The rest of us followed, in sudden ragged fear. For some moments there was this hut full of officers, the leaders of a proud division, ducking and crouching and shoving, a scene of undignified confusion. There was an explosion, loud, but not very loud. It was over. The whole thing had happened quickly and our actions had been instinctive. We regained our seats and slowly, with thumping hearts, and with relief at our own escapes, realised that no one was hurt. One of the overhead electric light bulbs had burst.

Bill Slim looked down at us with his square jowl and a faint smile. The laughter was subdued and shamefaced.

In mitigation I ought to add that most of the company had just been through many months of fighting, and their nerves were strained. It was not impossible that some disaffected Indian soldier might take this splendid chance to damage the

14th Army Commander and a good many of his officers with one easy swing of his arm. Everyone was conscious at the back of his mind of the Indian Mutiny, of the civil disobedience campaigns of Gandhi and the Congress Party, and of recent rumours of mutiny in a unit somewhere in Bengal.

In the years since the war Slim's reputation has grown, and some experts believe that he was the greatest British general of the war, perhaps of the twentieth century, perhaps since the Duke of Wellington. As to this I cannot judge, though I would not be surprised if later historians agreed. My own memory is that our General, caught as unawares as we, had not moved. No planned demonstration of nerve could have been more impressive.

The Nagas

We were in their country, and we saw quite a few of them from time to time. They did not wear much (Naga is supposed to derive from *nanga*, or naked); one could admire their splendidly developed bodies as they trotted along the track through our camp, carrying in baskets on their backs pigs and vegetables to the reviving market at Kohima. Our Nagas had cane rings around their legs, and necklaces of coloured stone beads. Other tribes dressed differently.

It is said that the Naga tribes, living for centuries within independent village communities, for the most part self contained, and physically separated from neighbours by mountainside, river and forest, have developed some thirty languages, each as different from the rest as the languages of Europe, and in an area the size of Wales. Differing languages were accompanied by differing customs and by firmly held mutual antagonisms.

It was fortunate for us that these anarchic warriors, proud, accustomed to fighting each other and everyone else, were against the Japanese and on the side of the British. Otherwise our training would have been dangerous, if more realistic.

The Nagas seem to have been well handled before the war, left on a loose rein, and we gathered the dividends. Earlier in 1944 they had been invaluable as guides and informants. Now the war had receded from their land and scores of Japanese heads were reported on display in the villages, legitimate head-hunting after decades of denial.

Naga men were strong and handsome, Naga girls were beautiful, and Naga country was wild, hilly and splendid. This would have been the place to spend one's life as a young man—except that for an Englishman the days for that sort of life were numbered. And after the war, when the numbering was done and the Indian Government took responsibility, something went wrong. The Indian and Gurkha troops who had been welcomed in 1943 and 1944 became enemies.

Latrines

We officers sat on a triangle of sticks with removable containers beneath, which the sweeper emptied, perhaps three such seats in a row, with a roof as well as walls if there was time to build one and rain was likely.

My first morning in the Battalion provided an embarrass-ment. I had discovered the correct hut, on the edge of a steep drop with a wonderful view over the valley, but was mystified to find only the sticks and no containers. I could not hold back and thought they must manage things differently here. On emerging, troubled but relieved, I saw the Indian sweeper, equally troubled, hovering between some tents, the containers in his hand. We passed one another as strangers, and for a long time I felt guilty whenever we met. The men called him 'Sanitation'.

Sanitation in a general way and in detail was a preoccupation of every officer and N.C.O. It had to be. We became so that the sight of a fly induced in us a Pavlovian reaction of horror. Flies carry many of the diseases that afflict tropical armies. We were always inspecting cook-houses and dining areas and latrines.

For their latrines the men dug deep narrow trenches which were quite a work of art, capped with a stout framework so that no one might fall in, and with walls and a roof. 'Heh, children,' called the N.C.O. with whom I was about to inspect H.Q. Company latrine: 'Any illegitimate son of a bullock in there? The Sahib is here.' There would be a desperate shout or two, and we would wait for the sheepish figures to emerge. The men squatted over a series of holes. Lime or some such substance was poured down at intervals. Eventually a new trench would have to be dug and the old one carefully filled in and marked. I once wrote an abortive novel whose main characters were all Gurkhas, and in it devoted a chapter to the digging of a new company latrine: the subject loomed heavily when my army years were still fresh in the memory.

In action, when in a place for a night only, we sloped off into the bushes hoping neither to be spotted by friend nor sniped by enemy.

Photographic Interpretation

In early December, when our training was to culminate in that brigade exercise, the Colonel sent me to Shillong on a ten-day course to learn to interpret air photos. I set off in the middle of the night with a jeep and a driver, down the stupendous, twisting, jungle-clad gorges to Dimapur, westwards on a course almost parallel to the Brahmaputra until near Gauhati, then south, climbing several thousand feet to the plateau on which Shillong rests. We took the driving in turns, and scarcely halted, and so arrived in the afternoon after covering over three hundred miles, mostly on narrow unmetalled roads.

Shillong is a pretty place of pine woods, rhododendrons, rolling moorlands and fires in December. It had often been the station of one or other of the Regiment's two regular battalions during the previous hundred years. In November 1940 it became the 8th Gurkha Rifles Centre. Here the 3rd Battalion was raised in October 1940, and my own 4th Battalion in December 1941. But with the conquest of Burma by the Japanese in 1942, and the need to use all the facilities in Shillong for hospitals and administrative organisations, the Regiment was shifted to Quetta on the North-West Frontier, across the entire width of India. The 1st Battalion, incidentally, was operating on the Assam–Burmese frontier a year after it was raised in 1824 (it was then called the 16th Sylhet Local

Battalion); and the 2nd Battalion, raised in 1835 as the Assam–Sebundy Corps, was part of a small garrison besieged in Kohima by the Nagas in 1879. Both battalions served for long periods in Assam. However unfamiliar India's eastern frontier may have been to most of the Indian Army, to the 8th Gurkhas it was once well known.

Photographic interpretation for an infantry officer was not too complicated or difficult, but required a certain knack that only practice could bring. We learned to interpret photos in stereoscopic pairs, and viewed through a stereoscope, so that the build of the land leaped up at the eye in sudden and detailed clarity, as though one was hovering above it in a helicopter with powerful field-glasses. Much of frontier Burma was not mapped when the war began, and maps of jungle country made from high-level photo reconnaissance, though useful, often did not disclose the detail needed. With a stereo- scope and overlapping pairs of large-scale photos, trees, trenches, tracks, huts, cliffs, streams, sandbanks, all stood out with three-dimensional force. We learned to spot signs of human occupation that no map could have shown. Even bunkers might reveal themselves under careful scrutiny. It was possible to pick in advance a good defensive position, and to be reasonably certain that the Japanese had not dug ambush positions beside the route one wished to follow. It was possible to inspect all sides of a position to be attacked with a thorough- ness that reports of ground reconnaissance by others could never quite equal.

Alas, all this was fine in theory, and I enjoyed the learning, but when I returned to the Battalion we had no stereoscope, and never managed to get one, and during our advance through Burma in the months that followed, we rarely had photos, and never had them in overlapping pairs. We moved too fast, or the planes were in short supply.

Jeeps

Jeeps were marvellous. I had never seen one until I came to the 14th Army. They were the first of a breed that has since become commonplace, but at that time their capacities were still a novel delight to us. I travelled thousands of miles in them. They were light, manoeuvrable, capable of high speed in normal gears, and of navigating a mud sea or a steep hillside in four-wheel drive. They would go where nothing else on four wheels would go, and were even adapted to become railway engines in Burma in 1945. I had a great affection for them, and loved driving them. But jeep travel could be hazardous. Their speed and manoeuvrability tempted the impetuous.

Peter Myers, returning from a party in the front passenger's seat, dozed off in an alcoholic haze, relaxed, unguarded. He had this facility for snatching sleep in the interstices of other activities. In dry weather most of our jeeps had their hoods and canvas doors removed, and so when the officer who was driving performed a particularly enthusiastic turn, Peter continued forward. For some distance the driver did not miss him. When he did, and returned in anxious search, he found Peter among the bushes by the roadside, undamaged, still asleep.

Once I nearly came to grief in a jeep. The driver and I were on a narrow muddy track that snaked along the side of a steep ridge east of Kohima. On a training exercise I had found the site from which some 25-pounder guns had fired a quantity of shells during the battles earlier in the year. The brass shell-cases, cut down and polished, make smart ash-trays. I had been instructed to pick up half a dozen good specimens for the adornment of our burgeoning Mess. There was no difficulty over this. It was turning the jeep that got me into trouble and I was broadside across the track, with a cliff behind and a chasm in front, before I realised that this was not a good spot to have chosen for the job. The track was slippery with mud and was not much wider than the length of the jeep. It sloped towards the drop and every time I let out the clutch to engage reverse, unless I was calm and timed the change perfectly with the release of the handbrake, the jeep and I slid forwards a few inches nearer. I was not at all calm: my driving techniques in those days were too recently acquired. What is more, the bonnet of the jeep masked the edge of the track, and all I could see was air and the tops of a few trees whose roots, I knew, were seventy or eighty feet below. I had a feeling of great insecurity. There was no room for the driver to push from in front. He hung on from the side. Eventually I sent him to cut down a substantial branch from a tree to jam in front of the rear wheels. All the time he was away I sat motionless in the jeep in case movement sent us slipping a few inches too far. If there was justice in the world, I ought to have been decorated for sticking to my sliding ship.

Mules

Do pay as much attention to animal management as you do to man management. It really needs more, as the animal can't complain.

I never had much to do with our mules. They were magical beasts, contrary, tough, invaluable. At Kohima, Walter Walker made us (all British and Gurkha officers) spend one day with them. We were to do everything the muleteer did: cleaning, grooming, feeding, exercising, loading, unloading. This was a nervous time, but educational. Muleteers work long hours, for they have themselves to look after as well as the mules, and are expected to be passable infantrymen, able to shoot and dig and move around in silence. While most of us might ride in motor transport from time to time, the mules and their drivers seldom did. I kept clear of my mule's rear, tried not to abuse his self-contained taciturnity, and thus survived the indoctrination.

Inspections

When we were not inspecting cookhouses and latrines and mules, we were inspecting something else. There was the daily inspection of the lines for neatness and cleanliness. There were periodic inspections of arms and ammunition, of clothing, boots, feet, bodies, mosquito nets, equipment of all kinds. If Orderly Officer for the day, there was the inspection of the Quarter Guard. There was the inspection of the turn-out of men on drill parades. There was the inspection of company records, of lists and forms, of the men's individual AB 64s, of ration returns, leave lists, sick-parade lists and of many other things which I have surely forgotten.

G

Indeed the army can be seen as a hierarchy of inspections and inspectors, with men at every level spending much of their time examining the activities of the levels below them, and more of their time preparing for examinations from those above. Perhaps only the physical limitations set by time and space give to the rifleman or private at the bottom a modicum of privacy.

A good test of a commander is his ability to spot the omissions and the errors of his juniors without the labour of total inspection. By the time a man comes to command a battalion, with its seven hundred bodies, he has many things on his mind besides the condition of the water-bottle cover belonging to Rifleman Purnabahadur Rai. But by that time, too, he has developed what seems an almost psychic skill at picking out that water-bottle cover during a swiftish walk down a line of men. Years of inspections, and of covering up weaknesses on his own account, have given him that skill. It would be surprising if, after ten or twenty years, a man had not evolved some quite special talents.

Were so many inspections necessary ? I think so. Few men will maintain the highest standards without some form of incentive imposed from outside. There is a tendency for the average to sink, to merge with the lowest, unless watched. And there is a tendency for slackness in one department of life to spread to others. We come back to the fact that the army is not a job, it is a way of life. You are a soldier for twenty-four hours out of twenty-four, or used to be.

IX

MEMORY

Not that even so the truth was easy to discover: different eye-witnesses give different accounts of the same events, speaking out of partiality for one side or the other or else from imperfect memories.
(Thucydides *The Peloponnesian War*)

. . . a story that was the subject of every variety of misrepresentation, not only by those who then lived but likewise in succeeding times: so true is it that all transactions of pre-eminent importance are wrapped in doubt and obscurity; while some hold for certain facts the most precarious hearsays, others turn facts into falsehood; and both are exaggerated by posterity.
(Tacitus)

Probably it is not possible to recall with accuracy how one thought twenty-five years ago. I suspect my own efforts. There are certain recorded facts, charted landmarks among the deceiving mists: on 30 July I was here and said this, in August I did that and disliked doing so, in November we moved there. Surviving documents, letters, notes in diaries, prove these, and such *facts*, because of this independent support, tend to acquire unwarranted importance. There seems a kind of magic about the confirmed date: I really was there, I did exist; look, this bit of paper says so. The rest is inference and reconstruction, for after twenty-five years what are we left with but the memory of memories, random, illusive, doubtfully authentic ?

The process of selection, mysterious and quite unpredictable, starts at once. Some mental images of places and of people remain, like snapshots, sharp, unchanging, to be recalled at will. These are particular images of an exact moment in time. I have no idea what I was doing five minutes earlier or an hour later. But some memories are composite, a merging into one another of many glances at the familiar scene, of much thinking around the same problems, of reactions more or less similar to a set of events more or less similar. During the merger foreign bodies may be absorbed, refuse from earlier incidents or later, or even from books or films. It is very confusing.

I never got to like drill parades. Although no memory of a particular drill parade remains, I am safe in stating that, as an officer, I was bored by them and longed for the dragging minutes to reach their term. If I try to recall all the parade grounds upon which I have stood, unnaturally stiff, counterfeiting the professionals, sometimes myself bawling the familiar orders, more often watching others do it, I cannot isolate an occasion and a day. The memories are blurred at the edges, are overlain one on another. Sweat trickles down the hollow of my back, the chin-strap of my felt hat is damp and mildly irritating, shadows from the blazing sun are sharp and dense, my own before me, more or less still; those from the squad striping the earth with hard abstract patterns as the men manœuvre like puppets to the strings of shouted vocables.

The background to this frenzied activity can drop precipitously to wooded valleys (Kohima), can rise over gentle jungle-covered hillocks to the peaks of a substantial range (Kuala Lumpur), is flat for a mile or two, then climbs abruptly three thousand feet to form the first great foothill ridge of the Himalayas (Dehra Dun), and so with a dozen other sites. The men are dressed in knife-edge khaki shorts, or in long jungle-green trousers and anklets. Their faces are a blur beneath the rows of tilted Gurkha hats, or shine unshaded under perched 'Kilmarnock' caps. The hour has gone at last. The Subadar brings them to attention and stamps towards me, halts, salutes, turns about, regains his place. 'A Company ! Company, dis . . . miss !' Away up the hill to the Mess tent. Off with the hat and belt, out with the mopping handkerchief. Shout for a beer. Relax. Lunch in ten minutes.

But there, I am in our pleasant camp on the rubber plantation of Mount Estate, outside Kuala Lumpur. The war is long finished. Even our brief adventure into Java is history. Time and demobilisation have made me one of the more senior officers.

Memory intrigues by what it keeps and provokes by what

it loses. Some things are lost so completely that even a proven reminder, though accepted intellectually, brings no glimmer of a feeling that they happened to you, were said or done by you, were felt by you, reacted to by you. Where have you gone, wandering self, that I must view you as a stranger ?

I have just discovered an example of this. I wrote the first pages of this book from my head, from memory. Weeks later I found the diary I have already mentioned once or twice, an intermittent and exasperating document for the historian. In it there is one entry while I was at the Great Central Hotel, Marylebone. Amongst other things it records a visit to London of my grandmother, our final meeting and parting, and the fact that I felt saddened. The words do not help. This is lost. I had not remembered and do not now remember one moment of this meeting. I would have sworn before a judge that we parted for the last time at her and my home in Wiltshire. I have not forgotten from indifference. I was fond of my grandmother and grateful for all that she had done for me; I would certainly have felt sad at the parting, which might well have been for ever. One ought not to invent incidents, even if they really happened, so I have not changed that chapter.

For much of life there are no diaries or other papers to shake the complacency of our notions about our own past. I have no diary for 1944, for example, while I was at Dehra Dun, Mohand and Kohima. I wonder what I did that others recall and I have lost ? If I can lose track so completely of my actions and my thoughts, how can I expect my memory to coincide with that of those who shared time and position with me ? Moreover, the sharing of time may be a true sharing, but the sharing of position is only approximate. My orderly beside me in the slit trench is two feet off centre from me, his eyesight is better than mine, his preoccupations are different, and anyway he and I seldom look in the same direction at the same time. I would not be surprised to have him contradict my account of an hour's vigil. Then perhaps my memory would take to itself details of his account that I had not seen at all, and serve them up as mine next day.

So memories die, and merge, and absorb foreign images;

they change. Later memories alter earlier; new experiences breed new ideas, new values. We are always at the business of re-interpreting our sense of reality, and the latest interpretation is apt to wipe out its ancestors, and to distort the memory of the evidence on which they were based.

X

THE JAPANESE

By the end of 1944 I thought I knew quite a lot about Japanese soldiers. My knowledge was theoretical.

We were told that they were quickened by a love of their country and a veneration for their Emperor which from years of childhood and army indoctrination were of a strength beyond anything we Europeans were capable of feeling. Wars were holy wars, much like the Muslim conquests of the seventh century, and the Christian Crusades that followed. To die in battle was to be sanctified. We thought this blind faith, this mystical patriotism, excessive, un-British, and in its place preferred to cultivate in our armies skill, initiative, reason and sound administration. Perhaps we could hardly do otherwise, since our armies were a muster of nationalities without land, climate, custom or religion in common.

We knew that the Japanese soldier was taught to prefer death to surrender. Death was a victory of the spiritual over the material. A man's honour was everything and surrender was the ultimate dishonour: a prisoner would have no rights, could never, so he was told, return to Japan. This was no theory, acknowledged on the barrack square, ignored in the field. Up to December 1944 the number of prisoners taken was so few that for an Allied soldier to have seen one was an 'occasion'. Not for us the luxury of capturing hundreds of our enemy. In two campaigns my battalion had not taken one. (We captured two in 1945, one drunk and one too sick for suicide.)

The contempt of the Japanese for surrender was extended, logically enough, to a contempt for our men whom they captured. Indeed, the counterpart of the Japanese love of his country, of his belief in Japanese superiority, seemed to be a

general disesteem for other races; and the counterpart of that
Japanese disregard for death was a disregard for life. No doubt
those attitudes were more to be found among soldiers than
civilians: you cannot teach a man to kill without brutalising
him, and all armies face this problem. The Japanese soldier
was treated so harshly by his own commanders that it must
have been natural for him to treat the dishonoured prisoner
harshly. Atrocities are another matter and what the explanation
for these was I did not know. We did know that to be taken
prisoner could mean a painful death, swift or lingering: too
many of our captured had been found tied to trees for use as
bayonet practice. This was a powerful encouragement to us
in our turn to abstain from surrender at almost any cost. There
was no easy way out of this war.

The Japanese attitude to the sick and the damaged seemed
to be of the same order as their attitude to surrender. We
Western soldiers cared for the sick and the wounded, believed
that a man should be given every chance of recovery; we
expended a high proportion of our resources in providing a
communications system that could speed the sick back to fully
equipped hospitals. Thus most of them returned to battle. The
Japanese ignored their sick for as long as possible, provided
few medicines and a rudimentary medical system. A man who
could not fight ceased to count. Japanese commanders used
their soldiers as their soldiers used bullets—until there were
none left. Soldiers were driven beyond the limits of endurance.
They were expendable. Thousands died who could have been
cured, and sometimes, as in the Japanese retreat from Imphal
while we were resting at Kohima, whole units disappeared from
a combination of disease, battle exhaustion and prolonged
starvation. The Japanese generals in Burma at last discovered
that will-power and discipline could not overcome all obstacles,
that spirit alone could not conquer.

I had learned to respect Japanese courage and self-discipline,
demonstrated in circumstances that would have disintegrated
the morale of most other armies. But we were no longer awed
by them. Indeed, they could be used to our advantage for our
enemy could be induced to squander his strength on heroic
but useless *banzai* charges. He defended positions to the last

man when a retreat to fight again would have been wiser. As General Slim was to write later in his account of our war: 'If five hundred Japanese were ordered to hold a position, we had to kill four hundred and ninety-five before it was ours— and then the last five killed themselves.'

When the battle was moving according to their plan, the Japanese fought well and intelligently. Their plans were bold, often original, and had brought them great success in 1942 and 1943. By 1944 the 14th Army had learned how to counter Japanese tactics: our troops were jungle trained, our administration and supporting arms had become superior. The Japanese found their plans no longer brought almost automatic success. Then they proved to be easily confused by the unexpected, slow to adjust, reluctant to change a plan. At the lower levels of the military hierarchy years of a too-strict adherence to orders, a rigid system of seniority, seemed to have killed initiative. The Japanese are a hierarchical people. At all levels to admit that a plan had failed was to admit defeat, which was to lose 'face'.

There were occasions, we learned after the war, when the real situation at Imphal was withheld from the Army Commander in Burma and from Imperial Headquarters in Tokyo. Senior officers and divisional commanders who knew that the offensive had failed could not bring themselves to advise retreat or a change of plan. So they reinforced failure to the point of disaster; incapable of surrender, short of ammunition, starving, ill and reduced in numbers to a desperate remnant, soldiers at the sharp end of the battle lay down and killed themselves. By 1944 there had been so many examples of Japanese blowing themselves up with grenades, and shooting their sick and their wounded when forced to abandon them, that our troops no longer wondered at the bodies as they found them. Physical courage the Japanese had in superabundance; of moral courage, of the kind that will admit mistakes, they seemed short.

I had learned that the Japanese Army prized mobility and kept its administrative 'tail' remarkably small. It ignored discomfort, poor food and scanty clothing. Japanese soldiers lived off the land to an extent that the British Army could not,

and the Indian Army did not, contemplate. This reduced
dependence on conventional communications—railways and
roads—and gave to the Japanese a literally overwhelming
advantage in Burma (where railways and good roads were
scarce and particularly vulnerable) until by late 1943 the
14th Army achieved air domination and developed air transport to compensate. Air supply gave to the 14th Army equality
in mobility, along with adequate rations, sufficient artillery
and ammunition for it, a splendid casualty-recovery system,
and a flow of human reinforcements. The Japanese system was
designed for rapid success. It disintegrated during protracted
battles of attrition such as Imphal became. And what was
true of individual campaigns was true of the war as a whole:
Japanese industrial capacity was proving unable to sustain a
long war against opponents like the United States. Though
none of us knew it, the war was won before I ever came near it.

By 1944 we had learned to be unconcerned by the favourite
Japanese tactic of sending wide outflanking movements through
the jungle to sit astride our lines of communication. We had
been taught how to use such moves as opportunities to cut off
the Japanese who made them, to surround and kill them while
they starved and ran out of ammunition, and while our supplies
rained down upon us from the heavens. The fighting was no
less fierce, for the Japanese always fought fiercely, but its end
was disaster for the Japanese, not for us.

I knew much about Japanese infantry tactics and weapons,
for in three years of fighting a fund of experience had been
distilled, and the Japanese did not change their methods.

In attack the Japanese were formidable but prodigal of
lives. They relied much on courage and on numbers. They
would attack the same part of a perimeter time after time,
despite frightful casualties, ignoring other sectors, so that we
could switch our troops to keep them comparatively fresh.
They had a taste for night attacks, and at night their terror
tactics—screaming, yelling, blowing bugles, banging cans—
could be very effective against unseasoned troops. Probably
also this supported their own courage, and was meant to
confuse us as to the numbers involved. Poorly trained troops
fired every weapon they had at this noise, uselessly consuming

fantastic quantities of ammunition difficult to replace, and disclosing the positions of machine-guns, which small parties of Japanese would then stalk and eliminate with grenades. After fire discipline had become a priority in our training, Japanese jitter noise did little but lose us sleep.

If the Japanese were formidable in attack, they were incredibly stubborn in defence. At the heart of their defence was the 'bunker'. Bunkers were placed in groups to give mutual support: troops attacking one came under fire from at least two others. Bunkers were strong points roofed with heavy logs and several feet of earth, and so well camouflaged that in jungle or villages they were invisible to any but close and persistent searchers. They were garrisoned with from five to twenty-five men and numerous machine-guns. They were usually impervious to bombardment by field-guns, and to bombing unless hit directly by a heavy bomb. Thus it was a common experience for our attacking troops to get on top of a bunker system and be blown off it by mortar and gun-fire called down upon themselves by the defenders.

The Japanese dug these bunkers with great rapidity, and fought from within them to the last man and round if told to. Bunkers seemed suited to the Japanese mentality. They felt at ease in them. British and Indian troops did not like to be in them, preferring the free use of their weapons from open trenches. Though we learned to make bunkers, we made them for individual machine-guns rather than as large inclusive strongpoints, and our supporting riflemen stood in slit-trenches, able to see in all directions. Bunkers in the end could become death traps. We evolved a battle-drill for dealing with them. If tanks were available, and latterly they generally were, and as Japanese supporting artillery grew scarce, bunker busting became routine and inexpensive. Artillery and tank fire would strip the jungle cover from a position. The infantry would locate a bunker and show it to the tank, which at point-blank range fired shot through the weapon slits. Once a couple of bunkers from the interlocking chain had been knocked out, the rest fell quickly, for they could be approached from a blind side.

Japanese mortarmen were good, and perhaps caused us

infantry the most casualties. They were quick to bring their
mortars into action, and were accurate. Their battalion
mortars outranged ours. Japanese grenades were lethal only
at very close quarters (the metal casing was thin-walled), and
were no match for our '36' grenade. The average Japanese
infantryman was a poor shot. I do not know whether this was
due to insufficient training, or a poor weapon, or weak eyesight. I once overheard a Gurkha reinforcement say: '*Aré*,
brother ! I would like to see these *Japani*. It is said that they
all wear spectacles.' And a great many of them did, which
somehow helped to diminish that early image of them as
supermen. But they made good use of snipers, too good use.
Individual Japanese would remain behind, perhaps tied into
trees, or concealed in undergrowth, and would wait for hours
until the right target came close. The right target was generally
an officer, revealed either by the colour of his skin or by his
giving orders (there was no saluting in battle areas). A sniper
who fired was hunted and shot; his mission was suicidal. But
the balance of the affair favoured the Japanese, for good
officers were not plentiful. On the march in close country two
of our men in every section were trained to look up, searching
the trees. Japanese snipers were an unnerving menace that
never diminished.

Each Japanese battalion had a number of 75 mm 'infantry'
guns that could be carried in pieces on mules. They were
effective as sniper guns: from some temporary fire-position the
crew of such a gun could let off a dozen shots, then dismantle
it and withdraw before counter-fire could be organised. There
was no equivalent on our side. The heavier artillery, 105 mm
and 150 mm guns, could shoot further than our 25-pounders,
but the Japanese seldom had enough of them, or ammunition
for them, to create a lethal barrage. On the whole we were
much superior in artillery.

Japanese tanks were no match for ours, and by 1944 our
tank crews had learned to bring their Grants, Lees and
Shermans into country which had been pronounced tank-proof
in the early days. Japanese tanks were thinly armoured and
carried a weak 37 mm gun. There were not many of them. I
think that nobody in our Battalion ever saw one.

We respected, even admired, our enemy, but did not rate his intelligence highly. For us the Japanese were like wasps, dangerous when disturbed, painful when they stung, but not too difficult to eliminate when the necessary techniques were learned and the proper materials were to hand.

I had no doubts at that time about the necessity for fighting the Japanese. In an ideal world we should not need to judge the actions of others, and increasing age brings for me an increasing reluctance to make judgements. I knew nothing then of the economic pressures upon the Japanese people. I did know that these people had allowed power to militarism, had acquiesced in government by the army which had embarked upon a programme of conquest by arms.

If the Japanese had truly 'liberated' the territories they conquered, liberated them from the rule of British, French and Dutch on behalf of their indigenous peoples, I might have felt less certain of my duty to fight. But it was evident that they were simply substituting their rule for ours. The Japanese behaved in Asia, at their best, like an intolerant and bad-tempered father, handing out kicks and slaps whenever his view is questioned or disobeyed by his children. Japanese arrogance, their casual brutality, their apparent insensitivity to the feelings and needs of non-Japanese, their inability to understand that other peoples did not consider Japanese ways of thinking and acting as best, not from perverseness or a desire to humiliate, but from a genuine preference for their own ways, all this made them bad masters of the countries they had conquered with such ease. The British, too, can be accused of arrogance and insensitivity, and of occasional cruelty, but the truth is that in those countries such as Burma which experienced the rule of both nations, and which at first welcomed the Japanese as liberators, the majority of the inhabitants came to look back on British rule as the lesser evil.

The Japanese Government granted formal independence to Burma on 1 August 1943, and talked encouragingly about 'The Greater East-Asia Co-Prosperity Sphere'. The Japanese Army carried on as it pleased, ignored the Burmese Government it was supposed to be protecting and supporting. Japanese soldiers too often based their behaviour on suspicion, force and patronage; they did the most barbarous things, sometimes deliberately, sometimes from ignorance of local custom. There must have been kind and tactful Japanese in Burma, but the good they performed was lost in the violence and insensitivity of the majority. It was easy for us to believe the worst of this majority because we knew of the large-scale brutality which the Japanese indulged in so frequently in China: the rape of Nanking became world news in 1937. We were to learn of many other examples after the war.

We judged the Japanese, on the evidence of their own behaviour, to be uncivilised and incapable of tolerant relationships with other people, whether Asian or European. We, as judges, were most imperfect ourselves, but despite our own imperfections—which were certainly greater than we realised —we thought that our values were better values and our behaviour less nauseous. We believed, however confusedly, in the importance of the individual human being and his right to have a voice in the control of his destiny. The Japanese apparently did not.

In that time of war it was perhaps natural that the unpleasant sides of the Japanese character were brought home to us; the better sides were displayed in peace and in Japan, and were hidden from us.

It was the soldiers of these people whom I was about to fight. I believe I can say truthfully that, although I was afraid of what they could do to me, I was not afraid of them. To that degree my training had been successful.

XI

KOHIMA: ENVOI

Order of the Day by Commandant 4/8th Gurkha Rifles, Lt-Col
W. C. Walker, 20 December 1944

1 The Battalion is once again about to proceed on active
  operations against the Japanese.
2 Most of us have had leave and most of us have undergone
  intensive training to fit ourselves for active service.
3 The results of our training have been excellent, and if we
  all not only remember what we have learned but put it
  into practice against the Japanese, we shall annihilate him
  on every occasion we fight him in battle.
4 We have had to face difficulties but all ranks have never
  given up trying, never lost faith and never forgotten the
  cause which has brought us together in this Battalion. And
  the result—the joint result—of it all is a real live regiment,
  with a morale and soul of its own.
5 Those of you who have not fought against the Japanese
  before have no knowledge as to what your real strength or
  weaknesses may be. Some of you, hitherto undistinguished,
  will come into your own and cover yourselves with glory.
  Only war itself can discover the qualities which count in
  war. But I am absolutely confident that the supreme Gurkha
  virtue—the virtue of holding on, and holding on, and holding
  on, until our task is accomplished—will not be found wanting
  in a single one of you.
6 The fighting in front of us will be tough and we shall have
  to exert every ounce of our strength. But we shall defeat the
  enemy just as we have defeated him before, and just as other
  Gurkha battalions have defeated not only the Japanese but
  the Germans also.

7 The reputation of Gurkhas as fighting men is unsurpassed. You are known throughout the world as the best fighters of any army, and the enemy respects you and fears you. The Gurkha Brigade has already received 7 V.C.s, the highest award that can be won for gallantry. We ourselves have received 2 I.O.M.s, 3 M.C.s, 3 I.D.S.M.s, 6 M.M.s and 1 Gallantry Certificate. All these have been Immediate Awards. There are more awards to come as a result of our fighting in the Arakan and Imphal area. As yet no battalion of the 8th Gurkhas has received a V.C.—let us be the first Battalion to achieve this signal honour.*

8 I know we shall kill and utterly destroy the Japanese whenever and wherever we meet him. As Commandant of this Battalion I pin my faith in you. You have character; you have grit and guts; you have supreme courage; you have high morale; you have discipline; you have pride in your race; and now that you have confidence as a result of our recent training you are all going to be an everlasting credit to the cause which roused the manhood of Nepal and the land which gave you birth.

So at last we were to march east, over the mountains and down into Burma. During these Kohima days the war had receded from us. It had not been so far away when Bill, Mike and I had landed at Imphal. But other formations had nagged and pushed at the retreating enemy until we were ready, refreshed, to close on the Irrawaddy and central Burma, territory which had been in enemy hands for more than two years. There was the scent of victory about.

I was now of the Battalion, no stranger to anyone. 'Those of you who have not fought against the Japanese before have no knowledge as to what your real strength or weaknesses may be.' A disquieting thought. Yet I was not deeply worried. I knew I should be frightened. I had read too much on the First World War to believe that I would be exempt from fear. But I thought I should be able to master the fear.

* In the Second World War. Three British officers of the Regiment had won the V.C. in earlier wars: one during the Mutiny, one in the Naga Rebellion of 1879, and one in Tibet in 1904.

For me Kohima had been a piece of marvellous good fortune. As I found out later, many active battalions were not the dedicated, happy entities of my imagination, yet the battalion I had joined fulfilled most of my hopes, and I had joined it at a moment which saved me from that nightmare of the reinforcement: to be sent too soon into battle with men who do not know or care for him. I had grown up in those five months at Kohima. I had shared an intensity of living, a total dedication to one object, that I had not experienced before, nor have since. Nothing had stretched me so far. The release of energy and will-power that follows from doing a job you want to do, and want to do as well as you are capable of doing, can be phenomenal. I was rising twenty, and now had a little insight behind me, some conception of my own capabilities, some knowledge of those around me, perhaps just enough. I will not swear that I faced the future with uncontaminated joy, but I did so with a proper reserve of confidence.

I knew that I was glad to be in this situation with Gurkhas. Identification with them was complete, unclouded by the smallest doubt that I might be happier elsewhere. It was always a pleasure, and often a joy, to be among them. They possessed many good qualities, and two which for me made them unique. First, they had an apparently inexhaustible fund of humour; their humour was not subtle, but it contained a quick sense of the ridiculous that spared no one, neither Colonel, themselves, nor me. If I slipped on a steep hillside and slithered twenty yards through mud, they would rush to pick me up, grinning so infectiously that self-pride had no time to consider that it might have been hurt. If a Gurkha slipped he would be the first to laugh. This natural feeling for the world as a place of comedy, rather than tragedy, was taken to its logical conclusion: death could induce ribaldry as readily as life. 'Eh ! If the Colonel could not make Bhimbahadur smart when he was in one piece, what will God do with him in six bits ?' Roars of laughter. This was banana-skin humour, but then subtle wit is probably a response to a complex social and cultural environment. I found Gurkha humour, with its cheerful deflation of the pompous, endlessly refreshing. It was good for us all. None of us could forget that he was a fallible human

H

being as well as Havildar-Major, Intelligence Officer or Commandant. No one of us could dwell on a personal misery for long. None could escape from the developed Gurkha art of mimicry.

Secondly, Gurkhas were honest. In a world where grand and petty larceny were habitual, distortion of the truth and self-deceit commonplace, the honesty of Gurkhas seemed unique. The quality of Gurkha honesty went much beyond a restraint from 'borrowing'. It was a quality of mind, of character, that permeated all their actions and reactions, a natural integrity, an inborn frankness. If you caught a Gurkha in the wrong he would not deny his guilt, or start to shift the blame elsewhere.* Gurkhas were quick to detect hypocrisy, they scorned equivocation, despised perversion of the truth. They seemed to issue from a mould superior to that of most other men. Probably their honesty, their honour, like their sense of the ridiculous, was derived from an instinctive realism: they seemed able to see to the centre of things. I have not met another people with so few illusions about themselves and the world around them, or who, looking at the world with this practical, objective, unromantic eye, found it funny. It was easy to command such people. It was a privilege to be allowed to do so. Living with them sharpened one's own character.

To humour and honesty must be added courage (the quality that Gurkhas themselves prize most highly), loyalty and toughness. I place courage third because it seems to me not so uncommon, though I acknowledge that a people without courage are nothing. Some Gurkhas had more courage than others, as you would expect; all of them had a great reservoir of it. Courage waxes and wanes in the same man, relative to hunger, health, fatigue, nervous exhaustion, and other externalities. Courage can be built up, like muscles, and gets run down. Courage, said our General Slim, is like having money in the bank. It is an expendable quality. If there are

* There was little 'crime' to be dealt with by the Colonel or the Company Commanders, when compared with that described by Robert Graves, in *Goodbye to All That*, as normal for the Royal Welch Fusiliers in the 1914–18 war.

continuous calls on a man's supply, he begins to overdraw. If he goes on overdrawing, he goes bankrupt, he breaks down. The army can develop courage, and wise commanders will husband its expenditure. But the army can produce neither humour nor honesty. It can only discourage dishonesty, a negative business.

As for loyalty, this has to be earned. We were loyal to our men, and in this giving of our loyalty, earned theirs. It was a natural process for me, for we were encouraged by every means to take care of our soldiers, and this had always seemed to me the only justification for being a regimental officer.

The toughness of the Gurkha race is well known. They led a tough life in their homes which well fitted them for the hardships of active service. They could march fast and far, and dig hard at the end of the day.

If you are beginning to think that I myself am practising neither courageous honesty nor realism with this panegyric on the Gurkha, let there be added a brief quotation from the enemy. In his book, *Prisoner of the British* (Cresset Press, 1966), Yuji Aida is scathing about the British, critical of the Indians, and not always complimentary about his fellow Japanese prisoners. The people he praises are the Gurkhas. 'The Gurkhas were transparently honest men, very brave, sticklers for regulations—the very model of sturdy, honest and simple soldiers—and as front-line troops during the war they had given the Japanese Army a really tough time.' Yuji Aida had both fought against Gurkhas in Burma, and, after the war, had been guarded by them. Guards who remain heroes to their prisoners must be special indeed. Gurkhas and Japanese (that is, peasant Gurkha and peasant Japanese) often look remarkably alike.

However, it would be dishonest to forget that Gurkhas had faults, even though we who served with them found their faults so little disturbing that for most of the time we could ignore them. In their own country they were said to be gamblers, sometimes to a degree that left the last outposts of common sense a thousand leagues behind. Gambling was forbidden by law in Nepal, and forbidden in the army. With us they used to play cards with splendid vigour, swearing and slapping down a card just as though a young second wife was at stake. They

were great womanisers, but I think not to the point of abnor-
mality. It is a matter for argument and of degree whether lust
is a fault or simply the common state of all humanity,
dangerously suppressed in many societies, recognised and where
possible indulged by Gurkhas. Gurkhas seemed to have formed
happy and stable family groups. If we learned of the infidelity
of some wives, and knew of the promiscuity of some husbands,
this was understandable when military affairs kept the two
apart for several years.

Many Gurkhas, by Western standards, were not intelligent.
I have no statistics, and an objective measurement of intelligence that allows for such variables as home environment
and lack of incentives has not yet been devised. A man's
intelligence will only be developed in those ways which are
relevant to his situation. Reading, writing and knowledge of
the internal combustion engine were not required by the
Nepalese farmer, and if, at the age of seventeen or eighteen,
he proved to be slower at picking up these skills than boys of
seven or eight in England, this is not surprising, for at that
advanced age the human mind is supposed to be already past
its maximum plasticity. So whether Gurkhas were truly less
intelligent, or had differently developed intelligence, is difficult
to prove. Some of them, bless their ugly flat faces, were
certainly very thick-headed.

They were fond of strong drink. In the hills they brewed
their own. In the army drinking was rationed by a man's
pay and more often by short supply. They were able to hold
their drink. The common sight at the closing time of English
pubs of half a dozen tipsy bodies staggering about the road and
pavements would have bewildered a Gurkha, disgusted him.
A man owes himself more control than that.

A further Gurkha fault, and the last of this catalogue, is a
certain insularity, a lack of interest in the world which his
military service showed to him. He killed enemies and ignored
allies. Burma, Egypt, Italy, Iraq, all seemed one to him,
foreign countries inferior to Nepal and of little interest except
for the drink and the girls they might hold. Officers had to
learn about the men, their customs and their country, and
enjoyed doing so. The men did not have to learn about us, and

only a few of them showed by their questions an awareness that England was not like Nepal.

I cannot remember that we wartime British officers spent much time in wondering why our men had enlisted. We took their arrival for granted, perhaps attributing it to the irresistible aura of our own collective personalities. Why did the Gurkhas leave their hills so readily in such numbers for so many years ? Why do they still do so ? Even before the East India Company's war with the Gurkhas had ended in 1816 the surviving garrisons of some forts were enlisting to fight for the rest of the campaign on the British side, an extraordinary *volte-face* to us Westerners, conditioned from birth to our various nationalisms, right or wrong.

The numbers of Gurkhas who have left Nepal, either temporarily or for ever, must be very great by comparison with the size of the country and its total population. For a start, enlistment into the old Indian Army was never confined to the ten Gurkha regiments. Gurkhas formed considerable parts of units such as the Kumaon Rifles, the Assam Rifles and the Burma Military Police. Wherever these regiments had depots, colonies of Gurkhas settled and spread. Much of the land around Dehra Dun, for example, was farmed by ex-Gurkha soldiers and their descendants.

Then Gurkhas have migrated to other places than the Indian Army. The origins of the British–Gurkha war lie in the attempted expansion of Gurkha rule by conquest south into territory controlled by the East India Company. They had already spread from eastern Nepal into Sikkim and Bhutan, and from western Nepal into Kumaon, Garhwal and as far as the borders of Kashmir. To the west they had been stopped by the Sikhs under Ranjit Singh, and promptly began to enlist in his army. At least once the Gurkhas invaded parts of Tibet, and thus came up against the Chinese, who defeated them. Although most of these conquests were subsequently lost, colonies of Gurkhas remained and have grown, reinforced by peaceful migration. Around Darjeeling, for instance, the girls who pluck the bushes on the tea estates are mostly Gurkha.

What has caused this Gurkha diaspora ? The evidence I have seen suggests that it must be due almost entirely to the pressure of economic conditions in their homeland.

Nepal is not a large country—a little over five hundred miles from east to west, and averaging about a hundred miles north to south. Much of the land is intricately mountainous. Close to the northern border with Tibet tower the Himalayan peaks, where no man lives. Inside the southern border is a strip averaging thirty miles wide of low-lying plain, the Terai, unhealthy, much of it thickly forested, shunned by the hillmen. The area inhabited by the hill tribes is thus a middle belt, but from this belt must be deducted the Valley of Nepal, some three hundred miles square, where are the main cities, and the far western and eastern districts, because in these areas live peoples who were not generally recruited for the Indian Army: the Newars, Dotiyals, Bhotes, Sherpas and others. These peoples are all Nepali, but they are not the martial tribes, the 'Gurkha' in the traditionally accepted sense of the word.

Thus the area occupied by 'Gurkhas' is much smaller than the total area of Nepal. It is an area of intensely cultivated hillsides with poor communications and little room for absorbing an expanding population. Communications in Nepal have always been slow and laborious, mostly bridle tracks ascending and descending in thousands of feet one ridge after another. There was no air service until 1950, no motorable road from India to Kathmandu until 1957, and there are very few miles of such road even now. The rivers are generally unnavigable.

Topographical and climatic obstacles to development and prosperity were aggravated by political history. The history of Nepal, so far as it can be disentangled from myth, is one of small kingdoms or tribal units fighting one another for ascendancy over greater or smaller areas until in 1768 Prithwi Narayan, tenth King of the House of Gorkha, said to be descended from the Rajput princes of Udaipur, completed his conquest of the principalities in the Valley of Nepal, and began to expand into the surrounding hills. His descendants did not hold power for long, though they remained as royal figureheads. For a century before 1951 (when the first of several experiments in democratic government began) there was a concentration of authority and wealth in one family, the Ranas, who discouraged foreign interference or influence. Their isolationist policy froze the economy at subsistence level. Britain's 1816 treaty with Nepal reinforced this policy, and so assisted in the thwarting of development, though no doubt the British Government's mind was moved by other considerations: the wish not to interfere with the internal policy of a people whose land would be expensive to conquer, and gratitude for an arrangement that brought a succession of splendid fighting men to the Indian Army. Rana rule kept Nepal cut off from the rest of Asia. The population apparently grew; the cultivable land, limited by topography and the mosquito, did not. Nor did the yield per acre, since discoveries elsewhere could not reach those remote hills.

Thus in every small self-sufficient village (and three-quarters or more of Nepal's population lived in villages with under a thousand inhabitants, and about 90 per cent were farmers) there came to be a surplus of landless young men who looked elsewhere for a living. It suited the Ranas to have this surplus profitably occupied where they could do no harm; it suited the British to employ them as mercenaries.

This is probably a simplification, but I believe it to be the main reason why the Gurkhas came to us. Gurkhas have a strong emotional attachment to their hills, yet life there can be so hard that they do not seem to need much persuading to try their luck elsewhere. In much of Nepal it is difficult to earn cash, and trade is still by barter. There are still villages too poor to buy fuel for heating and lighting, and villages riddled with malaria, tuberculosis and other diseases.

No doubt the economic incentive has come to be reinforced by tradition, perhaps disguised and overlaid by it. Probably many of our recruits came because of the examples set by fathers, uncles, brothers, who had enjoyed the life, had developed a loyalty to their regiments and perhaps to the officers of their day, whose stories would grow increasingly eulogistic as age left them with the highlights and lost them the routine. Probably many of these young men sought first adventure and a chance to prove their courage. But the value of a cash income would not be overlooked for long: sons need money to meet the expenses of marriage, and to buy land, and to build houses.

This argument—that Gurkhas left Nepal because of the economic conditions—would have been anathema to those British officers of the Gurkha Brigade who by training and by nature believed that only they could successfully command Gurkhas. These officers had come to feel such a depth of affection and loyalty for their men that they assumed a reciprocal feeling, and assumed that it must be unique to them. Up to a point that feeling did exist; had British and Gurkha not respected each other's qualities, and mixed well together, the Gurkha might not have come, or would have come in smaller numbers. But it was a feeling that did not go so deep as many of us liked to think.

To break the chronology of this story for a moment, in 1947, when it became known that six of the Gurkha regiments were to join the new Army of India and four were to join the British Army in Malaya, the men in the regiments selected for India were asked whether they were prepared to serve in India under Indian officers, or whether they preferred to transfer to the British Gurkhas. Here was an extreme test, a cruel one for many who genuinely liked the officers they knew and were apprehensive of those they did not. Nevertheless a very great majority opted for India, and in one battalion only one man volunteered for the British, and he recanted on discovering his isolation. Given roughly equal pay, ultimate loyalty was to the Regiment, to the community of men with whom a man served; it was not to the British or to particular British officers. This discovery hurt. But looked at from outside it makes sense, for the Gurkhas had not joined up in order to worship Lieutenant Smith, but to earn a living. The loyalty we gave and received was a bonus for both sides.

Those last days at Kohima were filled with inspecting, checking, double-checking, issuing items of missing equipment, packing up, tearing out roots. During this kind of detailed preparation and checking of a man's total possessions, an officer learns a good deal about him as a human personality, and about his

place at home, his social setting. A notebook survives in which
I jotted down the repairs needed in my small command, and
the gaps that had still to be filled.

87095 Sohabir Lama, a sniper, whom I had promoted to
unpaid lance-naik in October, when his kit was inspected had
nails missing from his boots, needed repairs to his P.T. shoes,
to one vest, to his pullover (holes in the arm-pits) and to his
towel and pugri; he was without grenade pouches and gauze,
his hat and kukri required cleaning and his large pack
stitching. Rifleman Sherbahadur Thapa, who was to be killed
by shell-fire in seven months' time, needed a new jersey pullover and a new pair of socks, his towel wanted stitching and
he was without grenade pouches and an infantry screen.
Sherbahadur had joined the army at the age of seventeen in
October 1941. He had passed his recruits test in 1942 and his
third class Indian Army Certificate of Education in 1943. He
had just returned from leave to his home in the district of
No. 4 West, part of Central Nepal.

My Intelligence havildar, 2389 Sete Gurung, was a regular.
He had joined the Regiment in 1936, aged sixteen. He came
from Shillong, the Regiment's old headquarters, and was
probably the son of an 8th Gurkha soldier who had settled in
the district. As I have said, Gurkha colonies were to be found
wherever the regiments put down roots. Children from such
colonies were known as 'line boys', and went to school, and
by sixteen were educated to a level that few young Gurkhas
from Nepal could reach. Thus many of the jobs that required
a high standard of reading and writing were held by grown-up
line boys. The British officers regarded them with mixed
feelings. We needed their skills, but found that an upbringing
in India often spoilt them. They were 'clever' in a way that
their kinsmen from Nepal were not. They had learned a thing
or two. Some officers condemned all line boys without distinction, put it down to education, and so by extension regretted
the need for Gurkhas to be taught anything beyond simple
training. This was unfair. It was not the formal education that
spoilt our Indian-domiciled Gurkhas. It was the environment,
the social conditioning of cantonment life in India. The morals
of the bazaar are not high.

By no means all line boys were 'spoilt'. Old Sete, for he seemed old by comparison with most of us, was steady, reliable, and charming, with one of those drooping moustaches that were favoured by the older men. He, too, had just returned from a long leave home. He had been a havildar since October 1941, and with his educational qualifications he was obviously in line for promotion. In fact he was made a jemadar and platoon commander in March of 1945, and I lost him.

My Intelligence naik was 85102, Khamansing. Like Rifleman Sherbahadur, he was a Thapa. The Thapa is the largest of the seven clans of the Magar tribe. Khamansing had joined up in October 1940, and was a boy of exceptional intelligence. His educational record was excellent. He was one of the few Gurkhas in the Battalion who could speak and read English (old Sete knew some). He, too, had just returned from leave. His district was Piuthan in Western Nepal. As did most of our men, he walked for a week or so from the nearest railhead inside India to reach his village in the hills. Khamansing had been made a naik in July 1943, and when Sete left, he was promoted havildar.

This is not the place for an extended account of the tribes of Nepal, but a brief foray into the subject is necessary, for a man's tribe was a fact of importance even in the Battalion, where such divisions tended to fade before the 'Gurkhaness' of our men as against the British, or the Sikhs, or the Punjabis, or the Japanese. In his own country a Gurkha was first a member of a kindred and a village, then of a clan, then of a tribe, and only finally, and often somewhat hazily, a citizen of the country called Nepal. No doubt these matters are changing, and schools and roads will be, as they always do, enlarging a national consciousness and diminishing local loyalties. In the 1940s Nepal was much as it had been when Gurkhas were first recruited by the British a hundred and twenty-five years earlier. In the army a man's clan or tribe was always part of his name. We British officers spent much time discussing the supposed relative merits of one and another. Our discussions had little scientific basis; our conclusions were soon upset by new evidence of somebody's behaviour.

In parenthesis, a man's army number often grew to be part of his name. Some men were known by their numbers. Any easily memorable part of a number tended to become a nickname. My orderly, Nandalal, had a number 85002. In Gurkhali two is *dui*, and he was called Dui as frequently as Nandalal. 'Eh, Dui, is the Sahib to be approached just now?' The use of numbers in this way was derived partly from the Gurkha love for nicknames. Physical peculiarities were quickly noted and succinctly described (*Kalo*, 'Blackie', for a dark-skinned fellow). But it was also probably because Gurkha first names do not have a wide range and tended to be duplicated in the platoon and company. It would not be surprising to find two Manbahadurs of the Gurung tribe together in the same sub-unit. Without their numbers they might be, for military purposes, one person.

We added to the elaboration of nicknames because we found it convenient to identify some men by a past or current skill, by some accident that may have befallen them, or by a habit for which they were well known. Manu the Drummer could never be confused with Manu the Tyre (the driver who had driven over the cliff and been thwacked by the spare tyre), or Danjit the Mule with Danjit the B Company Volley Ball.

Gurkha first names reflect their respect for courage. Many of them combine a suffix such as *bahadur* (brave) or *sing* (lion) with a prefix such as *Man* (spirit), *Dil* (heart), or *Bhakta* (loyal). Thus Manbahadur (Brave spirit), or Dilsing (Lionheart). Since names are given soon after birth, as with us, they reflect wishful thinking rather than observed fact.

Of the six Gurkha tribes most commonly drawn upon for recruits to the old Indian Army, the 8th Gurkhas generally enlisted Magars and Gurungs, the two largest tribes from the centre and west of the country. This is well illustrated by the men who passed through my Intelligence Section from September 1944 to April 1945. Ten were Magars, four were Gurungs, with one Limbu and one Chhetri. The Magars form a larger tribe than the Gurungs. For reasons which are unclear to me, Gurungs were nearly always called Gurung (hence Sete Gurung), whereas Magars were known by their clan subdivisions. Of my ten Magars, seven were Thapas, two were Puns and one was a Rana.

The solitary Limbu, Kale, came from eastern Nepal, as do the Rais. These two tribes were generally recruited into the 7th and 10th Gurkhas, but a few came to other regiments, particularly in wartime, when selection became less parochial. Scotty Gilmore's orderly, Nebilal, was a Rai, and typical of his people—small, quick-witted and round-faced. It was often impossible to tell by looks alone to which tribe a man belonged. But one made fewer mistakes with Rais than with most. When you saw a man for the first time and dared a guess and got him right, he was always delighted.

Lalbahadur the Chhetri happens to illustrate another facet of tribal history that became institutionalised in the army. The Chhetris are mostly reckoned to be descended from groups of high-caste Indians who in the twelfth century fled into the hills from the Muslim invasion and there intermarried with local women. They are Hindus of a much stricter order than the Gurungs and Magars—who wear their religion most lightly—are generally taller and finer featured, less Mongolian in their looks. Their social status in Nepal was said to be high. Because they kept more strictly to the orthodox Hindu taboos, they tended to be enlisted into the one regiment, the 9th Gurkhas. It was with the 9th Gurkhas that Dick Allen was serving.

There is a layering of culture and race through much of Nepalese life that is of great interest to the observer. Literature, art, music, the top-people's religion and social grading, and Gurkhali the lingua franca, came up from the south in comparatively recent times, and were Indian and Hindu or Buddhist. On the other hand the bulk of the people in the hills, their tribal languages and much of their local custom and social organisation, must have originated from north of the Himalayas, from Tibet or central Asia.

Perhaps it is this mixture and meeting of race and culture that gives to the hill Gurkha his refreshing independence of mind. He is in thrall to no person and no creed, owes nobody, god or man, a living.

So there he is, the Gurkha soldier, squat, thick-set, sturdy-legged, brown-skinned, with the high cheekbones, the almond-shaped eyes and the broad-based nose that gives the typically Mongolian appearance. The army made him shave his head, but the glistening scalp was usually covered by a hat; his chin and cheeks were naturally hairless. He comes to attention before you, and looks straight at you, certainly your equal, probably your superior.

It used to be well known that with whichever race a British officer of the Indian Army served, for him that race was best. I felt the same. For me Gurkhas were—and are—the salt of the earth. I would not have wished to go into battle with anyone else.

XII

TOWARDS THE IRRAWADDY

It was almost dusk. The line of lorries on the road above our camp was the final, the irrevocable signal. Tail-boards were lowered; the lorries were gulping men and equipment. The men were excited and happy. Round smiling faces disappeared one after another.

I stood beside my jeep and looked down. The tents that had held us for so many days and nights were struck, folded and stowed. Gone was the great Mess tent on the prow of the spur, gone the Quarter Guard and the Adjutant's office, gone my own small home. The neat fencing, the paths and the steps, the worn patches of bare earth, looked odd and sad without the tents and the men who had lived in them. For five months seven hundred of us had been here, pouring out energy and emotion so that the whole area—the hillsides, valleys, trees, the rolling cumulus, the lorries, mules, sentries, the squads at drill and P.T., the individual in singlet and shorts—the whole had grown its own atmosphere of which each of us was a part. We were part of the atmosphere, and it was part of us. We were nomads and expected no settled home. Yet to leave such a place, though you may have hated it, is always a little death. I had been happy. When I think of my four years in the army, it is to Kohima that the mind drifts most often.

The column was nearly ready and it had grown dark. I climbed into the jeep. There was no time now for regrets. We were off round the familiar curving track, and it was the needs of the present that occupied the mind, with now and again a thought for the future, a flash of wonder tinged with apprehension.

Most of that night and much of the next day (Christmas

Eve) we were confined to our transport, twisting down to the Imphal Plain, up and over the mountains to the south-east, where had occurred some of the fiercest fighting of the Japanese offensive, and down to Tamu, in Burma. There we stayed for more than a week.

We were re-invading Burma by the back door. In peace time this route, a mere track, had been used by no one but a few hardy traders and the occasional mad Englishman. Now from the railhead at Dimapur in India, through Kohima and Imphal to Tamu, there were 206 tortuous miles of an all-weather two-way motorable road, the only such road, beautiful, a feat of engineering, a tribute to Indian and Naga muscle, yet a quartermaster's nightmare. You cannot supply a largish army along one road. We should have starved or stayed in India without command of the air and the use of air transport.

And Tamu was the mere beginning of our journey. It lay in the notorious Kabaw valley, for half the year one of the world's most malarial districts, but in January idyllic (too cold for mosquitoes). We camped in the teak forest. Every morning there was a heavy dew and a thick mist. On the first morning I was awoken by the noise, like hail, of large drops falling eighty or a hundred feet from the canopy of enormous teak leaves on to the drum-tight canvas of my tent. I was momentarily petrified, unable to imagine any pleasant explanation. Later the sun dispersed the mist, sucked up the dew. For the rest of the day it was pleasantly hot.

That first morning at Tamu was Christmas morning. The year before I had been in Bareilly with my parents and sisters, and the Christmas before that in England. In Bareilly we had stayed in some vast tents in the grounds of the club, tents which I liked to imagine were those of an Arabian prince, for one led into another, and there were carpets on the floor, comfortable chairs, and oil heaters. My little tent in the teak forests of Tamu would not have suited the meanest camp follower of the most miserable prince in Arabia.

My parents sent me a cake which arrived the day after Christmas and turned out to be about the only Christmas fare we received, for something went wrong and our promised luxuries never came. But enough extra drink arrived for a

party on Christmas night, and Christmas Day saw an absence
of work, which was change and holiday enough.

After Christmas we continued with training. I practised
my snipers and intelligence sections on compass marches in
the forest. We divided into groups and by different routes
made for a rendezvous on the banks of a small river a few
miles off. There we caught fish by firing bullets into the water
beside them to stun them. Grenades are quicker, but we were
not yet so embroiled in war that I could write off grenades
without good military reason. We cooked the fish on the spot,
made tea, bathed, basked in the sun. In the afternoon I devised
another exercise to take us home.

Sometimes in the forest round our camp we came upon
burnt-out buildings: blackened rafters, charred foundation
posts, twisted sheets of rusting corrugated iron, already half
smothered by the encroaching undergrowth. Who had lived
here? Had they survived? I wondered whether soldiers had
fought at this spot, crouching behind that beam, shocked by
the blast of a mortar bomb there, perhaps where I stood falling
back to earth in that final blinding passage to death.

Tamu had changed hands several times, most recently in
August, when it was found to be a charnel house of dead and
dying Japanese, a town irrecoverably contaminated by
decomposition, disease and flies. It was cleansed by fire. The
monsoon and the murderously inadequate medical services of
our enemy had finished off what our troops back on the
Imphal Plain had begun. Of the Japanese soldiers who started
the 1944 campaign, ninety-two thousand did not survive, a
frightening total, each component a human being.

But in the reverse direction Tamu had already witnessed
disaster. During the 1942 retreat out of Burma the town had
been the last outpost of civilisation, the last place with shelter
and food and to which a few vehicles managed to drive, before
the long and killing mountain trek into India that faced the
troops and those wretched refugees. At Tamu cholera broke
out; dysentery, malaria and blackwater fever were endemic.
Privation and disease took a terrible toll. Months later, after
the monsoon, when patrols from Imphal re-entered Tamu, the
place was littered with rotting skeletons, men, women and

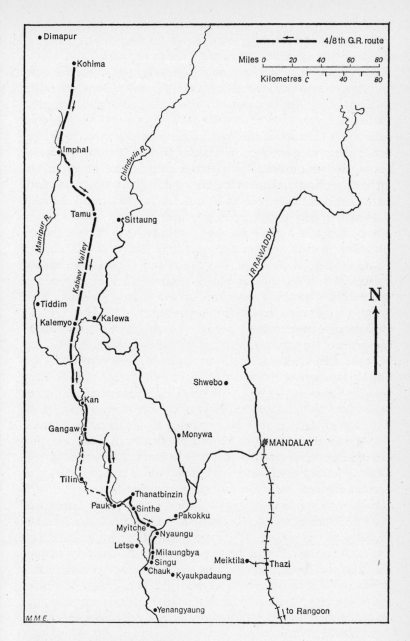

Map 1 Advance into Burma

I

children, just as it was to be again in 1944. Tamu was a
doomed place. It was good that we were some miles out in
the clean forest, and that it was January.

The Battalion's next move was 125 miles south, through
and out of the Kabaw valley. I left on 6 January in charge of
the advance party. We spent the day in a 15 cwt truck churning
steadily and bumpily through six inches of fine red dust. The
dust rose in clouds from each wheel of every vehicle using the
track, and the track was popular just then. The forest on
either side was coated with dust twelve feet up: each leaf,
each blade of grass, each twig and branch had thickened and
was coloured red, like a child's painting. We were soon in
the same state. I had to wipe my glasses every few minutes.
Handkerchiefs or scarves tied over nose and mouth kept most
of the stuff from our lungs, but not from the rest of our bodies,
on to which it settled like russet camouflage. We camped on
the banks of the Manipur river, and in it grew human again.
I had never been so glad to reach water.

Somewhere on this day's drive (I think it was this day) we
were halted for a time in the long line of traffic while several
men of the 28th East African Brigade, bothered by some
grudge against their commanders or the war, fired with a
machine-gun and with democratic indiscrimination on all
who came down the road. I never did learn just what happened.
Mutinous imbroglio are not recorded in the histories. Even a
unit's war diary deploys a discreet vagueness where it can.
But minor rebellion by Britain's colonial troops was not
uncommon. One felt amused and a little sympathetic so long
as the unit was not one's own. In my school histories a major
justification for Britain's occupation of India and Africa was
that of pacification. British rule, I used to read, brought *pax
Britannica*, and prevented all that uncivilised intertribal warfare. Now here I was, part of a large army composed of
Indians, Gurkhas, British and Africans (two West African
divisions and one East African fought in Burma), all of us
employed by the Government of Great Britain to fight war
on a huge and devastating scale—for the second time in
twenty-five years.

I spent my twentieth birthday, 7 January, with my five or

six men hacking down undergrowth between the trees near
the river for the various company and headquarter bivouacs.
We could not clear enough in the time, but when the Battalion
rolled in that afternoon, dust-free and late because it had
rained, we had substantial spaces ready. And there we stayed
for another week while other people moved forward and we
learned something of the plan for our Division over the next
month.

The plan was dramatic, bold enough to touch the spirit of
the least imaginative. It was a plan preferred by General Slim
as recently as mid-December. His earlier schemes had assumed
that the Japanese, who normally clung to ground as fiercely
as any limpet, would fight west of the Irrawaddy, on our side
of it. Our 7th Division had been destined to follow 19th
Division east from Tamu through the jungles and hills beyond
the river Chindwin and out on to the Shwebo plain well north
of Mandalay. When 19th Division's rapid advance, and other
evidence, made it clear that the main strength of the Japanese
was (uncharacteristically) retiring behind the Irrawaddy,
General Slim scrapped the first plan and substituted a very
different one.

He decided to isolate the Japanese armies in northern and
central Burma by switching two divisions, including ours, on
a sweeping hook to the south and east, to cross the Irrawaddy
near Pakokku, and to capture the nodal supply and communications centres of Meiktila and Thazi, ninety miles *south*
of Mandalay (see Map 1, page 115). Meiktila was the supply
base for almost all the Japanese forces in Burma. At Meiktila
too were some of the principal Japanese airfields. For these
places the Japanese armies must fight, or disintegrate. Our
Division was to lead the hook, which was to be kept secret for
as long as possible, with orders to force a bridgehead over the
Irrawaddy by 15 February. Others would come through us
and churn across the open country on the far side for Meiktila.
We were being sent into the desert of central Burma instead
of to the familiar jungles east of the Chindwin. The sudden
change of plan seems remarkable only in retrospect; what
excited us at the time was this daring reach behind the enemy
and the knowledge that success must destroy his hold on

Burma, and failure might destroy us. But I do not remember
that I contemplated failure. I had the confidence of half
knowledge, knew nothing of the administrative risks, and had
faith in Slim.

So on 14 January, with a month to go and no news of how
or when the Japanese would react, we began the foot-slogging
southward with a march of sixteen miles. Next day we marched
twelve miles and on the next fourteen. This brought us to the
village of Kan, which had become Divisional Headquarters
and rallying point. Here we shed our rear echelon—roughly,
those men whose primary task was not fighting. We changed
to a light-weight all-pack basis (no mosquito nets, no groundsheets, one blanket). The mules carried the wireless sets, the
3 in. mortars, the reserve ammunition and other essential
heavy stuff. Save for a handful of jeeps, mechanical transport
was left behind. On the 18th and 19th we covered another
twenty-two miles on the main southward track, which took us,
dust-coated, to the other side of Gangaw. On the 20th we
set off eastward into unknown country in the van of what was
called 89 Brigade's left hook.

The main track to the Irrawaddy went south from Gangaw
and at Tilin turned sharply east to Pauk, and on to Pakokku
on the river. It is 145 miles from Gangaw to Pakokku. At first
the track is through teak forest. Around Pauk the forests thin
out quite rapidly and the dry belt begins. Down this main
route, no more than a narrow cart track until the engineers
could get at it, the East African Brigade was advancing,
masking our 114 Brigade and Divisional Headquarters. We
of 89 Brigade were to march east and then south to cut in on
Pauk behind any retreating Japanese. Our third brigade, No.
33, which on 20 January was still at Kohima, 350 miles back,
was to motor to Gangaw and there plan and practise for the
Irrawaddy crossing.

The 4/8th set off twenty-four hours ahead of the main body
of the Brigade. With us was a mountain battery* and a

---

* Mountain guns could be taken to bits and carried on mules. Mountain
gunners had developed their skills among the hills of India's North-West
Frontier; they could assemble their weapons in minutes and fire them from
any small area of flat ground that a mule could reach.

platoon of engineers. The whole Brigade went on to air supply.

For the first time since I had joined, the Battalion was on its own; for the first time liable to meet the enemy; for the first time performing in earnest what we had so often practised in training—the procedures relevant to an advance along a jungle path, scouts of the leading platoon of the leading company clearing the ground well ahead, everyone on edge to employ counter-ambush drill. None of us knew this country. There were no guides. We picked a route from the map and ordered the day's advance according to the lie of the land, the availability of a dropping zone for our air supplies, and the presence of water. Water became increasingly scarce.

Each day we saw fresh country and each evening studied the maps for the country to be crossed on the next day. Quartering a map was always an excitement. New maps for a new stretch of country set me exploring: hills, valleys, towns, villages, rivers and tracks; which would I see and what would they look like? But as we advanced across a map it became infected with a rash of code-names, short and easy to transmit over wireless or on message-pad, and the euphonious Burmese names were brutally transformed. I have such a map before me now. *Mindandaw* becomes *Pin*; *Hmaikbingon* becomes *Toe* and *Shwehlan* is *Nail*. At *Hnetchaung*, where tracks met in a valley surrounded by 'dense mixed jungle', there was a rest-house; it looked an attractive place that did not deserve to be *Weep*. *Corn* and *Oats* disguised *Kyakhat* and *Kyaukswe*, and *Dolt* hid *Geyin*.

The actual marching, the movement across the land, was a pleasure, a lyrical start to the drama of my first campaign. The country we crossed was of forested hills and cultivated valleys, and the forest was open and fresh rather than impenetrable and steaming. We marched beside paddy stubble, through villages, over low wooded hills, across streams that sparkled in the sunlight. The villages were clean compared with those of India, and the Burmese villagers, those who did not prudently withdraw before the advance of us licentious soldiery, those who stayed to greet us, were clean too, and cheerful, and seemed little touched by war. There were chickens pecking at the dust, and even cows. The Japanese had been here, but briefly, and had not 'leaned' upon the inhabitants as they had in other areas closer to the centres of their activity.

In the history of war millions of men have marched to battle, and many of them must have enjoyed the marching as we did—the changing scene, the physical effort, the companion-ship, the shared dedication to an agreed purpose—whatever fate held for them later. Alexander's Greeks marched from Macedonia to India; Roman legions marched from Italy to Scotland, from the Tiber to the Euphrates; Napoleon's regi-ments tramped from Paris to Moscow. Our march might not equal these, but as we moved over the mountainous border of India down towards the heart of Burma, we knew that we were on no ordinary pilgrimage, but were sharing in the making of a minor epic.

And this march was the best sort of training. It enabled us as a battalion to establish routines of movement and defence that became instinctive and soon required no detailed orders. We left the night's perimeter early, after a quick meal, with the air cool and our bodies eager for movement. The leading company would be an hour ahead. Three or four hours later there was a long halt for a brew of tea with cold chupattis or biscuits. Then on again until the day's target was reached around 2 p.m., with the sun still high. Quickly the Colonel appointed company areas, and company commanders ap-pointed platoon areas. If this was a day for the Dakotas to fly in, the dropping zone was cleared and recognition signals prepared. Most days a little Auster came over with a sack of mail. Before dark each pair of men had a slit-trench dug, the spoil hidden. The evening meal was the main meal of the day. And before dark orders for the next day were given out, the password for the night circulated, maps marked with the code words for the villages ahead, repairs to equipment made, ration needs calculated, the sick doctored, the mules fed and groomed, and the dozens of minor bits of business conducted that go to keep seven hundred soldiers ticking contentedly. All this became routine. We got accustomed to administering ourselves on the move. A unit grows rusty at this after five months in one place.

Following the stand-to at dusk no one moved and no one talked until the stand-to at dawn. We slept in the open beside our trenches. Sentries relieved one another by tugging on bits of string tied to wrists, or by a gentle shake of the shoulders. For the first few nights the Gurkha habit of coughing and hawking through life like asthmatic tramps was a splendid advertisement of our perimeters. Pleas for silence proved useless. But when Walter Walker made coughing after dark an offence, and then punished one or two men that same night, a profound silence dropped upon us. God knows what suppressed convulsions were conducted at the bottom of slit-trenches.

The men carried packs. The British and Gurkha officers did not. This was one of the Colonel's most intelligent rulings, and against the run of opinion at the time. If a man is tired, really tired, he cannot think. An officer is no exception, yet it is his job to think, and other men's lives depend upon the quality of his thought. So for as long as we had enough mules or jeeps, officers packs went on them. In the majority of units, from a mistaken belief that officers should do all that their men do and more, officers carried heavy packs, and many of them, being no more like Hercules than the average Briton, arrived at the end of a long day's march needlessly exhausted, much less able to be sensible and active in reconnoitring and laying out company perimeters, in looking after their men, attending conferences, giving out orders. I was especially grateful for pack-free marching, for I could walk happily for thirty miles but did not have the build for carrying weights.

Another freedom was our abandonment of steel helmets. This was quite common throughout the 14th Army, and with the Japanese too. Steel helmets are heavy and awkward, almost unbearable in the heat of the tropics.

Throughout this time of marching no one in the Battalion saw a Japanese. It was a little puzzling, perhaps a little disturbing. Here we were moving steadily towards the heart of Burma, far south of those areas which had seen the fighting of the last two years. Soon we should be at the Irrawaddy, preparing to cross. It must be that the plans for deceiving the enemy as to the real weight of our advance on this flank had

succeeded. We were on wireless silence. Up north a dummy
IV Corps Headquarters was busy sending out and receiving
streams of signals to and from nobody. The attention of the
press, and of the Japanese, was also up north, deliberately
focused on the divisions advancing to the Irrawaddy above
and below Mandalay. Mandalay seemed the main prize at
which the 14th Army was aimed. The enemy reacted
accordingly. The first crossing of the Irrawaddy, by 19th
Division, had been on 11 January some fifty miles north of
Mandalay, and was followed by nearly a month of heavy
fighting as the Japanese tried to eliminate the bridgeheads.

Yet in our advance far to the south and east we kept expecting
some reaction, for sometimes we heard of small parties of the
enemy who had left villages only twelve hours ahead of our
entry. I do not know what our commanders expected. To us,
who could see the long lines of men and mules, the dust clouds
raised by moving vehicles, who watched the Dakotas roar
round and round to drop our supplies, it was difficult to believe
in secrecy. Perhaps because each day and night we had to be
geared for opposition, just in case, we came to think that
opposition was more probable than it was, and so were the
more uneasy about our free passage. Soldiers are conditioned
to be prepared for the worst. Perhaps we half felt that we might
have to pay in full later for present liberties.

Supply from the air was impressive. It was a familiar miracle
to the veterans of the Battalion. Those near to the open ground
chosen as dropping zone had to keep a sharp watch for free-
dropped goods. Large bags of flour or rice and fodder for the
mules came whistling down with tremendous velocity and
whammed into the earth. None of us wanted to depart life
beneath a bag of flour. There was a story, probably apocryphal,
of a loyal Sikh who did so because he thought it was his duty
to catch the bags. If the pilot was fractionally out on his course,
or the dispatchers early or late to unload, the goods came
crashing among the parties waiting to collect. Most supplies
were too delicate to free-drop. It was fascinating, almost
mesmerising, to watch the bundles tumble from the open door
in the side of the fuselage a few hundred feet above our heads,
then each bundle blossom to its own parachute, and then the

line of chutes sway and drift to earth. Sometimes a parachute did not open, and perhaps a crate of tins or a drum of petrol would burst against the ground like a bomb.

Parachutes were meant to be collected and returned. Many of them were. Some found other uses, chiefly as extra protection at night. Those January nights were chilly, and our single light blankets inadequate. The chutes were also coveted by the Burmese, for whom they provided cotton unobtainable for years. The Burmese 'borrowed' what we missed. We used the chutes as rewards for information.

From a village called Thanatbinzin which we occupied on 29 January I went on my first patrol. As I remember just three of us went: Naik Kamansing of my Intelligence Section, my runner Tulbir and myself. We were out for thirty-two hours. We left in the early morning and got back the evening of the next day, and were on the move for all but five or six hours of that time. We made a wide sweep north-east, then south, then back north-west, entering village after village to ask, with a mixture of signs and polyglot phrases, for news of the Japanese. We were now on the edge of the dry area of central Burma and most of our route was over and between low eroded hills, barren laterite country. Trees, except near villages and rivers, had disappeared. The villages were compact and surrounded by a thick and tall cactus hedge. At sunset the entrances were blocked and we kept away. River beds were generally dry. You could see for miles and be seen for miles. Gone were the familiar mountains and jungles.

I was very aware that a small body of retreating Japanese over the next ridge or in the next village would not have found us tough opposition. We did what we could to protect one another, moving well separated, entering a village one at a time, and so on. But the truth is that in real war, as opposed to practice for it, time and caution are in continual opposition. Paradoxically, it is often safer to move quickly, safer for the main body of troops. Scouts and patrols have another viewpoint. For them every defile, every blind corner, every village and river crossing, is a potential ambush. Because of the ground they have been told to cover, and the speed at which they must keep moving to cover it, the only practical way to

test such danger spots is to trudge through them, alert, well
spaced out, but in fact a living bait. Until the enemy's presence
is strongly suspected, infantry cannot wait to crawl, outflank,
watch patiently through field-glasses. In Burma this was
especially so. Burma was full of country which neither side
occupied, which both sides used from time to time. A fluid
war is a war of patrols. Thirty patrols meet nothing. Negative
evidence is valuable. The thirty-first patrol is unlucky. It loses
a man, two men, three men. Probably someone gets back to
give the news. For the loss of a couple of infantrymen a
hundred square miles of country is found to be temporarily
clear and the only body of enemy has been pinpointed. This is
good arithmetic. But the man on patrol can never rid himself
of the notion that this time he may be the statistic that pin-
points. You need luck as well as skill.

Kamansing, Tulbir and I were lucky. We covered thirty
miles or more but there were no Japanese and none had been
around for days. Another area of General Evans' map could
be marked clear.

It was on this patrol that I first went close to Burmese
pagodas, which are not like those of Japan or China. Every
village seemed to have its pagoda and its *hypoongyi chaung*,
its monastery. In time we discovered that the compound of
the *hypoongyi chaung* generally contained the best houses in the
village, with spacious courtyards and fine shady trees. As well
as the monastery's pagoda, others might crown nearby hillocks
and could be landmarks for miles around, gleaming white
above the trees and against the blue sky. To build pagodas is
to obtain merit; they are to be met everywhere, and often
far from human habitation.

The pagodas of Burma, even the simplest village examples,
were of such a satisfying form—bell-shaped, tapering con-
cavely to a high narrow finial of wrought-iron from which
hung bells and cymbals that tinkled in the lightest breeze—
that they must have pleased even the least sensitive of the
thousands of soldiers who marched past them, rested in their
shade, took cover behind their solid brick plinths. Indeed
they were generally solid throughout, and the shells that hit
them did no more than chip at the surface; few were destroyed.

The richer and larger pagodas might have arched wings each enclosing a figure of Buddha, perhaps gold-plated, impassive, larger than life-size. The spire, too, might be golden, or ringed with beaten iron, glinting in the sun. Round the base at the corners might squat the griffin-like *chinthés*, symbolic guardians. The monks of the monasteries were easy to distinguish by their saffron-coloured robes, but we did not often see them, for we were front-line troops, and where we were was apt to be dangerous for careful civilians. The monks were educated, ran the village schools, and they had a reputation for favouring the Japanese in the early years of the Burma war. By 1945 the Japanese were as much disliked as the British, and no doubt it was now a plague on both your houses.

The day after that patrol (2 February) the Battalion moved back to a position among some sharp hills immediately overlooking Sinthe, and here acquired from the air a second-in-command, a regular from the 7th Gurkhas, Major Watson-Smyth. Sinthe was an insignificant village near the Yaw chaung, a considerable river that flowed into the Irrawaddy forty miles to the south. Sinthe happened to be on the edge of an expanse of flattish paddyfield, and this had been selected as the next forward airfield. Supply drop by parachute may be necessary at times. It is not economical. It is better to land the transport planes on an airfield. Thus Sinthe gained fame and is mentioned in the more detailed official histories. Perhaps this is not a very fair exchange for the furious energy with which we and the divisional engineers and any local labour that could be persuaded to help, and guided by a Forward Airfield Engineer Group, proceeded to level the paddy bunds and fill in the ditches. With bulldozers and spades the job took just a week, and we had an airfield large enough to accept Dakotas and fighters which remained open until 2 April. We felt some pride as the first plane roared in and bounded along the earth runway safely. Soon the noise of aircraft became a trial. I was glad to leave on the next evening. The men of 114 Brigade had taken over the lead, had reached the Irrawaddy, and were meeting strong resistance. It was time for us to catch up.

XIII

PRELUDE TO BATTLE

I

The first sound of gun-fire, distant but unmistakable, came at night. To avoid detection we were marching through the dark, along sandy tracks over a range of low bare hills. In the early hours we began the descent to the Irrawaddy plain. The night had a cool warmth. The sky was open, starlit, and there was a feel of space everywhere. Then came that distant thud, thud, thud thud, sharper than thunder, ominous, exhilarating. The pulse quickened, heads lifted, and for a moment the grind of a long night march was forgotten.

We plodded on, tired, thirsty, straight towards the guns. After a while we could see faint on the horizon the flash of each discharge, like distant lightning. No one knew what was happening. We marched in silence, each within his cocoon of thought. Excitement, fear, curiosity, wonder at being at this place at this time, a sort of gay apprehension: it was possible to feel all these simultaneously, and more. I was marching towards those guns; I, Patrick Davis, the latest in a very long succession of individuals, a present summit of a particular evolution, a piece of matter unimportant in the perspective of millennia, yet all-important to me. To me, without me, the world would not exist. This ancient mystery was as fresh for me as it had ever been for any human who had preceded me. To enter battle was to put the world at risk. To die was to end the world. I was not invulnerable, from the beginning felt naked, soft, an easy target for rending metal. Some of us must die, and end our world. A difficult thought, unbearable really. Better not to think in that direction. As long as I could think, I was alive. If I was dead and could not think, then thoughts about the end of my world would not trouble me. There was some comfort in the word oblivion.

At the hourly halts I lay back on the warm night earth and watched the stars, stared into the immensities of space, aware of the insignificance of our crawl across the surface of this spinning planet. But the guns would not let the mind drift for long through the galaxies. Oblivion, that was bearable. It was the crossing to it that disturbed. Some of us would die in one blinding flash—so be it. Some would die slowly, in agony—not so good. Some of us would be mangled, and live—not good at all.

And there were mental wounds. There seemed no way of guarding against them. I had read of shell-shock and battle fatigue, but did not understand them. At Kohima I had come gradually to realise, from remarks and hints let slip, that at least two of my companions had not weathered well after the recent fighting. How would I bear up? Most people can control their fear for short periods. But the future would go on and on. Burma was a fringe affair for the Japanese, as for the Allies; a skin ulcer, not a cancer. The nearer we got to Japan, the tougher would be the resistance. The Japanese armies in Asia had scarcely begun to fight. There was river after river, mountain range after mountain range; Malaya, Siam, Sumatra, Java, Borneo, Indo-China, China itself, where one-third of the Japanese Army was deployed, endless vistas of rugged hills, jungles, plains, endless, endless. . . .

We marched on, over the plain now, the hills behind us, the Irrawaddy, unseen but potent, a few miles ahead. Step succeeded step automatically, ten minutes halt in every hour, the track too often of yielding sand, not often enough of sandstone. And at the end of the track lay Myitche, where hidden among the trees the bulk of our Division was gathering for the crossing of the river: infantry, engineers, tanks, rafts for the tanks, assault boats for the infantry, artillery, signals, mules, medical units, supply groups; men and animals and material moving in every night over the barren hinterland to concentrate briefly like a pent volcano, and then to erupt over the water to the unknown far bank, there to spread in widening arcs, and to send forth angry tentacles of fire to overwhelm our enemy. I hoped it would be like that. It had to be like that.

We marched on and on until the fear of fear was drowned

by fatigue. And before daylight the guns stopped and we reached Myitche. We had covered twenty-six miles. I remember Myitche best for the lemons we found in an orchard.

2

The Madrassi engineer, his black face glistening with sweat beneath a sagging bush-hat, heaved on the starting string of the outboard motor. Again he heaved. The flimsy assault boat shuddered, gathered way. We were off, other boats ahead, more filling up behind, off across the Irrawaddy. I trailed a hand in it, grey-brown water flowing swiftly among shifting sandbanks, a mile wide under a blue sky. This river was the aorta of Burma, rising far to the north in the wild mountain country of the China border, flowing south through gorge and valley into central Burma, past Mandalay, still in Japanese hands, past the other bridgeheads above us, past me now and on through this dry belt to the swamps of its own delta and the Indian Ocean. It was a great river, thirteen hundred miles of it. For months it had been a focus to our thoughts. It was a natural and formidable defence. On the other side was a reasonable road and rail system to give our enemy the advantage in quick concentration. On our side were long, winding tracks leading back over five hundred miles through jungle and over mountains to Dimapur, the railhead, itself a distant outpost of India. To cross the Irrawaddy was an act of faith. We had to believe that our aeroplanes could keep us armed and fed. We had to believe that the Japanese armies were so disorganised, their generals so misled as to our intentions, that we could cut through to Rangoon before the monsoon in May. When the rains came tracks would be washed out, aeroplanes unable to fly with such regularity or precision, and without Rangoon and its port we would be in trouble. We might have to withdraw, back across the Irrawaddy, back to Tamu, back perhaps to Imphal. There was no easy halt line in the middle.

We of the 4/8th Gurkhas had come all that weary way from Kohima without firing a shot. It was remarkable, and unexpected. Now, on the fourteenth afternoon of February, as we chugged over the water, everything was still peaceful.

We were part of the longest opposed river crossing of the war, one that made military history, and for us it could have been a jaunt at Margate. If there had not been the chance of air attack I should have been entirely relaxed, with difficulty recalling that on this innocent stretch, in boats like this, men of the South Lancs had died only that morning, threshing in agony, calling out, drowning. They had been machine-gunned from those cliffs we too were now approaching. Slow to start from the Myitche shore, dawn had come while they were still on the water.

Later I had watched our tanks and artillery from among the palm trees put down a barrage of fire on those cliffs, and aircraft dive-bomb the re-entrants, creating a hideous cacophony, as the 4/15th Punjabs of 33 Brigade tried again and found no one there. The Japanese, a patrol that had arrived only the day before, so the Burmese told us, had retreated into some catacombs in a hill overlooking Nyaungu, and there they remained for ever, since our sappers blew in the entrance. Now a column of black smoke was the only visible irregularity; it dwarfed the spires of Nyaungu's pagodas.

My fingers dribbled in the water and the sun was hot on the face. Here men had died a few hours back, countrymen of mine, two company commanders and a lot of other ranks. I discovered that I was not much moved by this. A soldier does not endure the pain of other units unless he knows them well, for they are almost as remote from him as are the enemy, sometimes more so. I was simply glad that I had not been on the river at that time.

My boat grounded on a narrow sand beach. We disembarked quickly, climbed the cliffs by an eroded gully. It was good to be out of the boats. Infantry are not at ease when they cannot spread. And there was a feel of adventure about our advance inland. We were boys trespassing on forbidden ground; someone soon must find out and get cross with us. Surely soon we must meet our enemy.*

* Unknown to our commanders we had crossed at the precise boundary between two Japanese armies, always a point of weakness. Together with some admirable and elaborate deception, this meant that we had little opposition for the first few dangerous days.

3

It was a gently undulating land, parched and barren, scattered
with a few small compact villages where tamarinds and toddy
palms gave shade, and wells water. Quite early the day
developed a white heat, compounded of a glare reflected from
the whitened sand that sent all of us trudging with screwed-up
eyes, and a vibrating sky drained of its blue. Thorns and cacti
grew profusely in places, were used as hedges between the
baked fields. The cacti were of many varieties, with fantastic
shapes; here and there red flowers lit the edge of some sculp-
tured and fleshy leaf, a knob of brightness in a landscape that
was mostly yellow-brown, brown and browny green. The
cacti were impenetrable, but they gave a little shade.

Into this desert we sent our patrols. For day after day we
sent them, and they met no enemy. To our right, nearer to
the Irrawaddy, both the other battalions of our Brigade had
been in action. The 1/11th Sikhs had been fighting with
particular élan around Pagan, defeating parties of Japanese
hurrying north. And the K.O.S.B.s had got into an unpleasant
battle near Monatkon, losing nine officers and sixty-seven
men (Map 2, page 133). We did not want this, but we needed
a battle, a successful one. For about six weeks we had been
on the move, and for the last four had expected almost daily
that we might bump the enemy. The peak of anticipation
could pass, morale could sag, and this would be dangerous.

But our first casualties were not by the enemy's hand. One
hot midday at Battalion Headquarters a series of shots sent
the heart thumping; a couple of bullets whined overhead. I
happened to be with the Colonel, standing near the top of a
slight ridge. My inclination was to lie flat. I assumed the shots
to be directed at us by some infiltrating Japanese. The Colonel,
by some instinctive process, divined otherwise. He strode over
the ridge, I following nervously, and towards a crowd of men
a hundred yards off. Our approach scattered them to their
duties and revealed two still figures. One was Jimmy Henderson, the Mortar Officer, and the other a Gurkha naik. The
Doc was already bending over them. Both were dead.

It seems to have happened this way. Each evening an officer of Battalion Headquarters or of H.Q. Company was on duty, responsible for checking that the various collections of specialists 'stood-to' in the proper manner on their sectors of the perimeter and afterwards obeyed the regulations about lights, silence, passwords, anti-malarial precautions, and so on. The previous night Jimmy had discovered this naik smoking in a trench. In his impetuous way Jimmy had roundly abused the man, witnessed by several riflemen, and had put him on a charge. Next morning the case came before the H.Q. Company Commander. Jimmy gave his evidence and started to march off. The naik shot him in the back, then fired two warning shots over the heads of the bystanders, reversed his rifle and shot himself.

There should have been no trouble. The man had been caught and had to be punished. The trouble came perhaps through the conjunction of a Gurkha and an officer both with unstable temperaments. Jimmy had used strong words. The naik felt himself to have been impossibly shamed in front of his juniors, a trust broken. He had the night to brood upon it. Jimmy's own men were used to him, accepted his language stoically, knowing that with the reverse of the coin they gained more care and love from him than many of us were capable of. This naik was not Jimmy's man.

It was sad that the first casualties had come in this way. They were buried that afternoon, a silent gloomy business: no bugles, no ritual farewell. As Intelligence Officer I had to record the position of the graves with map reference and sketch. And for the rest of the war we had no Mortar Officer. Havildar Prembahadur did the job, and did it well, to die himself in an ambush in Java next year.

Jimmy's was the first dead body I had seen. The sight of the flesh, recently so alive, still warm, yet now empty, neutral, silent, deprived for ever of further communion with us, the living, might have been traumatic. It was not. I accepted the revised situation within minutes and by evening it was almost as if Lieutenant James Henderson had never been.

Nor did this incident shake my faith in Gurkhas, though the killing of a British officer by a Gurkha might have been

K

expected to awaken buried fears. It was as if we all understood this to be a unique and unrepresentative happening, a
thrust of fate like a meteor or thunderbolt, unlikely to fall
twice on the same spot.*

4

It was Scotty Gilmore who saw what must have been one of
the great sights of the Burma war. To the south-east of our
position and two miles off a long, bare and broken ridge rose
abruptly seven hundred feet out of the plains. From the other
bank we had studied this ridge with distaste, for it dominated
the country for miles. But it was unoccupied, and Scotty and
a platoon climbed to the top and sat for several days round
a pagoda on the first sharp peak. From here one morning
they watched a vast concourse of tanks, artillery, armoured
cars, bren-carriers and lorried infantry deploy over the plain
and move east. Here at last the 14th Army was about to
exploit its superior mobility, fire-power and armour. We had
made the bridgehead. Now we held it while 17th Division
and 255 Tank Brigade churned across the eighty miles of
open country for Meiktila. On their prowess rested all our fates.
    Another great sight, not dependent on war, was the city
of Pagan, where the 1/11th Sikhs had been fighting. Pagan was
the ancient capital of Burma, destroyed by Kublai Khan,
deserted now even in peace. It was supposed to contain the
ruins of five thousand pagodas, which I wanted to explore.
Once or twice I glimpsed the spires. But the geography of
our fighting took me further and further away, and I never
saw them close.
    First we moved south to a line of villages west of Scotty's
ridge. On 24 February I took a platoon of D Company to
Kanbauk, a village where enemy had been reported. We went
at night in a long encircling sweep to approach from the

---

* It almost did. In Bangkok, soon after the war, for very similar reasons,
a Gurkha escaped from the guard-room one night and attacked an officer
in the room next to mine. The latter's life was probably saved by his
mosquito net, which entangled the kukri and blunted the force of the only
blow the man delivered before the alarm was raised.

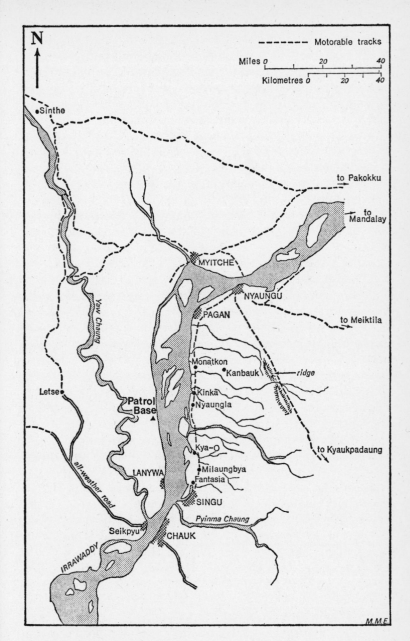

Map 2 Sinthe to Chauk

south, while another platoon under Bob Findlay came direct
to the northern edge to catch anyone we might drive out. To
spread wide in the dark means loss of control. People shoot
one another. We moved in single file. Close to the fringe of
Kanbauk I told most of the men to take up a covering position
and stay put. I and two others spent a couple of hours like
cats along the paths and among the houses, looking for someone
to attack.

It was nervous work. At night you must get very close to
places before you can know they are unoccupied. A rat or a
chicken moving in the dry undergrowth of a hedge can stop
one dead, heart thumping, ears and eyes strained. Bushes
take on strange shapes. They seem to move. Every darker
shadow menaces, could be the mouth of a bunker. There is a
background fear of mines, trip-wires, booby-traps. Our creeping revealed nothing. Before dawn I went back and brought
the men through to the protection of the earth banks of a large
water tank, in case we had missed any Japanese and had to
defend ourselves. But there was no one in Kanbauk. Perhaps
there never had been. The place had been shelled, had partly
burned, and was deserted.

This patrol set a pattern for me. It was the first on which
I went out with a complete platoon from one of the four
rifle companies. As the weeks passed I did this repeatedly,
and must have commanded at one time or another for these
brief expeditions almost every man in the Battalion.

Battalion Headquarters came into Kanbauk and that night,
the 25th, a fighting patrol to the village of Kinka met the
Japanese. Kinka was on the dry-weather road that bordered
the Irrawaddy south from our bridgehead towards the oilfields town of Chauk, twelve miles away. It was on or near
this river road that all the Brigade's fighting had taken place.
Bob Findlay took an infantry platoon and pioneers some four
miles across the Brigade front to reach the village. They
reeled out telephone line as they went. This time the reports
of Japanese in occupation were true. At 2 a.m. Bob came up
on the line to say that his patrols had pinpointed the Japanese
positions, and that he was going to attack the northern half
of the village. At Battalion Headquarters, waiting in sleepy

suspense, we heard nothing more till dawn, when the men walked in. They had fought a successful action, killing eleven of the enemy, blowing up bunkers, and escaping with no worse than several lightly wounded by grenade splinters as they retired. Bob Findlay was one of these, with five splinters in his right arm and back. Protesting, he was immediately flown out to a hospital in India. The telephone had been left hidden in a chaung (stream or river) while they attacked, and they had been forced to retire by another route. The two operators walked in much later.

This little fight finally reblooded the Battalion, and was exactly the right kind of fight—short and victorious. I wished that it had not deprived us of Bob, and for quite selfish reasons. He and I and Scotty were the three 'spare' officers available for patrols. Everyone else had jobs they could not easily leave. Bill Blenkin was now the Battalion's liaison officer at Brigade Headquarters. His successor as transport officer could not abandon his vehicles. Tommy Login's specialist knowledge of signals bound him night and day to wireless sets and drums of telephone cable. Company commanders had to command their companies. Bob's departure left just Scotty and me. He did not return until May and no one new joined us until the end of April.

5

Two days later the Battalion moved to Kinka. The village was now burned out by air strikes: splintered tree trunks blocking paths, charred timbers at all angles, twisted sheets of corrugated iron, a slim pagoda with red-brick patches like blood where the white plaster had been blown off, and everywhere the smell of destruction that we were to live with for months. This smell was a pungent mixture of burned things and putrifying flesh. The flesh generally belonged to cows, that quickly swelled to twice life-size and then burst, to become caves for maggots. There were also dead chickens, ducks, dogs, and occasionally a human body, perhaps a Burmese villager who had not escaped in time. The smell lingered indefinitely in this dry weather, unwashed by cleansing rain.

The wastage of life and property was sickening, even to us rough soldiery on whose behalf it took place. A few shots from a village, or a report from someone that Japanese had been seen in one (perhaps only a patrol passing through two days previously) was often sufficient for the place to be shelled or bombed. The ordinary houses of a Burmese village were made of bamboo matting or thin planking upon a wooden frame, with roofs of palmleaf thatch or matting, all of it tinder-dry. A few shells would set one or two houses burning fiercely. Villages were usually compact, with house compounds divided from one another by bamboo, cacti, or by wooden paling, also highly inflammable in the hot weather. A fire spread quickly until most of the village burned with a great crackling and loud reports like rifle shots from exploding bamboo. Thick columns of black smoke tainted the sky. The houses were raised two or three feet on stilts, and the space below was used for the storage of grain, tools and other property, and sometimes for penning smaller livestock (and by the Japanese for their bunkers). All this was lost as the burning houses collapsed. A house could be rebuilt, but food and animals could not be so easily replaced.

Kinka, though burned, was a good spot. We parked ourselves north and south. A wide clean side-channel of the Irrawaddy flowed below the bank by the battalion area. This was a rare treat, for the dry-weather course of Burmese rivers was often far from the outer banks. Sitting under the trees outside our Mess building we could see several miles of blue water stretching south into enemy-held land. The river was heaven. Since leaving Sinthe on 11 February we had been unable to bathe, or wash clothes. The odd well in our various positions had produced barely sufficient water for drinking. The weather was getting really hot, and sixteen days of slogging around central Burma in February without washing is enough. Everyone who could was in the water for as long as possible.

I was at Kinka for three days. Many stayed less. B Company moved forward two miles, and from B Company patrols went further south and east. With one of them Scotty was ambushed, but survived, and could not tell the Colonel exactly where he had been. Then Scotty had a thought. The naik from the Burma Intelligence Corps who accompanied him might be better with a map. 'Gee, Colonel, ask the B.I.C. naik. He's a good guy. He'll know.'

We had become the right forward battalion of the Brigade and bridgehead, astride the only motorable road in that sector. A few of us now had actually seen a Japanese. They existed somewhere a little way ahead. They would think we might wish to capture Chauk, the first considerable town downstream. We must expect them to attack us, to make continued efforts to dislodge the bridgehead or to contain its expansion. It was fourteen days since the first crossing of the river; time enough for them to have reorganised, time to bring up reinforcements, and to attempt to reverse the position which we had established by invading central Burma at a point where they had not expected us.

On our sector these elusive and formidable people seemed to be concentrating some six miles from Kinka in a village with the musical name of Milaungbya (*Milongbia*). Thither as if by magnets we all were soon drawn.

XIV

MILAUNGBYA

I

There's only one principle of war and that's this. Hit the other fellow, as quick as you can, and as hard as you can, where it hurts him most, when he ain't lookin!
General Slim quoting a Sergeant-Major in *Defeat into Victory.*

From six hundred yards everything was diminished but clear. Through field-glasses I could see individual men with disturbing clarity. Before us the ground sloped gently down for five hundred yards to the Yaw Chaung, which was dry, a miniature rift valley eight feet or more below the ground. On the far bank the battle had begun. C Company was attacking. They had come from the east, to our left front, through scattered scrub and palm trees. The Japanese were in the cover of a copse of palms ahead of us. We could not see them. The men I could see belonged to the right-hand platoon of C Company. The rest were beyond our sight, and with them Peter Myers. The men advanced parallel to the chaung in short individual rushes, kneeling to fire, racing to the bole of the next tree, occasionally lying flat. Bayonets glinted. One man fell and did not move. When they got into the copse the platoon of medium machine-guns (M.M.G.s) of the Frontier Force Rifles, in position near us to the right, ceased firing into it. The noise from those guns had deafened us, making the battle a silent film. Now we could hear, but no longer see. Smoke and vegetation obscured the actors. There were shouts, there was the sharp roar of exploding grenades and the crack of rifles, all muted by distance. Occasionally a bullet sang our way. I was glad to be watching from this safe vantage, yet

down there were men I knew and it seemed wrong not to be
helping.

Soon it was over. I had seen, as from a grandstand, a Gurkha
company in a formal attack, our first of this campaign. They
counted eleven dead Japanese. The rest of the enemy, about
a platoon, retreated to the village of Milaungbya, a quarter
of a mile to the south. We had captured what came to be
known as Bastion. It was the 2nd of March.

As we were to be occupied in the Milaungbya area for
nearly a month, a description may help the reader to follow
the narrative. The country along the east bank of the Irrawaddy here is open. The river flows from north to south, and
at intervals is joined by sandy chaungs, with low ridges between.
At this season the chaungs are dry. The area near the river is
studded with small villages and palm-tree copses, roughly a
village to every square mile. The villages are generally compact, surrounded by a protective cactus hedge. Each has its
pagoda, gleaming white through the trees. And there are wells.
For us the wells were vital: at this point the dry-weather
course of the Irrawaddy sweeps westward, leaving a cultivated
flood plain a mile wide between the bank and the water.
Once more water was scarce.

The area of Milaungbya village can be divided into four
sectors, all lying between the Pagan–Chauk road and the true
cliff bank of the river. The sketch map on page 140 may help
to form a picture. From north to south, from friend to foe,
there was first the outlying copse of palm trees and a low
ridge, between the Yaw and the Mu Chaungs, which C
Company had just captured. We called this Bastion. Some
250 yards south across the Mu Chaung was the village of
Milaungbya North into which the enemy had withdrawn, and
which we called Base. It was about two hundred yards square
with its western edge close to the cliffs. South of Base across
another chaung was a similar area, smaller, containing two
prominent pagodas and a few houses. With our customary
inventiveness this was called Pagodas. Finally, two hundred
and fifty yards south of Pagodas was the village of Milaungbya
South, two hundred and fifty yards square, known as Bottom.

On the other side of the road, east of it by three hundred

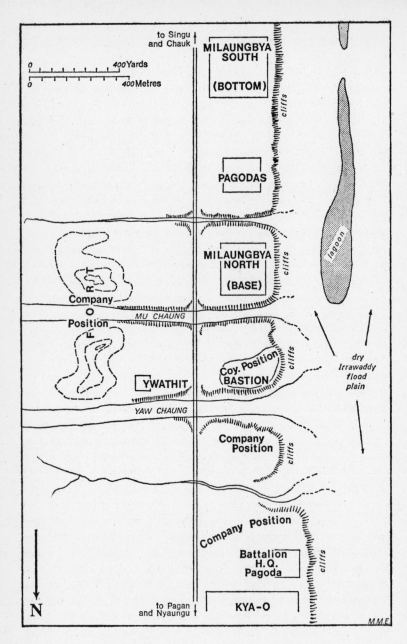

Map 3 The Milaungbyas

yards, in the open country, was a complex of low ridges that
overlooked the Milaungbya area and commanded both C
Company in Bastion and the Japanese in Base and Pagodas.
It was the key position for both sides. Both sides realised this
at much the same time.

On 4 March B Company was called up to occupy the area
and arrived on it soon after midday. Denis Sheil-Small had
his platoons in temporary positions and was in the middle of
his detailed recce when a large body of Japanese, perhaps
three hundred men, streamed out from the close cover of
Bottom and Pagodas, crossed the road, and made for Denis
and his men. The high ground gave B Company the advantage
of height, but little cover from view. It was quite barren.
75 mm guns and mortars opened up from Bottom, and
machine-gun fire from the flanks of the attack.

All this made a powerful noise. Battalion HQ, the operational
part of it, raced forward to our observation point of two days
before, now within A and D Companies' perimeter. Indeed
the Colonel had not long been returned from accompanying
Denis to his position. Again we could see part of the battle,
though more distantly. This was a different affair. It is one
thing to be attacked expectant, dug in, wired, with defensive
fire on call, reserve ammunition at hand, dressed for the part.
It is another to be caught *en negligé* in the open and by superior
forces. From the noise and the close approach of the Japanese,
it looked to be hot work. The Colonel asked for artillery fire
on Milaungbya and on the open ground between the village
and B Company. The gunners had to calculate from map
reference, for there were no observers with Denis, there was
no telephone line, and his wireless remained silent.

After perhaps fifteen minutes the Colonel turned and told
me to get into B Company's perimeter fast and to find out
what was happening and what might be wanted. Now I was
caught. From spectator I was turned actor. I took my runner
Tulbir and set off, with an outward confidence that was all
a mask. I did not like this first encounter with the sudden
confusions of war. We moved in a shallow arc to approach
the ridge from the north. There did not seem to be Japanese
on this side yet. From the high ground we could see far ahead,

but could ourselves be seen. In the Yaw Chaung we could not see nor be seen and I felt blind, trapped. It was extraordinarily hot. Sweat ran down me in a dozen simultaneous rivulets. Up and over another low ridge, watching sharply, and so safely to the Mu Chaung on either bank of which B Company was deployed.

I found Denis, hot but unharmed, in the chaung itself, whose south bank, seven or eight feet high, provided shelter from shells and bullets. It was Denis's first battle. The initial anarchic fury was over. He was taking stock. He showed me his wireless, wrecked by a mortar bomb in the early minutes of the battle. Against the bank in a narrow strip of shade were several of his men who had been seriously wounded, bloody, roughly bandaged, shocked. Some of them, he told me, had been hit by our own shells.

There is little you can say to a man who may be maimed for life when you are not. '*Kasto chha?* How are you?' '*Tik chha, Sahib*. I'm all right.' He is not all right, but something has to be said. The banal words perhaps convey the real concern, and an understanding of the concern.

In the chaung it was hotter than anywhere. The soft sand reflected the heat. There was no breeze. An occasional shell, the crack of a bullet close above, inhibited careless exposure, kept the nerves taut. At such moments in a battle you do not know whether you are in a pause, or have seen the end of the business. Denis was worried about ammunition. His men had started with what they carried, and now had fired much of that. Especially he wanted grenades. He was also concerned with his communications. The Japanese were in the small hamlet of Ywathit, not yet mentioned. From the map it can be seen that this was two hundred yards north-west of B Company, between it and the rest of the Battalion. The second of two attacks had come in from that direction. My own circular route had taken me clear of the place. From it the Japanese might attack again at any time. Left there they would be a perpetual threat. They would have to be removed.

I did not stay more than ten minutes. Denis was pre-occupied re-allocating men and ammunition. My job was to get back with a report. And I was glad to be gone before I

was caught in another attack, and while the route was still
clear. I walked back over the exposed ridges more blithely
than I walked out. As I went a rush of shells fell on Ywathit.
I learned later that these had been ordered by Tommy Login.
He and a line party of signallers had been plodding towards
B Company on a more direct route than mine, reeling out
telephone wire behind them, when they had spotted the Japs
in the village.

Tommy was always on this kind of mission. Signals were
so vital and needed such motherly care to keep them working,
that I seem to see him perpetually on the move, supervising
the installation of new line, tracing breaks across heaven
knows what isolated bit of countryside, tinkering with temperamental wireless sets in the middle of the night, persuading
company commanders and others far his senior that they must
observe certain rules if they wanted certain results.

Now his shells poured into Ywathit with sudden and frightful violence. Crrump, crrump, crrump. No more attacks came
from the village and when A Company assaulted later that
afternoon the remaining Japanese legged it back to their homes
in Milaungbya. So B Company's casualties were rescued from
the hot river bed, ammunition was replenished, and the men
dug themselves underground at record speed. They were
joined by Mike Tidswell's A Company, by a platoon of
M.M.G.s and an artillery forward observation group, and
during the next week transformed the area into such a warren
of interlocking posts that the position was code-named Fort.

As for me, I had been under fire at last, after a fashion.
Nothing had been directed at me personally. The few bullets
that had shot well above my head while I was with B Company
had been aimed at others. The possibility of another attack
had not materialised. My introduction to battle was being conducted with great gentleness. I thought this was a good thing.

The Colonel seized on this battle, which had been watched
by our Brigadier Crowther, to put in for a number of decorations. Awards for gallantry are generally taken to be splendid
for the morale of a unit, and uplifting for the individual or
his next-of-kin. On the whole this is probably true. In my
own experience no one got a decoration who had not earned

it, though there were others who deserved and did not receive. There are reasons for this. Whatever a man does has to be observed by senior N.C.O.s or officers, and those N.C.O.s or officers must survive the battle to tell the Colonel. Then decorations are nearly always given more generously in victory than in defeat, and especially if the victory comes after defeat. Third, there was reputed to be some form of loose rationing: if your battalion's battle was the only major engagement in the Division that month everything you asked for might be given; but if the battle was one of thirty, your requests might get sadly pruned. Fourth, something depended on how well your Colonel was regarded by his Brigadier, and he by his General: extreme bravery under a poorly regarded C.O. in a battalion with a bad record stood less chance of recognition than the same act under a well-regarded C.O. in a battalion with a fine reputation. Fifth, there is some skill in writing citations and on deciding how many to send. The Commander who shouts too loudly and too frequently is discounted and his real winners may fail. If he does not shout loudly enough, he makes no impact amongst the other citations that have accumulated at Divisional and Army Headquarters.

The Japanese, I believe, awarded no decorations for gallantry, holding that all their soldiers would die for their Emperor with equal courage. Each was given a campaign medal for being in a certain place at a certain time, and was by that fact a hero. There is much to be said for this arrangement, which avoids the risk of jealousy and of bitterness among those who miss out under the awards system.

Be that as it may, Walter Walker soon had his evidence and his citations, and most of them were accepted. Denis got an M.C.; so did the commander of his No. 6 Platoon, Jemadar Jitbahadur. Denis, apart from conducting his battle with considerable flair, had rescued a dangerously wounded man under heavy fire. Jitbahadur's platoon had borne the first brunt of the attack, and the Jemadar had personally given them covering fire with a bren-gun while they retired from the exposed position in which the unexpected opening of the battle had found them. A section commander received an I.D.S.M. (Indian Distinguished Service Medal) and another an M.M. (Military Medal). Two riflemen were awarded Gallantry Certificates. These were generally a poor consolation prize for the fact that the M.M. for which a man had been recommended was not to be granted. A man cannot wear a certificate, and it is the wearing of the medal ribbon that counts.

The next fight of importance was on 8 March, four days later. Patrols had established the Japanese positions in the Milaungbyas. There was evidence of a build-up for a counter-attack on the Battalion and the bridgehead we protected which the Colonel wanted to forestall. He decided to clear the entire area of Base, Pagodas and Bottom. The attack was to be by D Company and a squadron of tanks of 116 Regiment, R.A.C. (the Gordons). It was rehearsed on a sand-model—infantry and tank crews together. There was no shortage of sand.

I had no direct part in this battle and will simply say that it was successful. The Milaungbyas were cleared. Our casualties were light and those of the enemy quite heavy. Late in the afternoon I accompanied the Colonel on a quick post-battle tour of the field. Shattered trees and blasted bunkers displayed the powers of the 75 mm tank guns. The smell of cordite and of burning could still catch at the throat. I saw for the first time the litter of an abandoned position: empty cartridge cases, clips of ammunition, water bottles, mess-tins, torn and bloody bandages, the distinctive Japanese forage caps, trailing puttees, broken rifles, leather belts and grenade pouches, a helmet with a jagged hole and a scattered pile of canvas haversacks, and everywhere and always dust and flies and paper—paper currency, innumerable postcards, paybooks, operation orders, diaries, lavatory paper, scraps of paper blowing in the wind and covered with the beautiful Japanese lettering.

There was seldom anything worth looting. By 1945 neither Japanese rations nor equipment were worth having. Perhaps they never had been. By comparison with the stories we heard of our troops in North Africa and Italy, who every third day liberated cellars of wine and dumps of tinned cherries, olives and smoked salmon, we were again the poor relations.

As I followed the Colonel through our particular desolation I looked about nervously. I was primed with stories of Japanese

shamming death. No one else seemed concerned. I saw my
first dead Japanese and was moved only by curiosity. Their
values seemed so remote from mine that I could not comprehend them as fully paid-up members of the human race; and
whatever they were in private, in public they were trying to
kill my friends. I saw my first Gurkha killed in action. He was
tied to a stretcher on an ambulance jeep, bouncing slowly
along a rough track between the palm trees, with his trousers
torn away and his genitals exposed. Our Gurkhas were so
self-conscious about nudity before officers that automatically
I looked away. But he did not care. He was out of it. And if his
spirit saw me it would have laughed for an hour at fooling me so.

D Company Commander was Geoffrey Bull, the man who had
joined at Kohima from the Indian cavalry. I did not like him, but
after this battle did not doubt his courage, of which further proofs
came later. The tank crews, who were in the best position to see,
insisted that he should be put in for a decoration. He got an
M.C., the third of our four company commanders to do so.

After the battle we returned to the starting positions. The
object had been to kill Japanese. Protection of the Nyaungu
bridgehead was still our role and further dispersion outwards
simply lengthened the arc of the perimeter.

So the Japanese came back into the Milaungbyas, no doubt
hesitating and puzzled at first. They formed the habit of shelling
our positions with 75 mm guns from Bottom and with 105 mm
guns from Singu. This they did morning and evening with
between fifty and a hundred shells. Most of the shells fell on our
forward positions, but occasionally a series was directed on to
Battalion Headquarters, where the pagoda was a landmark.

I hated the shelling. With the larger and more distant
105 mm guns there was a lag between the sound of the discharge in Singu and the wail of the approaching shell. We sat
near our trenches and dropped inside if one seemed to be
coming close. They were formidable, but somehow elderly,
not totally alarming. With the 75 mm shells from Bottom,
however, the sound of discharge and explosion were practically
simultaneous. When the Japanese started with these you could
only fall flat as the bloody things shattered close by, and
anchor your stampeding heart.

Shelling caused few casualties. To troops well dug in it
seldom does unless concentrated at barrage scale on a small
area. But it did wear at the nerves. There was the natural fear
of the danger, and then the exploding shell makes a hellish
noise, battering and bludgeoning at the senses, slowly eroding
their capacity to give a man a balanced account of his life.

Our cook for the officers' mess, an Indian, was wounded
by a shell that exploded on the pagoda. This was a shrewd
blow at our morale, and a shame, for a non-combatant ought
not to be hit. He received a splinter in his backside and set
up an almighty racket about it. We thought he was dying
until some ironic comments from the Doc reassured us into
callousness. He returned a month or so later. Another shell
demolished Watson-Smyth's bunker, not far from mine, the
direct hit which you tell yourself is a million to one against.
At the time he was not in occupation.

My post was behind a stout three-foot wall that surrounded
the pagoda area. I was to the north of the pagoda, on the side
away from the enemy (and close to the village graveyard). As
the days went by my orderly Nandalal and some of the Intelligence Section transformed what had been a simple trench into a
stout bunker, with a thick roof of palm-tree logs and earth,
certainly splinter proof. Only that freak direct hit could have
harmed me. But I did not like sitting in the bunker. It was like a
tomb. The earth smelt damp. The bursting shells dislodged
crumbs and little lumps that fell into the hair and down one's
neck. Insects congregated. I went inside only when the shelling
was persistently close, and always slept in the open beside it.

The heat grew intense. March and April are the hottest
months. Temperatures up to 105 degrees in the shade were
normal. The men in Fort suffered most, for they were without
natural shade. Fortunately the nights were cool. We had a
water lorry, rotund, like a vast boiler on wheels, that trundled
its way to each company in turn, trailing dust that drew
enemy shells, and emitting complicated slurping sounds as it
bounced and tilted over the rough ground. We expected that
one day it would be hit, and would perhaps arrive inside

somebody's perimeter with a dozen water spouts gushing
from it. But it never was. For the forward companies water
had to be rationed. They had enough for survival, never
enough for comfort. At Battalion Headquarters we were more
fortunate, and were able to bathe regularly.

The dust which I have mentioned was a menace to travellers.
Towards Singu the ground rose in a series of low ridges to
culminate in the hills around Chauk. The Japanese could
overlook us and the road to our rear. For several hundred
yards on each crest every vehicle with its attendant corona of
dust was an undisguisable target. It is not easy to hit a moving
truck with artillery fire. But the Japanese amused themselves by
trying. They had the ranges worked out, and could get close.
Inside a truck or jeep an approaching shell cannot be heard
above the noise of the engine; all the time one anticipates the
final explosion. We evolved our own tracks to the forward companies, using hollows, slight valleys, the lee sides of chaungs,
so that exposure was minimal. Ignorant visitors trembled.

Dust was not merely dangerous, it was our intimate companion, shrouding us and our vehicles on any journey, always in
our clothes, often in our throats and eyes and lungs; almost,
it seemed, a constituent element of the air we breathed. Only
a bathe in the river freed us of it entirely for a short interval,
and river bathes were rare.

After D Company's battle on 8 March there were no major
fights for ten days. It was a period of intensive patrolling,
broken only by an oddly half-hearted night attack by the
Japanese on Fort, which left thirty-two bodies near the wire
next morning and a platoon of live Japs in Ywathit. The
Japanese soldiers we faced at this time were not first-class
troops. They belonged to 72 Independent Mixed Brigade, a
scratch force gathered from here and there and rushed to
Chauk and Singu with orders to drive in our bridgehead. They
could kill some of us individually, and could cause us much
discomfort, but they had no hope of dislodging us. We did
not fully realise this. Moreover reinforcements could arrive
at any time, and did. But they too were not highly trained
infantry units. Like a desperately keen but inexperienced
football team, they rushed at us piecemeal, hitting out wildly,

alternately pugnacious, then puzzled and panic-stricken when hit in return. Thus our battles with them resulted in dispro-portionate casualties. On this occasion one section of seven or eight Gurkhas went to investigate the movements in Ywathit, and for the loss of one man shot dead, hunted out and dis-lodged the platoon, killing eleven.

I have reason to recall that night. Soon after dark I had left the Fort perimeter with a dozen men of B Company and a section of D Force. D Force consisted of men armed with fire-works, explosives and a variety of gadgets with which they could simulate anything from a river-crossing to a battalion attack. We were going round to the back of Singu to look for Japanese positions and draw fire from them by making noises. We left Fort on the eastern face and moved up the Mu Chaung. After 150 yards we climbed on to the open plain and set off south-east for some low hills a mile off. There was no moon but the stars were bright and gave us enough light. We had scarcely got going, spaced well apart in a long line, with me at the head reading a compass, when the Japanese started the first of their attacks.

I knew what might happen as soon as the crackle of bullets and the shouting announced that Japs were present. Every perimeter had defensive fire tasks registered by the guns to the rear, and numbered. These were areas in which the enemy were likely to congregate during an attack, perhaps guided there by the shape of the land or the obstacles placed for that purpose by us. At night you had merely to whisper a number into the phone and seconds later a storm of shells would descend. I knew we were close to one of Fort's fire areas. I began to move away fast. The line of men behind me trailed beyond sight. Then I heard the sharp multiple crack, crack of a battery of 25-pounders firing, a reassuring sound normally, now most disturbing, and seconds later downright terrifying. The shells came at us through the dark with a great roaring shriek. We fell flat. They exploded fifty yards to the right. Bits of metal thudded into the earth about us. We got up and ran. Another batch came at us. Again we fell. They exploded further away. Again we ran. By the time I felt out of danger only four men were still with me. The rest were spread some-where on this wide dark plain and I would never find them.

We waited, while hearts quietened and the breath came more easily. There was no sign of another soul. I was not going back near Fort. Battles at night sound twice as noisy and around Fort now there was a manic row: machine-guns hammering, grenades and mortar bombs exploding with great flashes, and those salvos of 25-pounder shells still searching the area beyond the wire. Anyone moving back there, if not killed by our shells and bullets, or overrun by the attacking Japanese, risked being shot by the rest of my patrol, who must be scattered around in a highly nervous state.

Away from the Irrawaddy and the defended perimeters men could move over the plain at night with some freedom. I decided that I and my four men had better visit Singu. I could not go back to the Colonel in the morning without attempting something. We would turn ourselves into a recce patrol and see what we could see.

We trudged to the ridge ahead and moved into the broken hills behind and worked our way in a shallow circle round Milaungbya and Singu to the Pyinma Chaung, steering as much by the stars as by my compass. We passed several tracks and a couple of hamlets, but disturbed no one. The Pyinma Chaung runs into the Irrawaddy between Singu and Chauk (see Map 2, page 133). On our side the ground sloped gently down to the north bank. The bed of the chaung was dry. On the south side, however, it ran beneath sheer cliffs a hundred feet high, and beyond the cliffs the hills rose steeply for another two hundred feet. Here was a formidable obstacle. Capture Singu, a small town, and then immediately there was this wide chaung and the cliffs and hills rising from its far side. In the dark they menaced, looming above our heads, cutting out the southern horizon. To be beneath them was to defy every instinct of the infantryman. Looking at the map in the safety of Battalion Headquarters the Colonel had studied the colliding contours and had said that surely there must be defensive positions up there. He wanted to know if they were occupied. Without D Force, I could find out only by listening. Turning westwards towards Singu along the sandy bed of the chaung we moved very cautiously, straining to catch any revealing sound.

The road between Singu and Chauk was my second interest. It crossed the Pyinma Chaung near the main stream of the Irrawaddy, which was narrow here, squeezed between hills, without sandbanks or dry flood plain. And it was not until we were close to the road that we heard anything but the stars turning and our own stealthy shuffling. The cliffs were silent, revealing nothing, but on the road a vehicle of some sort wound down into the chaung from Chauk. The beams of its headlights, undoused and powerful, came sweeping up the chaung towards us and then away. We froze. The truck went on into Singu. I left three of the four men in a sheltered nook in the bank of the chaung and prowled the last hundred yards with one companion. On a recce patrol the fewer the better. I would always have preferred to go alone.

We reached the road, a much-used sandy track. It was an odd moment. I was six or seven miles from the nearest friend, squatting on the line of communication between the considerable body of Japanese in Milaungbya and Singu, whom we were fighting, and their base in Chauk. Apart from that one truck there had been no sign of people. The night was cool and very quiet. I was glad not to be moving for a while.

I began to wonder, as I often did at this time, how I, an ordinary person from nowhere in particular, had come to be mixed up in all this. I could, of course, trace the links back to the point where I had last touched normality, yet the gap was now so great that I felt mystified, a little awed, by my own progression. What was I doing here in Burma, thousands of miles from my home in Wiltshire, with Japanese soldiers nearby who would kill me if they could, and I them, and who were thousands of miles from their homes? At this moment in England my grandparents would be sleeping through a night that divided two 'normal' days during which they would have fed the chickens as usual, pottered in the garden, gone shopping, exchanged words with neighbours as usual, listened to the nine o'clock news as usual. My father was in Almora between two spells of hill touring. My mother was in Bareilly. My sisters were on a boat more than halfway to England. Their time and my time were the same, yet irreconcilably different. None of us knew what the others were doing. I could not properly believe in their time. I could only believe in mine, the vivid present.

The sound of another engine in the distance disturbed this unprofessional reverie and sent us retreating thirty yards to the cover of a pile of driftwood, flat against the warm, soft sand. Again the headlights swept down in scything curves, then moved steadily across the chaung and up the easy gradient on the north side. I waited for another twenty minutes. Nothing more came. There seemed to be no occupied defences here. It was time to go. There was a long trek back, a three to four hour journey, and already we were condemned to do the last hour in daylight. This would not matter unless we were to meet a larger force of Japanese on some flanking mission. Both sides had this open eastern flank which could only be covered by patrols.

The journey was uneventful. I stopped to study Fort with some care before we got within range. B Company might have been driven out. But all seemed well. I could see the familiar felt hats, and not the forage caps of the Japanese.

All night at intervals I had worried over the fate of the men who had been dispersed by that defensive shelling. It was a relief to learn that every one of them was safe. They had leaguered individually and in small groups, and exercising the soldierly virtue of patience, sat out the long, chilly hours till daylight.

The Colonel heard our story philosophically. I suggested that we try again that next night. He agreed. This time, knowing how long it would take us to do the round trip, and not to be caught twice in the same way, we left Fort in the late afternoon and moved a mile eastwards in the shelter of the Mu Chaung, set up sentries on either bank, and went to sleep until it might be dark enough to start. There was a young British officer in charge of the D Force detachment. It was nice to have a fresh face to talk at.

We reached the Pyinma Chaung about 11 p.m. after the now familiar slog, and moved down its bank to within half a mile of Singu. With so many men it was impossible to be as quiet as we had been the previous night. Yet no one challenged us. No shots came from those dark cliffs, no sudden beam of a searchlight, no shattering explosion of a grenade. D Force would take time to set up their pyrotechnics. Meanwhile we infantry arranged ourselves in suitable ambush positions between the site for the explosions and Singu. The plan was to simulate the noises of an attack beneath the cliffs in the hope of drawing fire from any Japanese who might be manning positions on top, and in the hope of catching other Japanese who might come rushing out of Singu to investigate or ambush our imaginary attacking force.

The D Force Lieutenant reported that everything was ready. Lighting a five-minute fuse he and his men withdrew well clear of the fireworks and of us, and went to ground. They had done a noble job. Even from our close distance it was a furious battle. The crackers were roughly like the whip-crack of bullets, other explosions imitated grenades and mortars. Till now we had been careful to be quiet. Suddenly and deliberately we had rent the night with noise. It was worse than whistling in a cathedral.

Nothing happened. No one fired from above. The last cracker cracked and the last echo rebounded from the cliffs. Silence came again. Lying on the ground I strained my eyes for the shapes of men moving towards us from Singu. There were none. We had agreed to wait in ambush for an hour. It grew colder and colder. I was less and less able to remain alert, more and more convinced that any Japanese who might be in Chauk or Singu were too far from our bait or too sensible to contemplate intervening.

At last the hour passed. I gathered everybody and we trailed towards home. I had to fight the desire to relax. We in turn might be ambushed. We might meet the enemy accidentally. And I still had to navigate. But no, we reached Fort unscathed. From there I plodded on wearily to Battalion Headquarters, with only negative results to report. I was very tired after two nights of tension and about thirty miles of footslogging, yet exhilarated. I was developing a taste for doing my work in the dark. This was my fourth all-night long-distance perambulation. A small patrol in this kind of country could go almost anywhere. Stars and compass, a memory for the map, a feel for the countryside, and a very strict discipline about noise, these were my weapons.

XV

MILAUNGBYA

2

While the month-long fight for Meiktila slogged on and on (and this was the campaign's decisive battle), we remained before Milaungbya, defending our part of the bridgehead. Between the set-piece battles there were 'offensive patrols' and 'routine chores'. The disinclination of the Japanese for surrender deprived us of an important source of information about them. Without live bodies to question, Brigade vented a continuous moan for documents. To satisfy Brigade someone had to kill Japanese. This the forward companies did with some success. There was a steady flow of badges, flags, notebooks, paybooks, identity discs, maps and diaries taken from the bodies of the dead. The flags were prized trophies. They were of white silk, with a large red sun centred, and beautiful red characters around. We asked for their return once the characters on them had been interpreted.

The companies sometimes captured useful weapons. A few platoons were using Jap L.M.G.s and ammunition to thicken the fire-power of their positions. We could no longer tell friend from foe by the noise of the firing.

The most bizarre trophy brought in by a patrol was the head of a Japanese officer which the N.C.O. in charge had removed from its owner with his kukri. He carried it back, so he said, as proof of his success. The Colonel had the head nailed by the hair to a tree-trunk near his bunker. It had a wispy beard and a drooping moustache, and hung there with a mournful air until it began to stink and was buried.

If this be thought an act of savagery, with the reader perhaps in some calm corner of our savage twentieth-century world, I can only suggest that when a man is fighting to retain his

life at the expense of someone else's, notions of what is and
is not 'savage' change remarkably. And soldiers instinctively
suspend feeling for a corpse, friend or foe. A corpse is a corpse,
impotent to help or hinder the living, and no deader for
being decapitated. Our Japanese officer's head was a two-day
wonder. Men came from all around to stare at it. Many of
them had never seen a Japanese, alive or dead. This was a
rare chance for fraternisation.

'Routine chores' continued whatever else was happening.
Each day casualty and ration returns were demanded of
companies, and in turn were sent to Brigade. Battalion orders
were churned out come flood, heatwave or high explosive. I
knew them stop only once, and that was in July when all
our records and equipment were lost, including typewriters.

There was the war diary to be written up by the Adjutant
(who was now Bill Blenkin) or the Second-in-Command. I
had to make Intelligence summaries. There were new code-
names to enter on maps. There was fresh information to absorb,
plans for the future to work on and rehearse. There was
equipment to check and replace, there were weapons to inspect
daily. A good battalion has good administration, and good
administration requires attention to detail, which eats time.

An advantage of being 'in action' was the absence of fuss
over getting fresh equipment and clothing. With daily shelling,
occasional battles and frequent patrols, destruction and loss
were expected. In the intervals between the fighting there was
occasionally a rather splendid sense of release, composed
perhaps of two contrasting elements: on the one hand release
from fear of imminent death, and on the other the continued
abeyance of that mechanical surface discipline to which
military life reverts, like water to its own level, when far from
gun-shot. The need to focus energies upon the enemy, and
our common lot of danger and discomfort, brought into our
personal relationships with one another, for example, a
simplicity and ease that I found refreshing; I had never liked
the strata and hierarchies of the rear areas. And then we did
not stick to scheduled weapon scales.

I was supposed to carry a pistol. Pistols are a trap for those
who are not experts with them. I was not. I was among the

majority who could miss a man at six feet. I tried a tommy-gun (sound but heavy), a sten-gun (light but unreliable), then settled for the rifle. The rifle was not too heavy, I was used to it, and it helped to merge me with the men I accompanied.

It is not easy to reproduce the quality of life at this time. Much of the detail has gone. My existence in Battalion Head-quarters, tucked snugly behind the pagoda at Kya-O, and some three-quarters of a mile from the nearest enemy positions, was relatively safe. There was the shelling. At night there was the chance of an enemy raid coming in from the open east flank. Otherwise we were free of the twenty-four-hour-a-day confrontation with danger of the forward companies.

Our headquarters Mess was in the *hypoongyi chaung* attached to the pagoda. After dark we blacked out the windows and lit hurricane lamps. There would be a basic half-dozen officers present, plus one or other of the company commanders, according to the rotation of duty in the forward positions. There was the occasional visitor. We had found a table and benches and some chairs—reasonable comfort. There was a wireless.

The rations relied heavily on tinned meats, tinned sausages, tinned fruits, biscuits with tinned butter and cheese. In that heat one was disinclined to eat unless tempted. Not much in the rations tempted us. Periodically we got bread, which dried out rapidly to become colourless toast. Sometimes fresh meat was flown in. Once we were assigned two huge tins of Sharp's toffees, and on another occasion, of all things, a large tin of crystallised fruit. The men's rations of rice and *chupattis*, etc., gave us variety: they were never so short (casualties and sickness were always a few days ahead of the consequent reduction in rations issued) that some could not be spared for a mendicant officer. Considering that the whole lot was flown in from India, the food was adequate if sometimes uninteresting. We never were hungry.*

* 'We discovered that, instead of the four hundred tons a day not considered excessive to keep a division fighting in more generous theatres, we could maintain our Indian divisions in action for long periods, without loss of battle efficiency or morale, on one hundred and twenty.' (Slim. *Defeat into Victory*, p. 540.)

Nandalal had built me a bathroom. The walls were chest
high of matting, or old sacking, with an overlapping entrance.
I had the usual canvas basin on three crossed sticks, so could
strip off in privacy to bathe. The morale-raising quality of an
evening bath was immense after the heat and fatigue of a
day in central Burma at this season. It was something that
the forward companies could not contemplate on their rationed
water.

I had got very fond of Nandalal. We had been together
now for eight months. My domestic arrangements were entirely
in his control. I did nothing. I cannot remember digging a
shovelful of my own trench except when a lone Jap plane
came over our position after the Irrawaddy crossing. Of
course, my job was not to burrow. On arrival at a new position
there were dozens of urgent matters for officers to decide and
supervise; it was right that they could leave their own safety
to others. For this reason they were allotted orderlies.

Rifleman 85002 Nandalal Thapa was from mid-west Nepal,
short and sturdy like his race, Mongolian featured, brown-
skinned. He had not been on leave for three years, and much
of this time had been active service. He had a son whom he
had never seen. Nandalal had a gentle smile and a wonderful
lack of small talk. His silence was companionable, not taciturn.
His movements were unhurried. However ill-tempered I felt
with the rest of the world, I could not sustain it against
Nandalal. He restored to one a sense of proportion. I valued
his tranquillity in those moments when I could retire from the
stress of life with the Japanese and Walter Walker. I would
find things ready without the need to use up energy on
commands: a change of clothes (yes, we had two of most
things), mosquito net slung, a bucket of clean water for
washing, perhaps a chair won from somewhere; after the
dawn stand-to a cup of tea and hot water for shaving. Wants
were neither complicated nor many, but it was good to have
them fulfilled by a man who was so especially easy.

Linked with Nandalal in memory is Tulbir, my runner.
Nandalal and I were equals. For Tulbir I felt a paternal
affection. He was another Thapa, but altogether different
from Nandalal. He was smaller, and thin. There are not many

thin Gurkhas. His paybook stated that his age was nineteen. It was certainly less. He looked fifteen, with his smooth-skinned face and bewildered expression. In Kohima I had appointed him my runner mostly from compassion; he seemed lost, perpetually nervous, and the others teased him. He had joined the Battalion soon after me, among a draft of six men chosen for the Intelligence Section. Whereas the rest had intelligence and some education, Tulbir seemed to have neither. He had passed no exams, not even his Recruits Test; he could not read; he took two minutes to write his name; maps, compasses, message pads, were nightmares from which he recoiled. His inclusion in that draft was an error on someone's file.

I saw little of him at Kohima. There was seldom work for a runner. He did the same parades as the others. When I spoke to him he was so shy that it was difficult to hear his answers. He never talked of his own accord. But as we moved into Burma his duties as runner brought us into frequent contact. The change was noticeable after a few days. I could hear his answers. He asked me questions. He and Nandalal began discussing the war, or the country we had passed through, or their work. During that first month of marching along obscure tracks towards the Irrawaddy they worked out a system of co-operative labour. At first Nandalal gave the orders. He never took advantage of Tulbir. But he was older, he had been longer in the Battalion, he had seen campaigns where real battles had been fought, he had more experience of my wishes, he was married, with a son, and Tulbir was a bachelor: automatically he commanded.

At the end of a day's march the conversation might have gone something like this:

'Eh, Tulbir, the Sahib wants the trench here. I shall get wood for the fire.' Nandalal's voice was slow, sure of itself.

'Yes, *huzoor*.' Tulbir's was almost feminine. For half an hour there would be the sound of his entrenching tool hacking at the earth. When Nandalal had collected some wood he would return.

'*Aré*, Tulbir, we must hurry brother. There is a good stream in this place. I have to wash the Sahib's other pair of socks.

I will do yours too. Quickly now, and we'll finish the trench.'
Nandalal would talk as they dug together, content with an
occasional word in reply.

The event which had crystallised Tulbir's emergence into
the world was that first patrol on which I took him, and which
I described briefly on page 123. We were out for a day and
a half and covered thirty miles of rough country. Though
we saw no enemy, there had been a chance of doing so. When
we got back I felt used up; Tulbir seemed very fit. I was
surprised. That evening I heard him telling Nandalal about it.

'. . . how dry this country is, Nandé! There's not enough
water for a monkey. For hours we marched and saw only dry
stream beds. Up over rocks and through the prickly bushes.
Babui! Have you mended the Sahib's trousers yet?'

For Tulbir this was garrulity. And next day, when I returned
from the Colonel's evening conference, I heard him arguing
with Nandalal as to the best way of camouflaging the newly
turned earth. Nandalal gave in to him. After that, although
Tulbir never lost his diffident manner, he began to have
friends, and to move as an equal amongst them. He had
protected me on a patrol; there had been grave responsibilities;
not everyone had been on a patrol such as that.

Tulbir's increasing independence was useful. I taught him
how to fire a sten-gun (which, I am thankful to remember,
he never had to use in my presence). He would follow behind
me on my outings, gripping it firmly, but failing in his wish
to look ferocious. When everybody else was flat behind cover
he would kneel peering in the direction from which the bullets
were coming. He had a peculiar little cry of his own whenever
he saw a Japanese, like a terrier that scents a rabbit. He
seemed immune to fear.

I was able to keep Nandalal and Tulbir in extra cigarettes.
My parents sent me tins of fifty at frequent intervals, which
arrived irregularly, but were on several occasions the only
cigarettes we had. I seem to have used my parents as an
extra-commissariat. As well as cigarettes they sent sweets,
biscuits, magazines, books, and on demand at various times,
gum (for joining maps together), drawing pins, a pair of
scissors, and dubbin (when the monsoon had set in)—all

essential weapons for fighting a modern war. These articles came in to the Sinthe airstrip (which in February we had helped to build) and then were ferried across the Irrawaddy and down the dusty track past Pagan to us. Opening parcels from India was better than any Christmas Day. Whatever they contained was likely to be a source of great pleasure. I would write to my parents, and perhaps two weeks later the order would arrive. My parents were in Naini Tal; I was over a thousand miles away across plain and mountain. It was like magic.

In exchange for a degree of extra comfort and safety, a junior officer at headquarters was plagued by scrutiny and interruptions. If the Adjutant, the unfortunate Bill, was the Colonel's administrative staff officer, the Intelligence Officer seemed to be his tactical or battle assistant. Wherever Walter Walker went he generally took me: visits to forward companies, visits to Brigade Headquarters, to conferences here and there. He sent me on missions to impart and collect information. Walter Walker was an admirable commanding officer. We would not have changed him. But he was a demanding one. He and Bill did not mix well, and Bill did not remain Adjutant for long. I had survived so far, at the cost of hard work, increasing fatigue and increasing irritability.

About now I began to feel in an acute form a longing for uninterrupted sleep. It is a longing which every front-line soldier of every army in history comes to feel above all else. I could sleep anywhere, on anything, but it was seldom I got five uninterrupted hours. Whatever may have happened in the night each man was awake for the dawn stand-to about six, waiting in trenches, weapons ready, while patrols cleared the perimeters. This was so at headquarters as anywhere else. During many a normal night there was firing somewhere from machine-guns, artillery, mortars. I am a light sleeper and, despite fatigue, usually woke. If we missed a night's sleep through being on patrol or being attacked, it was seldom regained by day, for the day had its own tasks. The most to be hoped for was a snatched hour, snatched against the noises of the others going about their jobs, and against demands from the Colonel (who seemed to require no sleep), the enemy, or anyone else claiming attention. I had become much thinner, and began to live on nervous energy. We all did.

I have read that the fighting man's war is mostly boredom. This must be true for many, since it has been so often repeated. I did not find it so. I had too much to do. Time! There was never enough of it. Battles against the clock were fought every day. The presence of the enemy merely intensified this time-war. 'Troops will be ready for inspection by 6.30 a.m.' 'You've got an hour to get that plan perfected.' 'Brigade need the information first thing tomorrow morning.' 'The one unforgivable sin is inaction.' 'Synchronise your watches.' 'Hurry, hurry.' There is no time . . . no time . . . no time. . . .

For the men, between and through all other jobs, there was digging. We had learned how to dig from the Japanese. A one-night stand meant slit-trenches only. Two or three days, and headquarters and the bren-guns had stout bunkers, the riflemen some alternative trenches, and the perimeter could be surrounded with wire, booby-traps and *panjis*.* A week, and every man might have roofed sleeping quarters, with crawl trenches between posts and back to platoon head-quarters. A fortnight turned a perimeter into a warren, proof against most kinds of attack that the Japanese were likely to mount at that stage of the war. This was not yet 1917–18 standard, but at Milaungbya we approached that.

The Battalion was probably at the peak of its fighting power during the Milaungbya period. We did not under-estimate the Japanese. We were simply very sure of our own ability to deal with any situation that a battalion is normally asked to handle. We had faith in our skill and that of our commanders. That we might land suddenly in an untenable situation was always a possibility—a private dread at the back of every mind—for in the vast distances of Burma surprise for either side was easier to achieve. But here at Milaungbya we sensed our strength and the weakness of our enemy.

* *Panjis* were stakes of sharpened bamboo, hardened by fire and of varying length, set in the ground at forty-five degrees. They were generally placed among trees and uncleared undergrowth, waiting to pierce ankle, knee, thigh or stomach. Each man carried some; they could be fixed in place very quickly.

Research into Japanese records after the war has shown that we were right. It was against 17th Division in Meiktila to the east, and against the East Africans and our 114th Brigade to the west, on the other side of the Irrawaddy, that the enemy was concentrating his most fierce counter-attacks.

The next of our set battles came on 18 March, a Sunday. My pocket diary for that year tells me it was a Sunday, but there was no imposed rhythm to distinguish Sundays from other days of the week. Each day was equal in its potentiality, as it must have been for early man, and we were ruled by other rhythms: phases of the moon, dry season and monsoon, the building up of supplies and the spending of them, the psychology of morale, of keeping your own soldiers in good shape while wearing down the enemy.

On 18 March we attacked the Milaungbyas for the second time. It had become obvious that the Japanese were feeding men and guns into Pagodas and Base. We wished to forestall their plans, to catch them off balance. Mike Tidswell, Scotty Gilmore and A Company went out, with the same squadron of the Gordons. Mike had been commanding A Company for a week or two now since the departure of Frank Crouchman. For a prelude there was an air strike, and artillery and mortar concentrations, to disorganise the Japanese and to cover the noise of the forming up and approach of the tanks.

I was out on the right (west) flank with a platoon of D Company. Our job was to shoot up any of the enemy who might try to escape across the flat Irrawaddy flood-plain (see Map 3, page 140). We were to advance more or less in line with the main attack up on the cliffs. Spaced out on the plain we were under good observation from the Japanese. For the first hour they had a couple of guns firing at us in a desultory way. We could hear the discharge and the approaching shells, and flattened ourselves in good time. It was unpleasant, but not one of us was hit. As the main battle worked to its long climax, the shells stopped falling on us. We had nothing to do but watch the shimmering plain and listen to the wireless from time to time. All day under a boiling sun there was no target, and too much time to brood upon thirst.

In Base, the first objective, A Company had met stiff

opposition. The Japanese were concentrated in unexpectedly large numbers, on the point of launching their own attack, and they were entrenched in deep bunkers and in foxholes, many sited on reverse slopes which the tanks could not touch. The heart of their defence was amongst a series of re-entrants that led in from the cliffs. It took six hours of continuous fighting, most of it with hand grenades and bayonets and tanks firing into bunkers at point-blank range, to clear Base. By then our men and the tank crews were tiring. The heat was still intense, and had hastened the natural fatigue of battle. The tanks were running short of petrol and ammunition. So the advance onwards into Pagodas and Bottom was called off. A Company withdrew, as planned, into the battalion perimeter. We trooped back across the plain, aching for shade and water.

The results of this battle were surprising. They showed what highly trained infantry can do with skilled tank support against a fanatical but less skilled enemy. Ninety-four enemy dead were counted. It can be assumed that others were wounded and escaped, and that a few more were buried in bunkers or blown to bits by artillery and tank fire. Three 75 mm and two 37 mm anti-tank guns were captured or destroyed, and several machine-guns of varying calibre. Our price was six killed and thirteen wounded. This was an extraordinary result, for in the normal way troops attacking a well-entrenched enemy can expect to lose heavily, and against the Japanese frequently did so. Our Japanese refused to leave their bunkers. Once a bunker had been spotted and shown to a tank, or once it had been outflanked by events elsewhere, killing was skill, patience and time.

A word here about the counting of enemy dead: the Colonel was adamant that totals should include only those dead bodies that could be seen to be counted. No possibles or probables were allowed, no guesswork about bodies removed (the Japanese always tried to remove their dead, often at great risk to the living). Counting was done by an officer or senior N.C.O. Thus our totals were, I hope, reliable.

Two days later the Battalion attacked again. C and B Companies were detailed. Once more I had a flanking platoon

M

(from B Company) out on the plain. This time the main force circled round to the east and came in to sweep northwards back towards our own positions, while I went much further south than before, and west of the lagoon (Map 3, page 140), until I was opposite Bottom, where the lagoon ended. I had a tank with me. It rumbled slowly forward in a splendidly prehistoric way. Again we attracted a few shells. Opposite the main Japanese positions we came under long-range rifle fire. On the move the whole platoon walked on the lee side of the tank. When we stopped the men spread out in a defensive arc, like pilot fish around a shark. I had told them that at all costs no enemy should be allowed to reach our monster.

I was nervous that the Japanese, taken from behind by our main force, might decide that we were the lesser evil, and that we might be faced with a charge of several hundreds of enemy. Our three L.M.G.s and the guns of the tank would have killed a great many, but probably not all, and then it would have been hand-to-hand fighting.

Lying on the hot plain I scanned the line of palm trees on the cliffs to see who was firing from where. The trees were about three hundred yards off, and the shadows under them too dense and distant. I could see nothing. At intervals I jogged round to the back of the tank to discuss our next forward bound with the tank commander. There was a telephone housed there, but with the noise of the tank's engine and of the battle in Milaungbya it was difficult to hear what he was saying. We got hotter and hotter and ceased to care whether the Japanese came at us or not. The metal sides of the tank grew unbearable to the touch; inside it must have been an inferno. Bullets zinged past to keep us from relaxing. Occasionally they whammed against the side of the tank. Overhead the artillery's spotter aircraft droned round and round like a blue-bottle in a heatwave.

Nothing happened. Again we never fired a shot. Nor was any of my platoon hit. Warned by the noise of the tanks the bulk of the enemy had retreated south from Bottom before our men closed in, and they suffered badly in that open country from our artillery. The few who remained (including whoever

was firing at us) were killed. A 105 mm gun was found knocked
out.

I list these guns individually because in our war we counted
guns in ones and twos. It was seldom that our battalion was
supported by more than a battery (eight guns). The Japanese
were less well off. So the capture or destruction of a gun was
a significant event to us. The Japanese were good with their
few guns.

So ended the third and final raid on Milaungbya. It was
also the last time we fought along with the Gordons. They
were a splendid and co-operative lot. I admired them, cooped
in their metal boxes in that heat for hours on end, and never
knowing when a concealed Jap gun might not turn their
home into a volcano of fire and exploding ammunition. They
said that they admired us, who had to move in the open
without protection. Well, I had chosen my way long ago, and
nothing I saw subsequently made me want to change. I
preferred to take my chance in the free air.

We returned to our perimeters, to 'offensive patrolling'
and 'routine chores'. A week later we withdrew into Brigade
reserve, relieved by the Sikhs. The men in the rifle companies
needed a rest. The strain of shelling, of attacks and patrols,
of night watching, begins to tell. It was six weeks since we
had crossed the Irrawaddy, and over four since our first clash
with the Japanese at Kinka. Brigade promised us two weeks
of peace.

XVI

PATROLLING

Most of the Battalion went back four miles to the village of Nyaungla, beside the main stream of the Irrawaddy, to rest, bathe, fish and refit. I did not. Two days before the move, on 25 March, I embarked with the Colonel in one of those ageing assault boats with their temperamental outboard engines, to cross the Irrawaddy. We were to select a patrol base on the other side which I, with a platoon from B Company, was to be the first to occupy. Our task was to watch the Japanese in the Lanywa and Seikpyu areas to the south (Map 2, page 133). The nearest Allied troops on that side of the river were fifteen miles to the north-west in what was called the Letse Box. They were under heavy attack. The enemy had reacted more strongly to the advance of this force than to our own. Perhaps they judged it to be the greater threat, for undoubtedly they wished to keep open the tracks running westwards to their forces retreating from the Arakan. Or it may have been simply that they had a more energetic commander on that side, or better troops. Their commander on our side got the sack, so we afterwards heard.

We chugged over quickly, partnered by the swift current. The main stream left Nyaungla on a diagonal course until after three-quarters of a mile it curved south against hills on the far side. Just short of some cliffs we disembarked. There was no sign of life. We crossed a ledge of flat stony ground, climbed steeply into a maze of broken hills rising five hundred feet above the river, and selected the best defendable spot. This had to be close to the landing-place: every piece of equipment, all ammunition, food and water, would be carried up by hand. It was thought that the nearest enemy were four or five miles downstream. No one was sure. We re-embarked, and the voyage back against the current was a crawl. There was ample time to admire the sandbanks, the blue water, the hot sky.

Next day I crossed with B Company's 4 Platoon. The engine of my boat broke down and for ten minutes we drifted rapidly towards the Japanese. I kept a straight face while thinking furiously. There was no military answer to this. Most of the men could not swim. I was not sure that I could have tackled this broad swift stream. Ahead the river narrowed and both banks were held by the enemy. There *was* no answer. Then the engine restarted. I half relaxed. On other trips the same thing happened, but no one ever reached the Japs.

We landed and set about making this forsaken spot defensible and habitable. Hereabouts the western side of the river was barren. This was a moonscape, a confusion of sharp ridges devoid of soil, vegetation or trace of human activity. Where we had landed a wide though short valley penetrated into the hills. We perched high on the edge of this. At our back was the river. Northwards the rocky slopes fell sharply to the valley. These two sides were safe. But west and south were miles of ridges, re-entrants, cols and little pointed peaks, all at about the same height. The Japanese were somewhere in or beyond them. We could withstand probing from patrols. A serious attack must destroy us. We had nowhere to go, no one at hand to help us, and could not have held out long for lack of ammunition, water and safe cover. I felt most uneasy, and was only temporarily relieved when the first recce patrols reported the neighbourhood empty.

4 Platoon of B Company was commanded by Jemadar Manbahadur. He was a Gurung, a likeable fellow, squat, with the squashed, flat face of an ape, truly simian. He could not give his thoughts the thinnest coating of tact, was disconcertingly direct when he felt I was wrong. I knew Manbahadur, as I knew all the Gurkha officers by now, but this was the first time we had worked together. I grew to admire him immensely, to like him perhaps more than any other of the G.O.s. He possessed great courage, and in my opinion controlled the best platoon in the Battalion. On this baking

afternoon on this burning rock ridge I drew comfort from his presence. Like me, he thought we were in a pestilential position and said so. He also remarked that there weren't any Japs around yet, our tour of duty was only three days, and at least we were on our own, free of interference. He drove his men up and down the almost vertical path from beach-head to perimeter with a fierce persistence that I should never have dared to impose. Soon all stores were up and he set the men about constructing as best they could their individual rifle and L.M.G. posts. We could dig down scarcely anywhere. We had to rely on natural outcrops of rock, tiny re-entrants, splits in the surface, slight hollows. Against heavy mortar or shell-fire the position was untenable. There was nothing we could do about that.

I moved over the nearer hills myself, and sent small patrols encircling wider. Old prints of a Jap party (the revealing zigzag pattern of the Japanese patrol boot) were noticed on a track a mile to the south-west. Otherwise nothing. It was abominably hot, worse than Fort had been. We made sun-shades out of groundsheets and lay beneath them through the hottest hours. Flies gathered; I spent a lot of time killing them with a knotted handkerchief. I grew quicker than they, for they were torpid in the heat and I was driven to fury by the discomfort of their tickling. From my narrow ledge on the rock, where there was just room to stretch out, I looked straight down into the valley, and across to the sun-shaken slopes on the other side. By standing I could gaze over a shoulder of rock at the river sweeping towards us between its massive sandbanks, blue between yellow; and at the distant undulating plain on the far bank, with patches of green where the villages sheltered; and at the low bare hills on the horizon. It was a splendid view, but a graphic reminder of our isolation. Everything stayed quiet. Sentries were relieved each hour. Those of us not on duty lay supine, exhausted by the heat until evening brought relief.

In the late afternoon I descended to the river to bathe. The sand dropped rapidly into deep water. Six feet out I had to swim. The current swirled by with silent power, a little menacing. By swimming hard against it I could just keep my place. But the water was deliciously cool, and a fine cure for worry. Alas, climbing back brought on a fresh sweat and lost half the benefit of the bathe. That night, with a full moon shining on this lunar landscape, and not a sound anywhere, I felt that I might be the last human being.

So our tour of duty passed and on 29 March we were relieved. Scotty Gilmore had the pleasure of my sun-baked ledge. For two clear days I was at Nyaungla. On 1 April, Easter Sunday, I went back with a platoon of C Company. Scotty's men had established that there were Japanese of unknown strength in Lanywa, opposite Milaungbya, about five miles to the south. Lanywa was an old steamer station. On the map there were shown a brief flurry of metalled roads and a number of houses, surrounded by our same uninhabited hills. Lanywa must have been an extension of the Burmah Oil Company's operations at Chauk.

I was ordered to visit Seikpyu, much further to the south. Seikpyu was a village. It lay opposite Chauk, where the river was narrowest, and was the base for the Japanese forces who confronted our troops on the west bank. An all-weather motorable track gave them a firm line of communication. Between Chauk and Seikpyu was a recognised ferry service. Chauk itself was at the northern end of a considerable system of metalled roads.

Thus on Easter Monday I and three men set off. We were to cover twelve miles there and twelve back, skirting Lanywa and crossing the wide Yaw Chaung, which in February we had met further north. To do this in a night, allowing for a cautious advance, and for a couple of hours at Seikpyu, we left in the afternoon. It was still light as we moved down a valley that led to the Yaw Chaung. High on a ridge to our left was a prominent two-storeyed red house, an outlier of Lanywa. There were supposed to be Japanese up there, but the house was half a mile away and in the interests of speed and conservation of energy we ploughed straight on. Sure enough, as we came opposite, there were distant shots and a scurry of bullets zinged overhead. We ran smartly for several hundred yards to reach cover round a bend in the valley. It was too hot for running. Protected and shaded by the bank of a stream bed, we sat down to recover, hearts pounding like drum-beats, salt sweat streaming into the eyes, and my Gurkhas cursing softly at the whoring sons of illegitimate Japanese blockheads. And to have this lot so close to the route home was unsettling. It would be easy for them to ambush us. I would have to detour or return this far in the dark to reduce risks.

Close to the Yaw Chaung we lay up until the last of the light was gone. I did not wish to advertise the direction of our further progress. The hills on either side were steep and broken and would make slow going, even in daylight. I proposed to bum down the middle of the chaung, which was perhaps a quarter of a mile wide, trusting in the dark, and in the space available for running, to avoid trouble. The Japanese might have posts anywhere, but were less likely to have them in the middle of the chaung.

The chaung still had pools of water. This was luck. We could drink from our water-bottles now, refill from the pools and leave our purification tablets time to do their work before we got thirsty again. We could have done our twenty-four miles and our eighteen hours on one water-bottle, but I am glad that we did not have to try. The water we drank was warm—it nearly always was—and smelled of the tin that held it; it did not refresh, but it was a guard against dehydration.

When the dusk was almost dark, and the hills about us were invisible, we shot into the middle of the chaung and knelt round a pool, splashing water over faces and necks. It was fresh life. Even to travel this far had dried us out.

We set off down the sand expanses, and after two hours of cautious but steady advance passed between the hamlets on either side where the chaung widened to join the Irrawaddy, and mounted the right bank to enter the outskirts of Seikpyu. There was a track leading in. For ten minutes we squatted, listening. Nothing. We moved on. Beside the first house I left the other three with instructions to remain until I returned, unless they heard violent noises. If dispersed, our rendezvous was where we had lain up waiting for the dark.

The Japanese here were surely confident, or careless, or

both. Perhaps they felt safe twelve miles from our patrol base (if they knew about that) and fifteen or more from the Letse Box. I crept from the shadow of one house to another. Palm trees added to the dense shade over much of the village, and the moonlight now shining penetrated in patches only. In some of the houses I could hear steady breathing but had no way of telling whether the breathers were Japanese or Burmans. From start to finish I *saw* no one. Possibly there were no Japanese. I had to suppress an inclination to toss a grendade into a house to see what happened. When you have been under a strain of silent suspense for some hours there is this desire to resolve it suddenly in noise and action. Moving slowly and with long pauses, I reached the main road through the village, a metalled road, the first such that I had seen since leaving the Imphal Plain in early January.

Up this road were several thousand Japanese. Maybe round me were hundreds more. At my back, out of sight in the dark, was the river, and across the river was another host of the enemy. Somewhere out on the river now I could hear an engine. Probably the Japs did their ferrying at night to avoid our aeroplanes. In a patch of moonlight beside the road I examined the dust and made out tank tracks. The tracks were still sharp and therefore recent, a useful piece of information. Then a few yards away I noticed a bunker dug down, from which the sounds of restless breathing were perfectly audible. The inhabitants might have been villagers. It was unlikely. Suddenly I felt that I had pushed my luck far enough. I wanted to get out. I ought to get out. It was more than an hour since I had left my three companions. How quickly the time had passed! I did not take so long to return to them. They had begun to be anxious: waiting is worse than doing. We crept away.

The Yaw Chaung was well lit by the moon now. We returned up it quietly but smartly, spaced well apart, and trusted that the Japanese were as absent or as sleepy here as in Seikpyu. I could clearly see the hills on either side, but knew that we four small objects in the middle of the sand would not be seen so easily. All went well. At the place to turn off we had another long drink, a splash, and a ten-minute break to eat. We had been on the move for over twelve hours.

It was still dark as we threaded up the valley beneath the Red House. They had not laid an ambush for us. I ought not to have returned by the same route. To do so was against all the rules. I took the risk because any alternative would have added miles to our journey, we were very tired, and the Japanese in Lanywa had displayed a commendable lack of offensive spirit. I was even fairly sure that they had not been to look at our base and did not know exactly where it was.

For the last hour it was daylight and good to see where to put aching feet. Partly we walked on a track, which did the route selecting for us. I was beginning to know these hills. A close-range ambush was possible in a few places. Between these we could jog on with reasonable safety.

Over those final miles, with the air heating up once more, I remember sucking a lump of rock-salt. It had a reddish tinge and was delicious. Rock-salt was in the rations and was meant for cooking. But on' these long patrols our bodies sweated out more salt than was replaced by salt tablets in the drinking water. Our green uniforms had bleached white under the armpits, across the back and round the waist. I found that lumps of raw salt, a portable salt-lick, which ordinarily would have made me sick, became wonderfully palatable.

Along with water and salt I lived on concentrated chocolate at the patrol base. Some of the men disliked it, so there was plenty spare. My appetite for the rest of our rations dwindled. Only the chocolate and the tinned fruit were easy to eat.

Soon after our return a boat arrived to take me to the Battalion. General Evans, the Divisional Commander, was visiting the Brigade to meet officers and men, and the Colonel wanted me to report personally about Seikpyu. So I lined up with the rest and was presented as still hot from behind the enemy lines. I would rather have had a few hours' sleep, but did get a decent lunch in the cool Mess building, with enough cold drink to sink a camel, before chugging back over the river.

Next day it was Scotty's turn (he too tramped to Seikpyu) and I recrossed to the flesh-pots of Nyaungla. Those gentle intervals on the water were relaxing. They would have been perfect but for the mutinous habits of the engines. In Nyaungla between tours all was not roses. My Intelligence bodies must not be left out in the overhaul of equipment that was in progress. Repair or replacement was much needed after three months of movement and six weeks of battle. Boots wanted resoling, sweat-soaked clothing had rotted, things got lost, or damaged or used up. There was the Intelligence situation to catch up with. Then I remember a concert by a troupe of local Burmese dancers. I remember it because it was the occasion for one of those useless tragedies that punctuate life, and end it for some. The concert was about to start and we were settling on our seats when there was a shot two or three feet to my right, and a jemadar sank back to the planking of the verandah. Squatting down to enjoy the show he had jarred the butt of his sten-gun and set it off. The bullet went through his groin and stomach. He never regained consciousness. After that it was difficult to appreciate the stately Burmese dances.

I was back at the patrol base on 7 April with 6 Platoon of B Company, whose commander was Jemadar Jitbahadur Ale. It was he who had been recommended for an M.C. when B Company was so unexpectedly attacked on 4 March. Jitbahadur was an intelligent, cheerful soul with a considerable knowledge of English learned as a boy in India. His intelligence had gained him rapid promotion, so that he was younger than the average Gurkha officer, and not always quite sure of himself. The older ones appeared never to have doubts, which was reassuring to a Johnny-come-lately like me. Jitbahadur and I had this in common: that we were both stretched to the limit of our experience and beyond by our present responsibilities, whereas others seemed to work well within themselves. I liked Jitbahadur, but was never at ease with him as I was with Manbahadur.

This tour at the patrol base was my last and most eventful. Brigade was still agitating for live Japanese to interrogate. The Colonel thought that we might be able to abduct one from the Red House positions at Lanywa. Since the captured Japanese soldier thought himself lost to his homeland, irretrievably disgraced, he was often a willing respondent under interrogation. He would tell all he knew. At this junction of

our affairs, when the Division was poised for an advance out
of the bridgehead (as I will explain later), everyone was
desperate for accurate news of Japanese dispositions and
intentions. What was going on in Chauk? And further south
in Yenangyaung? Where would the enemy resist most fiercely?
How could we best ensure that none escaped? The pressure
for a prisoner was so great that Walter Walker promised me
promotion if I got one.

There were two clear days in which to achieve this. The
plan was to do a close recce of the Lanywa positions on the
night of the 8th, and to return on the next night with a platoon
to effect the capture. An extra platoon, No. 5 of B Company,
came over for the job.

So the afternoon of the 8th saw me making the familiar
preparations: pockets emptied of papers, rifle and ammunition
cleaned and checked, grenades primed in their pouches, torch,
map, compass, Very pistol, water-bottle and sterilisation
tablets, emergency rations, first field dressing, rubber-soled
patrol boots (they were still called jungle boots, and were
splendid; I was on my second pair). We all knew our objective
and the route to it; we knew what to do and where to go if
ambushed; we knew the password. At dusk I was off with
Havildar Sunbir, I.D.S.M., and three men. The hot and stark
position we left was like home, grown safe through familiarity,
though never comfortable.

Following the Seikpyu route we arrived below the Red
House, invisible above us on this starlit but moonless night.
Very slowly we crept up the hillside, steep and bare. At the
top, nothing. Just below the crest a path led along the ridge
towards the house. We moved on it, cat-like, expecting
momentarily the challenge or the bullet. Somewhere up here
there were Japanese, somewhere close. We crept beneath
trees, no doubt planted years before by my fellow countrymen
of Burmah Oil. Among the trees we came on a tarmac road
leading to the house. I consulted with Sunbir. We left the
riflemen here as cover, and together moved very slowly all
round the house. Nothing. No wire, no trenches, no Japanese.
I seemed fated to creep over Burma without finding the
enemy I looked for.

The house was on the end of a spur that dominated not only the valley out of which we had just climbed, but also the Irrawaddy valley to the east, and Lanywa below. From the map it seemed as though it probably overlooked Singu across the river, where I had twice wandered in the dark. We could sense the space around us.

Where were the Japs? They had fired on me six days before. Other patrols had noted them since. They might have gone, but it seemed improbable while their fellows were active at Milaungbya on the far bank and on our side up at Letse.

The tarmac road led from the house down the reverse slope to Lanywa: Sunbir and I moved along it. The virtue of tarmac to patrolling infantrymen is that in our rubber-soled boots we could be silent without effort. After about a hundred yards, just clear of the trees, we heard voices. I lay flat to look for silhouettes. There was nothing until we got very close. Then the mound of a bunker was just discernible. From within came animated conversation that sounded exactly as I supposed Japanese ought to sound.

The bunker was partly dug into the ridge above the road. If I was going to surround it in the dark with a platoon of men, I needed to know more. Sunbir covered me while I inched along until I was crouching on the roof itself. Where were the sentries? Did they not bother with such trifles in these parts? Of the odd situations into which the army led me, this was the oddest. In a way it was exhilarating. There was a ventilation shaft beside me. I could hear the voices clearly: the voices of men at their ease, laughing frequently, picking their commanders to bits perhaps, or retelling scabrous stories. It would have been simple to drop a grenade among them, and perhaps my patrol could have caught one of the bodies that would have poured out. It was tempting. Then I grew cautious, perhaps mistakenly so. There might be other bunkers. I would return with more men tomorrow, as planned.

I rejoined Sunbir and we padded back up the road and round to the rest of the patrol. Our careful progress had eaten time. We all returned to the point on the ridge where we had climbed up. The others were descending, and I had just stepped on to the slope, beginning to relax, when someone below slipped and sent a scurry of stones bounding downwards. There was a swift and unexpected reaction. Five yards from me a voice called sharply. I was so startled that I lost my footing and rolled some way down the hillside. A shot cracked above me, and then another. I came to rest upside down with my rifle jammed beneath me, and the remainder of my brave band sliding and rattling far below. Between my feet I could see the dozy Jap sentry silhouetted.

Upside down, with no immediate means of defence, you do not feel aggressive. If the sentry had rolled down a speculative grenade I could have been scuppered. I kept brooding on this as, with infinite caution, I turned myself about on the steep rocky slope, and retreated slowly sideways and down. Sunbir and the others were at the bottom, unhurt and anxious. I described my recent position, *ulto pulto* in the graphic Gurkhali term; we set off home in better humour.

I wondered now how best to capture our Jap. I did not fancy going round to the bunker upon whose roof I had rested, with this newly discovered post athwart our communications. On the way up we must have been exceedingly quiet, or the sentry heavily asleep. Perhaps we had best try our luck with this post, which I presumed to be another bunker. There was no wire that we had seen. I could send two sections up the side we had just come down, but further away, to spread quietly across the path and cut the retreat of the Japanese in the post. I would take the third section to the other side and, by making some kind of demonstration, hope to flush out the terrified occupants into the arms of the waiting captors.

So it was. Next evening I set out again with Havildar Asbahadur and the men of 5 Platoon to cover the familiar miles to the valley below the Red House. Halfway up the hillside we split: the Havildar and his two sections, guided by Sunbir, to the right; and I with six men to the left over unknown ground. I waited fifteen minutes to let the others get into position. All seemed well. I heard nothing. When we set off I found myself crawling up the crest of a steeply ascending ridge, and assumed that at the top I should find my post. I was nearly there, moving with commendable silence, and followed closely by the next equally silent man, when from

behind and lower down there came the sounds of a Gurkha
in a tearing hurry to catch up: unsilenced footfalls, the rattling
of small stones, heavy breathing. Who it was or why he was
acting like a stampeding buffalo I never found out because
in the press of later events I forgot to ask.

I turned round to the man behind to hiss at him in fearful
anger so that he would hiss at the man behind him, and so on.
But it was too late. There was a hoarse challenge a few feet
above, and a shot whammed past my head. The flash of the
discharge was very close. I sweated and cursed. The plan
was not destroyed, but I would have to put it into operation
before I was ready. I had meant to get my men into a half-
circle round this side of the post before the people in it woke
up. Now I should have to move fast. A succession of men on
a descending knife-edge ridge, even in the dark, are a vulnerable target when it had to be assumed that the enemy might
have a machine-gun trained down it, and when grenades
could be rolling among us at any second. I had no wish to
get anyone hurt in exchange for the Jap.

After that shot the night had become quieter than the grave.
Neither the Japanese above nor my Gurkhas below made a
sound. For a few seconds while my thoughts raced one could
have heard the worms turning. Then almost instinctively,
following the maxim that any kind of action, even the wrong
action, is better than inaction, I extracted a grenade, slid up
the rock a few feet further until I could see quite clearly the
outlined roof of a bunker, and threw at where I hoped the
weapon slit might be. The grenade had a four-second fuse.
There was time to slide back and down before it exploded,
sending showers of muck around us. In the interval between
throw and explosion I had a terrible fear that it would hit the
side of the bunker and roll back on to me. In fact, though I
did not know it then, it must have exploded in the opening.
I got another grenade into my hand. By this time two men
were up beside me. That made me happier.

Immediately after the explosion the Japanese in the bunker
began yelling, and then there was the thud of running feet
receding into the dark. Then a brief silence. We waited. I
hoped to hear some kind of noise to show that they had run

into my cordon. Instead, after a few seconds, there was a fusillade of rifle shots, many of which came whistling close over our heads. That did not sound too good. There ought not to have been the need to fire. Then there was silence again, a silence that went on and on. There was no sound from the bunker above, and none from beyond.

I crawled up to the level of the bunker. I lay still, thinking and listening. Should I investigate the inside? I decided not to, mostly from sheer funk. I might get shot by my own men on the other side. I might get involved with any Jap who remained, though it seemed unlikely that one did remain. I might get blown up by and along with a wounded Jap: we all knew of their predilection for holding on until we arrived, then letting off a grenade. To see anything in a bunker in the dark you shine a torch inside. If you shine a torch you are a good target. My courage did not feel up to this.

So for about fifteen minutes we crouched on the hillside, and I held a whispered dialogue with my section commander. Then I fired a red signal cartridge towards the stars, the sign for the return to our rendezvous in the valley. It seemed probable that we had failed, but I could see no way of redeeming the failure without taking risks that I was not prepared to consider. We had no plan for further action, the enemy was alert and in unknown numbers, and my personal fears were reinforced by the sound guerilla rule of hit hard and get out quickly.

At the rendezvous it was as I expected. The fleeing Japanese had not followed the track towards the Red House which Asbahadur had blocked. They had escaped at right-angles over the ridge. This more direct route to their other post or posts might have been covered by my own section if the alarm had not gone off prematurely. Never mind. We were all alive and the Japanese must have been at least as frightened as I had been. Our only casualty was a naik who had twisted his ankle coming down the hill. I bound it up and he managed to hobble back with us.

My active military career seemed condemned to recce patrols on which I saw nothing, and fighting patrols on which we failed in our objectives. I reported our failure over the

wireless. No promotion this time. It was Scotty's turn to come
over that morning, so I went back to Nyaungla. For a post-
script, we heard two days later from a local Burman that our
patrol had killed two and wounded three. The Burman said
that the Japanese in Lanywa had been very angry, and had
accused him and others of betraying them.

I now had three days in Nyaungla. On the second of them
I ceased to be Intelligence Officer (and was succeeded by
Bill Blenkin) and joined Denis Sheil-Small's B Company as
Second-in-Command. I was very tired, desperate for sleep.
I was so tired that I tended to argue when I should have kept
quiet. I got hauled up before Watson-Smyth for this. It was
as well that I now left Battalion Headquarters for a rifle
company.

N

XVII

SINGU

This is an egocentric account. The rest of the Battalion was also fighting a war. They too were tired, and some of them edgy. In my own speciality there had been scores of patrols led by naiks and havildars and Gurkha officers. Every day someone somewhere went out, if only to make the dawn patrol around the perimeter to see that the night had not left a gross of Japanese at our gates. Some patrols brought in valuable results. Naik Chankhebahadur, out from our trans-Irrawaddy patrol base during one of Scotty's tours, lay on a hill-top near the Yaw Chaung and watched hundreds of Japanese and dozens of mules file past below him, withdrawing from before 114 Brigade. This was news of consequence. But I am not writing the story of the Battalion. I mention events in which I was not involved only if they were of prime importance.

I had been engaged more and more on 'infantry' tasks, and less and less on 'Intelligence'. Perhaps in transferring me to B Company Walter Walker was simply legalising this. Perhaps he wanted me to gain experience with a rifle company. For weeks only Scotty had been available as a reserve company commander. This was too narrow a margin. Whatever the reasons, I was glad to go. I needed the change. And I was pleased to be joining Denis and B Company.

The move coincided with the end of the Battalion's rest. I joined B Company on 12 April. On the 14th we took over from the Sikhs in front of Singu (they had occupied Milaungbya during the two weeks that we had been in reserve). Our orders were to capture Singu.

At this point I ought to give a short résumé of events beyond our horizon. Three months had gone since our 7th Division

began its advance down the Gangaw valley. We had crossed
the Irrawaddy and held a bridgehead while the mechanised
17th Division concentrated, then drove through to capture
Meiktila, the air base, supply centre, and nodal point of the
Japanese 15th Army's communications. To the north the fall
of Mandalay to other divisions was a matter of time and hard
fighting. South from Meiktila, and well to the east of us, the
17th and 5th Divisions were now swarming down the direct
road and rail routes to Rangoon (see Map 6, page 230),
racing the monsoon due in May. The need for a firm bridgehead was gone. We were about to move south down the axis
of the Irrawaddy towards Chauk, the more extensive oilfields
at Yenangyaung, and eventually Prome, the largest port on
the river. For the next two months the Division was to operate
on its own. We were still on air supply. The three brigades
worked independently, and within brigades each battalion
was often alone: airdrops were organised in penny packets
and on occasion came in at company level. If anyone doubted
the value of air supply we did not. Almost all that we asked
for came down on the next drop. It gave us tactical mobility;
relying on those planes we could plan to move anywhere.
It was marvellous.

The forward Sikh positions were on an isolated hillock a
mile north of Singu. The Japanese, who had perfect observation, objected to their presence and used them daily as target
practice, both for artillery fire and for harassing attacks by
infantry. This hillock was known as Fantasia, and to it B
Company was sent on the morning of the 14th (Map 2, page
133). We motored through our old positions, through the
battlegrounds of the Milaungbyas, and out to the open country
beyond. It seemed almost irreverent to pass by so casually
where we had toiled with such intent. Well short of Fantasia
we disembarked and crept forward, section by section, to
avoid attracting attention from the Japanese guns. Even so,
occasional shells were falling on and near the road as we
came in. I was glad that the immediate plan did not ask us
to remain in Fantasia, but to advance into Singu that night.

Movement by day would have been costly, so we were to
capture the town by night infiltration. Singu was divided in

two by a chaung, and I had seen from the map that just
north of the chaung (our side) on the eastern edge, there
appeared to be a semi-isolated group of trees and buildings
gathered around a pagoda. If we were to capture Singu by
stealth rather than by formal attack, then the way to do it
might be to file quietly into this area, which we could reach
from the open east flank where I had tramped in March.
Should it be occupied we could retreat into the night. If
empty, we were in, and with artillery and air superiority,
ought to be able to hold on.

This plan was agreed and elaborated. As a battalion we
preferred the indirect approach, generally less expensive in
casualties. I would start with my friend Jemadar Manbahadur
and 4 Platoon. We were to reel out telephone line behind us
and call up Jitbahadur and 6 Platoon as soon as we reached
our objective. Finally Denis, Company Headquarters, 5
Platoon, and a platoon of medium machine-guns would sneak
in. By dawn we ought to have the complete company assembled
in the town, in a position that could be reinforced by night
over the open plain, and which on two sides (plain and
chaung) would be difficult to attack.

I left Fantasia with Manbahadur and his men in the early
afternoon. We were to do a little patrolling and deception
before the night's work. About three hundred yards short of
Singu was another small chaung. Well to the right (west) of
the road and on the far bank of the chaung was a hillock
with trees on it. We moved on to the hillock at about 3 p.m.
It just absorbed a platoon comfortably, though I did not
trouble to disguise our movement. I sent a couple of three-
men patrols into the outskirts of Singu on the west side. I
wanted to find out if there were Japanese in this northern
half of the town, where and in what strength. And by probing
from this side I hoped to distract them from the eastern
approach we were about to use.

The patrols reported Japs in small numbers. One of the
patrols was fired on and followed. This was good, but as the
afternoon drew into evening I could not help being anxious
lest the enemy might react too quickly. I did not want an
attack, which I might not be able to beat off, before dark.

I thought there would be an attack. The enemy's dislike of the Fantasia position suggested that our further advance must provoke them. I studied Singu through field-glasses. It was an easy rifle shot away but I could see no movement in the outer layer of huts and palm trees.

At last it was dark. Everyone had their orders and was ready. We wasted no time. We slipped off our hillock back into the chaung and moved up it as quietly as we could straight between Fantasia and Singu. I was relieved to be away, and rightly. We had not gone half a mile when a fearful racket opened behind us: rifle- and machine-gun fire, grenades, faint yells, the lot. They had been creeping up as we crept out. The thought of their assault upon nothing kept me smiling as we tramped on, a long line of dark shapes against the sand.

North-east of Singu by half a mile or more we turned out of the chaung and began our circle round to the next chaung, which we could then follow to the town. It was impossible to move as quietly or quickly as I would have liked. The drum of telephone wire creaked as it revolved, and the two signallers who held it could not stride out. Men who individually can move in silence, in the mass tend to blunder on behind the fellow in front without much care. It took us an hour to cover the next mile. Anyone about must have heard us. There was no one about. I wondered what the Japanese who had charged our hillock were doing. I hoped they would not find the telephone wire. Then the chaung bank was suddenly below us and we turned west for Singu. These chaungs were a splendid help to night navigators. Soon we could see the dark tree-fringe of the town. We lay down in silence while a patrol went in. After half an hour they were back. No one around. We moved quickly into the trees and I did a short circle about the pagoda, the chaung bank and the buildings nearby. They were empty. I got on the phone to Denis and told him to send Jitbahadur.

Our job now was to keep quiet so that the rest of the Company could join us before we were discovered. We took up an all-round position, set sentries and dozed off. Two hours later Jitbahadur arrived. He had taken a direct route from Fantasia, and unencumbered by drums and signallers had made good time. I telephoned the news to Denis. It was now past midnight. Unfortunately he could not start at once. The company that was to relieve him had not arrived—through some misunderstanding it was lining a ditch five hundred yards back waiting for orders. When at last he set off, accompanied by a gunner O.P. party, more telephone cable to reel out, heavy wireless sets, and the M.M.G. Platoon, he was far behind schedule.

I did not know this. I now had two platoons and felt happier. We enlarged our perimeter to include the pagoda, its compound and outbuildings, and I took some care in sighting the six L.M.G.s. We still could not dig or make any kind of noise, but there was plenty of good cover. Beyond the pagoda to the west and north, so far as could be seen in the dark, there were no buildings to block our immediate field of fire, and the trees were thinly spread.

It was a long time before I found out what had gone wrong. Dawn came, quickly as always, and with it instead of Denis came the sound of heavy firing half a mile north of us, where no one was supposed to be. It seems that not only were Denis and his group late, but that they strayed too close to Singu. At first light the Japanese saw them and with great speed had them pinned around a cluster of small pagodas with machine-gun fire, accurate sniping from tree-tops, and then with shelling.

This left me and my two platoons a little isolated. We were deprived of our main potential fire-power—the M.M.G.s and the wireless with which to summon artillery. But the men were cheerful, and in daylight the position still seemed a reasonable one, provided that no major assault hit us. We began to dig like madmen. I needed a couple of hours free of interference, and I got them. By the time the Japanese found us and had realised that we were not going to move, everyone had a slit trench or was behind a substantial wall, and everyone was familiar with his surroundings.

The day began to hot up in every way after that. From the thick cover on the far bank of the chaung, which was a mere fifty yards wide, the trenches near the bank came under accurate sniping fire. I had a man killed here; his companion and the occupants of two other posts were pinned inside their trenches for the rest of the day. They got hot and increasingly thirsty. Several of us tried to spot the snipers through the upper windows of a brick house that overlooked the chaung. I could see nothing through field-glasses, and all the time I searched there was the nasty feeling that perhaps a sniper could see me and was about to put a bullet between my eyes.

Then I tried to direct the field guns on to a house that might be sheltering the snipers. Since the gunner O.P. was with Denis, I had to be my own spotter. This proved to be difficult. There was only the telephone to Fantasia. I started on a map reference. I gave this over the phone and then ran thirty yards to a position from which I ought to have seen the shell burst. I had to run if I was not to be a sitting duck for the sniper. There was a dull roar somewhere behind and to the right. I ran back to the phone. 'Up two hundred yards.' I ran back to my observation point. There was a dull roar somewhere among the trees to the right. Back to the phone. 'Left one hundred.' There was a dull roar well ahead, somewhere among the trees. I had seen no sign of an explosion, was streaming with perspiration, and was convinced that I would soon land a shell on top of myself or the men. I tried twice more, running to the phone and back: the shells just vanished into the trees. I gave it up, and looked with respect upon the next gunner officer I met.

We started to receive harassing fire from light mortars and grenade dischargers. This was not heavy but the bombs were apt to catch us unaware. I had a narrow escape. As I stepped under the stone porch of a building which we had made into a first-aid post, and where a couple of lightly wounded men were being dressed, a mortar bomb exploded on the roof of the porch, and showered the space I had just left.

The Japanese made no serious attempt to attack us. A few probing patrols through the trees were easily discouraged. Perhaps they were content to keep us on ice while they pre-vented reinforcements getting through. Denis had much the worst of the deal. Throughout the morning I could hear eruptions of firing to the north where I supposed him to be. The sounds grew no closer, so I knew he was stuck.

About midday Walter Walker came on the phone. 'You all right, Pat?'

'We're fine, sir.'

'Good. Hold on as you are and we should have Denis to you during the afternoon. We've got the gunners' carriers here, three of them, and Geoffrey Bull is coming out in them with rations and ammunition. He'll go to Denis first and then on to you. I don't think the Japs are about in much strength. The carriers will discourage them.'

'O.K., sir.'

'Oh, and Pat, I'm making you a captain with immediate effect.'

He rang off. That was a good moment. It was like those stories of the Crusades I had read as a boy, in which the last Saracen is still gouting blood and the fierce cries of battle still ring in the ear when King Richard commands the young squire to kneel and be knighted. Even in our vaster wars there cannot have been many who were promoted over the telephone while cut off and under shot and shell. It was certainly a morale-raiser. I moved around in a mild euphoric daze, a combination of fatigue and good spirits, and waited for the promised junction with Denis. I was almost sorry when he made it late that afternoon. I had lost my independence.

Denis had had an unpleasant morning. Several of his men had been killed (two of them beside him) and others wounded. Unlike us he'd had no water. His ammunition had dwindled alarmingly. When the carriers set out to reach him, all three had broken down in the open close to the Japanese positions. Still, they had got themselves going again and here he was. I showed him our perimeter and into it we absorbed the fresh men. We sited the M.M.G.s, and the gunner O.P. was able to accomplish what I had failed to do—bring down a rash of shells along the opposite bank of the chaung—and as soon as it was dusk I was able to rescue the unfortunate men on our side of the chaung who had been sniped into crouching all day in their trenches.

We lay down to sleep, wondering whether the Japanese would now put in a serious attack upon us. They ought to have done. We expected them to. I slept as though drugged and woke for the dawn stand-to in the slow realisation that I was still alive, they had not attacked, and I was a captain.

We stayed put all that day, trying to locate and eliminate snipers, and harassed now by a machine-gun that appeared to fire from that same house on the far side of the chaung. We had to be very careful how we moved. On the 17th A Company relieved us and we retired to Bastion and more shelling. The Japs continued to snipe A Company during the morning, and resisted C Company when it moved to the high ground east of Singu. But the end was unexpectedly close. From further east down the metalled road from Kyaukpadaung to Chauk our 33 Brigade had come storming in, and on the night of the 16th/17th had found a vital hill feature unoccupied. On the 17th the 4/1st Gurkhas reported most of Chauk empty. We had been delayed by a thin screen while the main body of the enemy withdrew in the least expected direction, across the river to Seikpyu. We should not have to attack over the Pyinma Chaung and up those hostile barren cliffs I had crept beneath five weeks earlier. The battle which we had expected would be difficult, and perhaps costly, vanished. On the 18th we were all in Singu and that night there was a considerable celebration in our Mess. We had seen enough of the Japanese now to be grateful for reprieve.

That obscure little fight at Singu, which rates only a couple of lines in the Divisional History (without mentioning the 4/8th), a short and inaccurate paragraph in the Regimental History, and nothing in the official *History of the Second World War*, was the climax of my war. It was the last time I went confidently into battle, the last occasion I was in full command of my fears.

In war fear is inevitable. It accompanies all but a very few for all but very brief moments of their time in action. It is possible to forget fear in the stress and heightened emotion of close fighting, but such moments are rare and short. Even in the toughest battle too much of the time is spent in waiting, or approaching, or outflanking an unseen enemy, for battle-fever to supplant fear. I never felt this fever of battle. But if fear is certain, it is at first controllable. It is one element among many that together make an exhilarating tension. If a soldier is well trained and well led he remains for a long time mentally robust, confident, curious—anxious but master of his anxiety.

Then, after weeks, or months, or maybe years, there comes a moment when mind and body have had enough. People differ in how quickly they reach this moment according to the intensity of their experiences and their physical and mental constitutions. They may try to conceal their condition for as long as possible. But like a tree with worm, their core is no longer inviolate. They are hollow men, hearts gnawed by the worm of fear. If they are unlucky the final breakdown is spectacular and dangerous. If they are lucky the condition is diagnosed; they will be gently pensioned off, posted back perhaps to a training unit where hard-earned experience can be taught to others.

It is not easy to describe this change in oneself. At Singu nothing new had entered the situation. The chances of being wounded or killed were as before. It was as though something had worn out or broken. I suppose I had exhausted my store of nervous energy. Perhaps I had done too many patrols too close on one another. Physically all of us were on the down-grade. We were short of sleep and of nourishing food. It is difficult to eat properly when very tired, very hot, under strain and the food is not appetising. During those two days in Singu I could not eat anything. Yet so far my encounters with the Japanese had been remarkably unbloody. I had not fired a shot in anger, though some had been fired at me. I had thrown one hand-grenade. I had been shelled and mortared a few times, though never with intensity. Many of our men had gone through two campaigns against the Japanese, each more severe than this, and were still serviceable.

Nevertheless, whatever it is that keeps us going willingly and ardently into battle had for me run out. Will-power and pride bore me along after a fashion. Maybe no one noticed the difference. But from now on I never volunteered. I shrank inwardly at the news of fresh assignments. I most wanted to be where the Japanese were not.

XVIII

PURSUIT

Now began a confusing and unsatisfactory kind of war. The glamour (and much hard fighting) was with the divisions racing south for Rangoon. It is their operations which fill the histories. Our role was supplementary. We were to destroy the Japanese in the Irrawaddy valley, prevent them from interfering with the drive on Rangoon, and to cut off and destroy the Japanese now retreating eastwards towards the Irrawaddy from the Arakan. Apart from the river port of Prome, which I never saw, there were no important physical objectives: no cities, no mountain ranges or river lines to capture. We were after bodies, and bodies can be elusive things.

On 22 April we climbed into trucks and jeeps, an unexpected luxury, passed through Chauk, which we had seen in the distance for so long (bare hills, oil derricks leaning at all angles, rust-red and desolate), and after some pleasant dust-free motoring on tarmac roads, and two nights on the way, recrossed the Irrawaddy in a variety of small boats at Kyaukye, a village of no significance eight miles north of Yenangyaung (Map 4). 33 Brigade kept east of the river; ourselves and 114 Brigade quartered the west.

One of those two nights on the way to Kyaukye provided the first of my two snake encounters during four years of the tropics. We had arrived at our bivouac in the afternoon. While I was at a conference Nandalal arranged my belongings under a tree in the middle of a field, and found for me a piece of flat woven matting as a bed. When I returned and pulled the matting a few inches further from the trunk of the tree a large and beautiful snake emerged and slid rapidly towards some of the men. Gurkhas will chase any living object at the drop of a

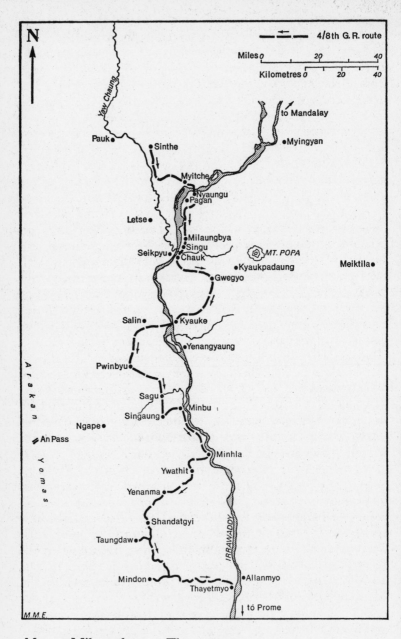

Map 4 Milaungbyas to Thayetmyo

hat. Their hunting instincts are uninhibited by concern for the hunted. There was an immediate pursuit. Yells, whoops, sticks and stones soon dispatched the poor snake. The Doc, who studied snakes for pleasure, and to whom the men took every snake as the Greeks offered chickens to the Delphic oracle, pronounced mine a Russel's viper, very poisonous. It was wonderfully marked with a series of light brown circles, ringed in black and white, like links in a chain, on an orange-brown background. Earlier, back in Tamu, Denis had a similar experience, waking one morning to find that he had spent the night warming two kraits beneath his sleeping-bag.

The second snake to meet me was in south Burma just after the end of the war. B Company was in the middle of a platoon exercise. I wanted to cross a patch of secondary jungle, and was hurrying alone down a narrow footpath bordered by thick tall bushes, with trees meeting overhead. Rounding a corner I faced a large dark-coloured snake sprawled on the path. With reactions sharpened by nine months of active service I was running in the opposite direction before my eyes could register details. I never knew what snake had routed me.

Snakes were plentiful in the dry belt of central Burma, so we were told. Not far to our east, when we were before Milaungbya, was the 5,000-foot Mount Popa, reputed to be swarming with king cobras (and Japanese). Perhaps it was. I never met anybody who was on it. We saw very few snakes. One night a rifleman crawled inside his mosquito net and, having tucked it carefully down, found that he was sharing the space with a snake he could not see. Both became desperate to escape; neither was damaged. Another man was bitten when he jumped on a snake that had fallen into his slit-trench. He suffered no worse than a painful swelling. Once a python was spotted high in a tree. It was doing no harm, but people felt nervous about it up there, so it was shot. According to the records, in the whole 14th Army, from 12 November 1944 to 19 May 1945, only four cases of snake bite were admitted to hospital. Three of them died.

But to return to our war. The object of crossing the Irra-waddy where we did was to cut off the Japanese who were withdrawing before 114 Brigade. The Sikhs and the 2nd

K.O.S.B.s had crossed at night before us, without opposition
except from soft sand, swamp and leeches. As we crossed there
was a tank stuck on a sandbank. Then we were turfed out on
to a sandbank ourselves, and marched a scorching thirteen
miles with full packs over shifting sand, over plough, through
six-foot spear-grass, deep chaungs and then swamp. We arrived
at our objective, some high ground inland, exhausted. Neither
the tanks, nor the artillery, nor our transport carrying food,
bedding and ammunition, could make it that day. Nor did
the Japanese, because they had already passed.

The next two weeks were spent on a series of southward
bounds, occasionally in transport, mostly on foot, and often
at night. We and the Sikhs were leapfrogging one another; the
K.O.S.B.s were off to the west. In this way we passed through
Pwinbyu, Sagu and Minbu, and reached Minhla on the
Irrawaddy on 4 May. The K.O.S.B.s had several sharp brushes
with parties of Japanese; with one exception we did not. The
Japs were avoiding the obvious routes along the river plain
and were keeping to the hills. The exception was D Company,
which at one point did a four-day solo sweep westwards across
some low hills and was attacked, losing the popular Jemadar
Nathu Gurung and several men. Nathu took a wrong turning
in the dark, walked out of his own perimeter, and was
bayoneted by some Japanese who were closing in for an
attack. He died seven days later.

It was during this period, on 27 April, that three new officers
joined us, the first officer reinforcements we had received since
Kohima. They were Quentin Kennedy (a close friend to
Mike Tidswell), Peter Dickenson and Douglas Farnbank.
Quentin Kennedy was posted to D Company under Geoffrey
Bull, and found himself next day on the diversion I have just
mentioned—a sharp introduction to battle. Douglas Farnbank
was an old acquaintance, for he had left England with me, and
we had been commissioned on that same distant October day
eighteen months ago. He became Intelligence Officer in place of
Bill. Peter Dickenson went to another of the rifle companies.

Although these days were often hard work, and for a few of
us were dangerous, I found them restful. Much of the time I
had no more to do than get myself from a to b. Denis did the

thinking and the worrying. I was sent on one patrol: by jeep
along an open road beside a canal which ran through pleasant
cultivated country where only in the villages could the enemy
hide. In a rifle company I found little of the tension always
present at Battalion Headquarters. I was now part of a limb,
rather than of the heart. We led an almost pastoral existence.
Indeed this little enclave of Burma, bordered west and south
by the forested Arakan Yomas, and with the Irrawaddy and
the barren hills beyond to the east, was the antithesis of the
Milaungbya area. It was a green land even at this fag-end of the
hot weather. The larger chaungs carried water the year round
and fed a network of irrigation canals. Villages and people
abounded, physically unmarked by war. The people laughed.
We had come in from the desert to the land of milk and honey.

Some of the anxieties persisted, like Sinbad's burden. Each
day or night as we marched towards a new objective it was
expected that we might have to fight. Each evening at the
Colonel's conference we heard of clashes just outside our line
of advance, and of reports of large bodies of enemy in the hills
to the west. Nevertheless, though the night marches kept one
short of sleep, there was time to relax. I got into the rifle
company routine: march, arrive, reconnoitre, site platoon and
section positions, site headquarters, dig in, mug of tea, orders
from the Colonel, orders to platoon commanders, food, final
rounds, tot of rum or whisky with luck, sleep with luck. I merely
had to know what was going on, and to be ready to help. On a
routine day no help was required. Everybody knew what to do.
They had been doing it for months across half Burma.

I got to know Denis better. I described him earlier as short
and neat and soft spoken, as almost diffident. He had a neat
black moustache that well expressed his personality, for he
was exact in his thinking and brisk in his actions, like a robin,
and dead honest. When he was amused, which was often, his
eyes sparkled. He had joined the Battalion as a lieutenant only
a week or two before me, and like me had just missed the
Imphal campaign. But he was considerably older than most of
us. He had been a Territorial Army soldier before the war,
had been mobilised in 1939 (as a rifleman), and had been
serving somewhere or other ever since, including a year at

the 8th Regimental Centre in Quetta. There he had achieved a captaincy and command of a training company. He had dropped rank to join the 4/8th. So it was not surprising that at Kohima Walter Walker had soon promoted him to company commander and major. And everyone was delighted when his M.C. for that first Milaungbya battle was announced.

I liked Denis and wished that I had been in better shape to help him.

When I transferred to B Company, Nandalal and Tulbir came with me. They too soon carved spaces for themselves in the company hierarchy. Indeed, until I had been there some weeks they were in the privileged position of being interpreters of my actions and thoughts. 'When the Sahib says this he means that,' they would probably explain. 'He pulls at his nose when he is angry. It is better to ask no favours until he has drunk his tea in the morning.' Tulbir had developed a degree of assurance that was astonishing. He required no mothering from me.

After Minhla this happy state of comparative relaxation began to change. We marched inland almost due west. The country changed, the weather began to change and the enemy changed. It looked as though we might intercept a substantial number of the Japanese from the Arakan. These had been moving back into central Burma over the An Pass to Ngape. Our move west would cut the hill-tracks south from Ngape, and would catch both them and the remaining forces who had been keeping the pass open for them. These Arakan Japanese belonged to 54th Division, a tired but experienced crew who would combine the usual Japanese fanaticism with the skill gained of several years in action; they were a tougher proposition than the troops of 72 I.M.B. whom we had recently opposed. With them would be their motor transport and perhaps artillery. If we were in time to block those tracks they would have to abandon both and break into small parties. They would cease to be a formed military body, and they would fight to prevent this happening.

The change in the country helped the Japanese. We now entered a land of forested hills. The hills were not high by Asian standards—they seldom stretched to a thousand feet—and the forest was not generally thick; but the combination was enough to restrict movement off the tracks. It cut back on the advantage we had been enjoying of superior tank and artillery support. It made air supply that much more difficult. It favoured the foot soldier in small parties. It prevented the concentration of large formations quickly. The mobility we had been able to exploit on the plains was lost. We were back to the jungle war for which we had been trained, and because of which even our vests and underpants were dyed a jungle green.

Although I liked the jungle—the light and shade, the green mystery at every step, the sheer triumphant vegetable growth —and during training had enjoyed working in it, now that I was to fight in it I was not so happy. Perhaps it was that I came first and fresh to fight in the open: unlike love, war does not improve with experience. Perhaps in training it had been easy to ignore the instinctive dread of the dark forest that probably lies deep in us. Perhaps I was just too tired.

As for the weather, we were in the pre-monsoon steam bath. The nights were still cool; the days were a trial, hot and humid, so that we longed for yet dreaded the first rain.

On 3 May Rangoon was captured. So was Prome. In Britain this must have seemed the end of the campaign in Burma. For us it was satisfactory, but almost irrelevant, a remote victory that made no immediate difference to our lives. We did not celebrate.

We set off from Minhla on 5 May, one day behind the Sikhs, on a ten-mile march to Ywathit (every fourth village in Burma seems to be called by this name), and next day did the seventeen miles to Yenanma. On both days, on the afternoon of our arrival, I did jeep patrols. From Yenanma I left as mortar bombs exploded on our dropping zone, which B Company was defending. There were several skirmishes with Japanese patrols during my absence.

These jeep patrols had not been unpleasant in the open country. You sped along where no enemy could hide, dismounted before bridges and villages, spied them out on foot, and covered ten or twenty miles quite quickly. Along hilly forest tracks they were very different. These tracks were seldom straight or level for a hundred yards. They were narrow. Ambushes were possible anywhere. It was difficult to turn quickly between the trees. The noise of the engine deprived us

o

of a major protection, our ears, and gave to an enemy long warning of our approach. I sat beside the driver, eyes straining at the jungle on either side ahead, always tense, always ready to leap for cover, and hardly mollified by the knowledge that most Japanese were poor shots, and that they should not have had time to lay mines. The suspense was continuous. It might last for several hours as we roared up and down and round ten miles or more of narrow trail, halting only for the obvious dangers such as chaungs, a cross-roads or a village. In a village, if it was empty of the enemy, we could question the inhabitants, and feel happier if they had no recent news. The return journey was only a little less anxious, for it would have been quite possible for Japanese to come fresh on to the track behind us: they were on the move south, as we were. Or a party might have let us pass going out, and hoped to catch us coming back. In this fluid war, with a huge, wild no-man's-land around small bodies of troops, we had to use jeeps to cover the distance.

On the second of these two patrols I let exhaustion and fading courage win. Short of the village which was our final objective we stopped, and backed the jeep into the trees ready for a quick retreat. I then sent the naik and his two men to look through the village and myself fell asleep. This was wrong. I knew it was wrong. But I couldn't take any more. Fortunately for my public reputation the village was empty of enemy and the men returned safely an hour later. I do not like to think what they thought of me. I thought nothing of myself, and the incident still troubles, twenty-five years later.

I was not the only one to have become nervy. There was at this time a marked reluctance with many of the men to press home patrols. A few shots from an enemy outpost would not have deterred people four months ago as they did now.

We spent three days at Yenanma with Brigade Headquarters while the Sikhs at Shandatgyi, in the next valley fourteen miles to the west, got involved more and more heavily with the main body of the rearguard to the retreating Japanese divisions, and while 114 Brigade pressed down from the north. Here on a night patrol Scotty fell down a well and survived undamaged. Here also I spent a night miles out with a platoon of B Company in ambush on a track down which it was thought

some enemy would come. I realised then how lonely is the
position of a front-line infantryman in our sort of war. Hitherto
I had slept within Battalion Headquarters, protected by a
rifle company or two and by our H.Q. personnel; or I had
slept inside a company perimeter, with three platoons between
me and the outer night; or in positions such as our patrol base
on the bare hills opposite Nyaunglya, where no one could
easily get close. This night was different. With dusk the forest
grew twice as tall, and malevolent, as in childhood nightmares;
it was full of noises, inexplicable, menacing. I lay awake in the
dark, listening and listening. The night was a prison and we,
a small band of twenty-five souls, were in the condemned cell.
Between me and the Japanese if they came, hundreds of them for
all I knew, there was one post, two men in a trench. None came.

My rebellious nerves might have been calmed by a more
frequent meeting with the enemy. Many soldiers have recorded
that anticipation of battle is worse than the fighting. In our
war you could not relax. Almost every day and every night
held the possibility of action. Yet the times we clashed compared with the times we might have clashed remained small.
We were condemned to almost perpetual anticipation.

We were at Yenanma when the war in Europe ended. My
cousin Minna wrote: 'Pat, out there in the sweat and toil of it
all, can you get a glimmer of what it means to us here that the
wholesale slaughter and the continual smash, smash, smash is
finished for Europe?' Her letter made me pause. Who among
us had cared about the happenings in Europe, another planet?
It was difficult for us to appreciate their reliefs. We should
benefit from their victory—in the long run. It made no difference now; and it somehow accentuated our fate. How many
in England knew or cared about our remote corner of an
unknown country? We had developed a pride in our isolation;
in the enigmatic and unpronounceable Burmese names of the
places we attacked and defended; in the criss-cross quartering
of the land by our units, north, south, east and west simultaneously, that no layman could have made sense of; in the
fact that, while we killed Japanese by the tens of thousands,
others elsewhere got the publicity; in the knowledge that we
did all this on a poor man's diet of weapons and equipment. VE

Day made us smile. There was a lot more of our war to come.

On 10 May we marched the fourteen miles to Shandatgyi to join the Sikhs, who had managed to block the desperate attempts of the Japanese to break south, and who were in need of relief. Soon after the war I wrote bits and pieces of a narrative that was intended for a novel. Little survives but one short section that was based directly on this march to Shandatgyi. I reproduce it now, slightly edited, as it gives the kind of detail which time expunges from the memory.

The Colonel gave out his orders just before dusk. The Sikhs were heavily engaged with several hundred enemy. They were five hours' march ahead, over a range of small hills. C Company was to start that night, arriving at a village behind the Sikhs by first light. The rest of us were to march at dawn. Depending on events during darkness, we would attack tomorrow. The enemy must be destroyed.

Questions were asked and answered. Details were checked and rechecked until everybody was satisfied. Then we returned to our companies to explain the orders to the platoon commanders. This did not take long, for we knew the procedures thoroughly. Order of march, formation, equipment, these were automatic. Only the time and place changed.

It was dark now and we lay down to sleep. Beyond the familiar forest noises there was no sound. Silence meant life. For a few minutes I lay and worried; worried about the morrow, about what we should find, who would be hurt, was there anything I had forgotten, was Naik Dhaniram seriously sick or would he come back in a day or two. But I was very tired and was soon asleep; it seemed that only a few minutes had passed when my orderly was muttering in my ear.

All around dim forms were moving. There was a continuous rustle of clothing, a clinking of mule harness, scarcely audible whispers. Beside me a mug of hot tea was steaming. I laced up my wet boots between sips, and shivered. The pre-dawn air was cold. My orderly rolled up my blanket. There was little for me to do. I slipped on belt and pouches and checked my rifle. Suddenly all this muffled activity was stilled. The men were in their sections, equipment on, ready to move. Platoon commanders came to report. I looked at my watch.

We were half a minute late. Denis gave the signal to start.

The first section moved off, the second, then the third. That was No. 6 Platoon on their way. Jemadar Jitbahadur looked as jaunty as ever. Now Company Headquarters followed, and I with them. It was getting lighter. I could see the whole Company now. Most of them, as usual, were still half asleep. They stumbled a lot at the start. But the dawn chill made marching a pleasure and the leading section set a good pace.

Those forest tracks were very beautiful in the early morning. A blue mist drifted through the tree-trunks, sometimes so thick that the man two ahead was lost, sometimes stretched in long ribbons, curling round a tree, uncurling, swirling in a current of air, gathering itself around a dripping bush, seeping through and over, passing on. The mist covered our clothing and equipment with beads of moisture. When thick it caught at the breath in our throats. As the sun rose, the mist turned from blue to rose pink. Then it would begin to stream up through the trees into the clear air where it vanished in the growing heat. And suddenly we, too, would find ourselves steaming, and another day of heat and sweat, worry and fatigue had really started, and the beauty and the mystery of the track was gone.

Like this, no doubt, we marched off to Shandatgyi, towards what everyone felt must be the climax of our present efforts. Sometimes battle comes unawares, and its climax is upon you and past before you are sure of anything beyond the need to fight as skilfully and bravely as you can. It was not like this now. We had recrossed the Irrawaddy on 24 April, and ever since had been trying to bring the Japanese to battle. Now we knew that they were almost in our net. The Sikhs had killed a large number at Shandatgyi. There remained only one more valley, twelve miles further on, containing a track that could be used by a military force with trucks and artillery. Westward was a wilderness of forested hills impassable to vehicles. The Japanese had recoiled from the Sikhs, whose patrols were following them over and into that last valley, the valley of the Mu Chaung. And into that valley B Company was sent. We were to be the centre of the climax, and knew it.

XIX

THE TRAP

The efforts of 33 Corps to prevent the Japanese forces on the west bank from regaining the east resulted in two considerable engagements. The first, some thirty-five miles north-west of Allanmyo, lasted from the 11th to the 15th May. In it, troops of the 7th Division destroyed Yamamoto's rearguard, and, what was perhaps more important, captured seventy-five of the enemy's rapidly diminishing stock of lorries.... General Slim, *Defeat into Victory.*

From the col on the ridge the track dropped quickly, slanting across wooded slopes to the open valley. From the edge of the forest we stared at the village through field-glasses. There was nothing to be seen, no movement of any kind. Out on to the bare fields went the scouts, live bait. The leading section followed. The rest of us lined the edge and covered them. The forest now seemed a friendly sheltering place. The scouts reached the village and disappeared. The section reached the village and waited among the first houses. No sound. No movement. Five long minutes. A Gurkha reappeared and waved. On your feet. Let's go. No time to lose. Driven by an urgency that infected every man, we moved fast across the sun-stricken earth. We had got there first. But by how long?

The valley was half a mile wide, almost flat, with the village, Taungdaw, nearer the far side (Map 5). A little north of the main village was the *hypoongyi chaung*, surrounded by trees. Close by this on the west was the stream and the ford by which the track from the north crossed it. Down this track and over this ford the Japanese must bring their guns and bullock carts and vehicles. Beyond the stream the ground rose steeply for several hundred feet, forming the valley's western

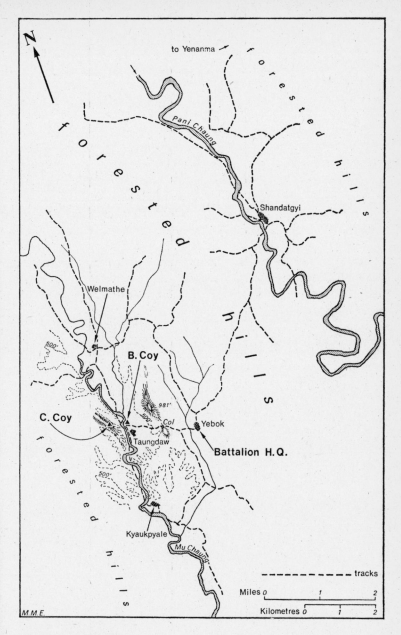

N

to Yenanma

forested hills

Pani Chaung

Shandatgyi

forested

Welmathe

500'

hills

B. Coy

981'

C. Coy

500'

Col

Taungdaw

Yebok

Battalion H. Q.

forested

500'

Kyaukpyale

Mu Chaung

hills

– – – – – – – – – tracks

Miles 0   1   2

Kilometres 0   1   2

M.M.E.

Map 5 Taungdaw

boundary. This ridge was covered in trees and undergrowth. Denis sent a patrol up there, and another north towards the next village upstream.

Surveying the ground, Denis and I were puzzled. Our orders were to block the track. The safest place to be was on the ridge across the stream, which would be difficult to capture; from it we could block the track with fire by day. Could we block the track at night? It seemed unlikely. On the other hand, if we sat by the track, covering the ford, we would be massacred by enemy on the ridge.

Walter Walker had asked Denis to phone back if he thought a second company was needed. Clearly it was. Denis asked for it and at once C Company set off to join us. Denis decided that with a company on the ridge we could survive in the valley. If there was to be a position in the valley, the sooner somebody dug trenches for it the better. Up on the ridge, with its steep sides and limited avenues of approach, delay was less serious.

This decision to sit in the valley was thought to be unsound by the rest of the Battalion. Certainly we did not feel easy down there in the days to come. Yet I still do not see how else we could have stopped the Japanese from moving past at night.

Anyway, rightly or wrongly, we committed ourselves. The men began to dig furiously. And within two hours a messenger from the patrol up the valley returned with the news of Japanese only a mile away. We had come just in time. By the afternoon when Peter Myers and his men trudged past to file up on to the ridge, it was too late to change. The Japanese patrols were sniffing around us. I felt like the cow that was tied up as bait in tiger shoots: the tiger killed the cow and the hunters killed the tiger.

The position Denis had chosen, if it had not been for the high ground close by, was quite a good one. To the west and north Jemadar Manbahadur's platoon defended the curving waters of the chaung. An attack would have to wade through them and climb a four-foot bank to reach his posts. Tucked inside this curve, forming a rough square, was the *hypoongyi chaung* and its compound, our home, with trees and several buildings to give concealment. To the east and south was open flat cultivated ground. The nearest cover here for the enemy was the village of Taungdaw, 150 yards off.

Company Headquarters was close to the edge of the southern perimeter beside the vital track, looking towards Taungdaw and up to C Company's ridge. Near us, by the *hypoongyi chaung*, was a gunner Forward Observation Party of 136 Field Regiment, Royal Artillery, with a 22 wireless set, commanded by a young Lieutenant, Gilbert Gentle. We had a telephone line back to Battalion Headquarters. Another F.O.P. under Lt. Bark accompanied Peter Myers. It was comforting to know that sixteen 25-pounder field-guns were on call, and that we could summon air support. We could have done with wire, and time to fix up booby-traps.

That evening the battle started. From somewhere to the north-east came the staccato rap, hiss and echo of a single menacing shot. Everyone tensed. There was a series of explosions to the south-east, out in the valley. For a few minutes we were mystified. Then Peter Myers came through to say that his 2 in. mortars had dispersed some forty Japs who had been forming up to attack us. As dusk cut down visibility, we settled in for what seemed certain to be a grim night. Neither Denis nor I said so, but we knew that if the Japanese concentrated a large enough force to rush us in the dark, they could overwhelm us. Without wire, without the medium machine-guns that had provided such a solid weight of fire for our Milaungbya positions; without 3 in. mortars, without defensive fire zones ranged about us, our position was not secure. Neither food nor ammunition would last a prolonged fight, for we had come only with what we could carry. As the last of the light faded I fixed the bayonet to my rifle, had a round in the breech, placed my kukri near me and stretched out beside my trench. There was nothing more to be done but to sleep while the chance of sleep remained.

The Japanese were oddly hesitant that first night. They jittered us, sending shots into the perimeter and calling out. We could hear them up on the ridge before C Company, whose forward platoon on the northern spur held the key to that position, and so to our own. But they made no attacks. This was unexpected. Generally they were quick to react.

It is easy to forget the difficulties of one's enemy. In detail such difficulties can never be known at the time. They can only be surmised. Up the valley to our north there were supposed to be between a thousand and two thousand of these unknown Japanese soldiers. That seemed a lot of men to us, with our hundred or so down by the ford, and the same number on the ridge. We imagined that it should have been simple for several hundreds of them to collect and rush us. But no doubt it was not simple. Their men were probably a good deal dispersed. They would all be tired, even exhausted, perhaps hungry, certainly battle weary. They had already fought with the Sikhs and had lost. They had sick and wounded. They had supplies and trucks and guns to move and to guard. Perhaps the track had to be improved, bridges strengthened. We knew that we were tired, needed sleep, were always short of it. We forgot that our enemy must sleep. We thought of him as perpetually hurrying towards us, desperate and energetic.

It is only now, as it becomes possible to read here and there of what was felt by the Japanese who were fighting in Burma (little enough has been translated into English), it is only now that our enemies shrink to human size. Long since I have accepted other Japanese as human beings. But the Japanese army of the years of war, those ugly, grinning, toothy fanatics of the newspaper caricatures and the government propaganda posters, the enemy, 'them', whom one hardly ever saw, and whose trademark was grenade, bullet, shell and that peculiar smell which remained in every position they had occupied, 'they' did not easily tire or hunger, seemed immune to fear and never surrendered. 'They' were not truly human.

Then years afterwards I read this in a book, and the true proportions of what we all endured grew clearer. Here is a young Japanese lieutenant talking to his platoon before they go into action for the first time (at Kohima in 1944):

'You see,' I said to my soldiers, 'keep your heads, keep cool. If you want to find out just how cool you are feeling, put your hands inside your trousers and feel your penis—if it is hanging down, it is good.' I tested mine, but it was shrunk

up so hard I could hardly grasp it. More than thirty soldiers
did the same thing, then looked at me curiously, but I kept
a poker-face. I said, 'Well, mine's down all right. If yours
is shrunk up, it's because you're scared.'

Then a young soldier said to me: 'Sir, I can't find mine
at all. What's happening to it?' With this everyone burst
out laughing and I knew I had got the confidence of the
men.'*

Any soldier of any nation will recognise the truth of this
physiological fact, though maybe a British platoon commander might have hesitated to make use of it. That platoon
went into action and by nightfall only eighteen out of thirty
were left. It is impossible not to feel sympathy for them. Both
sides were up the same bloody creek.

On our side we stood to at dawn like men reprieved from
the gallows. By day we could hold our own.

It is difficult now to remember the order of events. Indeed
my memory of the Taungdaw battle is much less sharp than
my memory of earlier engagements. But around midday the
Japanese were shelling us at close range with 75 mm and
'infantry' guns. B Company got the first dose of this, and it
was a most unwelcome surprise, for we had hoped that our
enemy might be without artillery after their long mountain
trek from the Arakan. An even more unwelcome surprise was
that our own artillery somewhere over by Brigade Headquarters
was unable to drop shells close to our positions in the valley
because the high ridge in between intercepted the necessary
trajectory. The Japanese shells were aimed at the *hypoongyi
chaung*, whose roof was probably a fine landmark. They burst
on the building with frightening suddenness, or wailed past
and out of our perimeter like insane ghosts. Crouching in our
headquarter trenches we could hear pieces of metal tearing
the leaves about us, thwacking into the earth. Smoke thickened
and drifted among the tree trunks. We were on the fringe of
the zone of fire; it was the gunner O.P. party who were in real
danger and they moved elsewhere at the first lull.

* Lieutenant Seisaku Kameyana, 2nd Battalion, 58th Regiment, quoted
by Arthur Swinson in *Kohima*, p. 69, Cassell, 1966.

In the middle of the racket a young British gunner appeared before me, blood streaming from a torn artery in his upper arm. With an imperfect memory of first-aid lessons from my Home Guard days in 1942, I tied a tourniquet. The wound was clean, no bones damaged. Later I loosened the tourniquet and bound up the wound itself. Then a column of mules arrived with rations and ammunition; it was unloaded at speed, for the occasional shell was still falling, and with it the gunner was able to return to Shandatgyi.*

The Japanese guns turned on C Company, and proved more effective because a number of shells burst on the tree tops, shooting fragments down into the slit-trenches. There were several casualties. And it was on this afternoon or evening that the Japanese discovered our telephone line and cut it. But we still had the two wireless sets. Then our B Company artillery set was knocked out with a sniper's bullet through its guts. This left the set with C Company. And that evening the two Sikh operators of this set were wounded by a shell-burst. One died during the night. The other, despite a painful foot wound, carried on, a brave performance.

We in B Company must have been able to communicate with Peter Myers, for we got news from him regularly. I have forgotten whether we did this through our short-range battalion wireless sets or through a telephone.

By late afternoon the enemy were in strength on the 900-foot ridge between us and the rest of the Battalion, the eastern boundary of our valley. They were also in Taungdaw, behind us. We were cut off. Again C Company spotted a bunch of them forming up to attack us. Again some accurate 2 in. mortar fire broke them up, while our men joined in with rifles and machine-guns. Some twenty-five were killed and lay a hundred yards from our perimeter for the next three days.

So came another evening stand-to, another dusk, and once more the careful arranging of personal weapons against the

---

* In September, shortly after the war had finished, I was walking through a camp outside Rangoon when suddenly this young gunner reintroduced himself. He wanted to thank me. He was quite recovered. I sometimes think that binding him up was the only constructive action I performed during my war.

probability of attack in the warm dark. Surely by now the enemy had concentrated his troops and would make his supreme effort to dislodge us. He could not wait to starve us out. Time was our friend. For a day, perhaps two days, the Japanese would have superiority in men. This would not last. The rest of our brigade was closing the trap. We were the trap-door, the cork in the bottle, the keystone of the dam.

Mosquitoes whined. We rubbed the protective oil on faces and hands now filthy from forty-eight hours of unwashed toil. A stillness had come over our world. The guns were quiet. Not a rifle-shot broke the silence which seemed to grow more and more menacing as it was prolonged. Around me were the men I knew so well: Denis by his slit-trench six feet away; his orderly and mine, Nandalal, sharing a trench scarcely more distant on our southern perimeter; the men of the platoons, some along the river's edge listening above the murmur of the flowing water, others facing the open night of the valley that might at any moment erupt with charging figures. Some would be trying to relax into uneasy sleep; the sentries would be straining for the suspicious sound, the hint of movement. Were they all as deeply apprehensive as I? 'I shall not forget that night at Taungdaw', wrote Denis to me many months later, 'when Peter said the Japs were massing for an attack on us and you and I both had our kukris out and both thought that it was the end but would not admit it to each other. Do you remember?' I do remember. I did not seem able to bolster my courage with anything. To lie in silence and wait and wait is difficult. Each man is alone with himself.

The first alarum was at midnight. A few yards off, from where our orderlies lay, a single rifle shot woke us brutally. So I must have slept. The orders against shooting at night were strict; the men would not have fired without good reason. What had they seen? Although so close, I could distinguish nothing. Nor did we call out to them. I had taken up my rifle as I woke, and now sat with it peering into the night, sensitive to every sound, abnormally aware of my own body, of rapid heart-beats, of fingers round the rifle barrel, of elbows and feet and skin pressed against cloth. A faint shifting of the shadow close by showed me that Denis was alert. I felt for my two grenades on the front edge of my trench and touched the pins. Heart-beats quieted. I began to distinguish the silhouettes of tree-trunks and bushes, and after a while, as always happens, these began to shift and waver, to change their shapes, to simulate men, men crouching, stalking, crawling. It was time to look away, to relax, to try to regain sleep. Whatever had disturbed the orderlies seemed to have stopped. Or had they been lured into shooting a shadow?

The next disturbance was in the early hours, about one o'clock, and came to us more distantly, from the ridge above. There was a sudden flurry of rifle-fire that grew quickly into the sustained sound of a major battle, with machine-guns yammering, the dull roar of exploding grenades, and just occasionally, through moments of quiet, human shouts. It was not us the Japanese had attacked, but C Company. The noise went on and on, with crescendoes and diminuendos. We lay and listened. There was nothing we could do, though our fate lay in the outcome of the battle up there. We could see the flashes of the bursting grenades; random bullets whined above our heads. The fighting seemed to stay roughly in the same place. If this was so, then 9 Platoon under the redoubtable Jemadar Padamsing, C Company's forward platoon on the ridge, was holding out. The ridge was narrow and steep, and the number of enemy who could attack at one time was limited.

Sleep was a lost hope now. Indeed we must not be diverted by the battle above lest there was an attack still to come on us. There was a lull on the ridge. They would be bandaging wounds, discovering the dead, taking stock of ammunition, staring into the dark to know if their ordeal was to be renewed. Around five o'clock it was renewed, and seemed more violent than ever. I was glad that we were not involved, yet it was terrible to be unable to help. On and on went the battle until, above that other ridge to the east that divided us from the rest of the Battalion, the sky paled and the firing petered out.

We slid into our trenches for the dawn stand-to. Gradually the now familiar landscape was revealed: bushes, trees, the watching heads of silent men, glimpses of the open valley. This was always an anxious yet joyful moment. Night was being banished, but daylight might reveal that the enemy had seized some advantage. Apprehensively we peered at the ridge. If the Japanese had even partly succeeded we must expect to be sniped and mortared. They would look down into much of our perimeter.

Tentatively men began to move. Nothing happened. Nandalal slouched off to make tea.

We now discovered the cause of that single jolting shot at midnight. Sprawled on the track not ten yards away was a dead Japanese. Denis's orderly had shot him. From the marks in the dust it seemed, incredibly, that he had crawled right through the Company from north to south until he had been killed as he was about to leave. Did he know what he was doing? Was he on reconnaissance or simply confused? How had he escaped detection further back? We never solved the mystery.

Nandalal brought the life-restoring tea. Peter came through to say that all was well with him, more or less. They had killed many Japs, and had a dozen killed and wounded themselves. Padamsing's platoon had fought superlatively: thirty-eight bodies were buried in front of it later that morning.

I forced myself to leave the shelter of my familiar patch of earth to look round our positions. While with 4 Platoon by the stream I was called urgently by a rifleman who made me peer between the bushes by his trench on to the hillside below C Company. Clearly visible about two hundred yards off was a solitary Japanese. He was crouching behind a tree and looking up the hill with rifle at the ready. I had never seen our living enemy so close. I could have laid down and shot at him. He was not a difficult target. But I told the rifleman to do so and moved on. My store of courage was so sadly depleted that I did not wish to be where reprisal firing might arrive. The men round the perimeter were surprisingly cheerful. At least it seemed surprising to me. I was ashamed and tried to take a grip upon myself. We had been lucky: not a man in B Company had been hurt since our arrival.

It was now the morning of Sunday, 13 May. Much happened on this day, though for us it was mostly a sitting and a waiting day. On the other side of the high eastern ridge the rest of

the Battalion had concentrated at Yebok, a little village
through which we had marched two days earlier. Some
Japanese had attacked one of D Company's platoons during
the night. This attack was a typical Japanese reaction to
desperate circumstances. It was made by ten men led by an
officer armed with a sword. All were killed. The officer killed
one of our men. Why did they throw away their lives? It is
unlikely that a superior officer ordered the attack, for there
was no co-ordinating movement elsewhere and ten men on
their own could not achieve any possible advantage. The
answer can only be that this small group, perhaps all that
remained of a platoon, grown desperate with the long retreat,
had decided on suicide with honour. What a people! We had
still to capture one.

It was on a D Company section too that the second bomb
from a Japanese heavy mortar landed. Momentarily caught
grouped close, six out of nine were killed or wounded.

During the morning D Company probed to the north,
intending to relieve pressure by coming in behind the Japanese
attacking us. They were blocked by strong forces three or
four miles from us, and were fiercely attacked. They could
make no headway, so the Colonel withdrew them to Yebok.
Indeed the Japanese seemed everywhere, and there were
plenty of them. The two sides were circling round each other,
searching for the opening for a mortal blow. In this country
of broken thickly forested hills it was a deadly game of blind
man's buff.

It was on this day too that we learned about Douggie
Farnbank, one of the three officers who had joined us on
27 April. The Colonel had made him Intelligence Officer.
We heard via Peter Myers that he had been badly wounded
the day before. It seemed that he had been sent on a jeep
patrol south of Yebok, with four Gurkhas and a Burma
Intelligence Corps naik. They had discovered about twenty-
five Japanese bathing. Although Douglas was on a reconnaissance and should have confined himself to observation,
the story we heard was that he charged the Japs in Crimean
War style. The bathing Japanese had not neglected sentries,
and a burst of L.M.G. fire hit Douggie in both legs. He

apparently owed his life to the B.I.C. naik, who carried him
to safety, hid him from the Jap patrols, bound his wounds,
stayed with him overnight, then reported his position to D
Company in Yebok, who brought him in. The four Gurkhas
with him seemed to have faded out.

Poor Douglas. His period of active service had lasted
seventeen days. Sitting with B Company on that morning of
the 13th, and hearing only the outline of his unfortunate
adventure, I remembered that he and I and Derrick Norris
had performed an absurd sketch at a concert at Mhow. On
that occasion Douglas had played the part of both hero and
heroine, wooing himself with much vigour before an imaginary
B.B.C. microphone. Why had he charged so impetuously,
against every rule of our training? He recovered fully, and
rejoined after the war, but I did not like to question him on
the subject.

Up round C Company's perimeter the Japanese were still
active. C Company now had a number of casualties who
needed attention from doctors, and as the day progressed,
shelling and sniping caused more. The most serious of these
was Ken Bark, the artillery lieutenant with 136 Field Regiment's O.P. A sniper sent a bullet through his stomach while
he was directing the guns. Peter came through to tell us, and
it was decided that Gilbert Gentle, our counterpart, whose
set had been smashed, must replace him. Half an hour later
he set off with a two-man escort to cross the stream and climb
the steep forested hillside. It was a potentially dangerous
journey, for no one could tell just where individual Japanese
had got to in the night. We were profoundly relieved to hear
of his safe arrival.

The Japanese made no major assault on us that day. They
were content to snipe and shell. Indeed they seemed to have
placed a large proportion of their fighting infantry on the
ridge between us and Yebok. Patrols from A and D Companies,
probing these positions, found them to be held in strength.
Walter Walker decided they had to be shifted, and organised
an attack for the next day. Meanwhile the 1/11th Sikhs from
Shandatgyi began to circle round to the north to attempt
what our D Company on its own had found impossible. We

P

in the surrounded positions knew none of the detail of this. We knew only that we were not alone, and that we must exist until help arrived. Individually each of us was busy—improving defences, organising the rationing of our diminishing food, digging latrines, on patrols to locate our immediate enemy and to remove troublesome snipers, simply keeping watch to guard against surprise attack.

The night of the 13th/14th passed quietly for us. Neither we nor C Company were attacked, so far as I recall. Nevertheless on the 14th morning the atmosphere was tense. Our supplies of food, and of mortar bombs and grenades, were uncomfortably low. The wounded up in C Company required evacuation to hospital more urgently than ever. Though Peter did not say so, it was obvious that Ken Bark was dying, and that only rapid surgery might save him: everyone knew that stomach wounds had to be treated quickly. Peter's perimeter must have been very unpleasant: it is difficult to remain undepressed by the sight of wounded for whom you can do so little.

During the morning Mike Tidswell and A Company started an attack to capture the col above Yebok where the track crossed the ridge. They climbed the ridge to the south and began to work north towards the col against increasingly heavy opposition. We could hear the firing, distantly, and I hoped that today the Japanese would break, would abandon their transport and get out. No doubt this was not a 'correct' wish. The longer they stayed around us, the more of them we should kill. The more we killed now, the fewer there would be to kill later when they might be rested and rearmed. But to hell with the longer view. I did not like to be the cheese in a bait.

By eleven o'clock A Company's leading platoon was stuck, halted by heavy and accurate fire from positions fifty yards ahead and above. Movement on these forested ridges was always difficult, and always favoured a resolute defence. Several men had been hit; the rest had gone to ground. Mike went forward to see what was holding them up.

Our British officers were discouraged from taking avoidable risks. It was our job to command, not to get killed. But Mike was faced with the one situation which we had agreed required personal leadership. The Japanese had to be driven from the col and the high ground on either side. Casualties had to be accepted. The men amongst whom the bullets were cracking and whining, who were beginning to receive those casualties, who could advance only over a narrow strip of upward-sloping, rough and forested earth, were not enthusiastic. They were hot and tired and afraid. It was the classic situation where the British officer went forward to lead in person.

We do not know exactly what happened. Apparently Mike reformed the platoon under cover, and then led them in a charge that was successful in capturing those positions immediately before them. The Japanese left ten dead behind. But in the charge Mike was hit at close range. A bullet went through his right arm and into his body, emerging at the top of his spinal cord. He was immediately paralysed, though conscious and able to talk. He died about an hour later, in the jeep taking him back to the Advanced Dressing Station, when paralysis reached his lungs.

Down in our valley we heard at first that he had been seriously wounded. When much later Denis came over to tell me that he was dead we both felt a great depression of spirit. Only one other death in the Battalion affected me so deeply, and that was yet to come.

I am conscious that in this account I have failed to bring to life my companions. Partly this is due to attrition of memory and insufficient skill. Partly it is because the British officers were not as much together as might be expected. Work kept us physically apart. The bulk of our active time was spent among Gurkhas. At Kohima we had evenings in common: we talked, sang, drank, read books. Such casual talk, which I do not intend to re-invent as a novelist legitimately might, gets forgotten. Since Kohima we had been much split, and in particular I had seen little of the officers with the rifle companies. So I am left with nothing out of which to draw a portrait save a kind of essence from the man, a distillation of spirit, of character, divorced from the revealing detail of speech and action.

I had known Mike since the days of the 38th Gurkhas at

Mohand a year before. With Bill Blenkin we had together
joined the Battalion. Mike was gentle, kind and nice; a civilian,
not really a warrior. Although he was competent as a soldier,
or Walter Walker would not have kept him, he did not lose
his amateur status. Everyone liked Mike. For most of my
fellow officers I could feel affection. A rough life of shared
experience brings all sorts into that much communion. But
only with a few was the bond of a quality to outlast the
dispersions of peace. Mike would have been one of those few.

When he was carried off, Scotty took over. By late afternoon
he and A Company were overlooking the road at the col, but
could get no further without the certainty of heavy casualties.
Beyond the col the ridge rose steeply, almost a cliff, and was
well defended. So there they consolidated.

Meanwhile we in B Company had our distractions. It was
on this afternoon, I think, that a flight of Hurricanes attacked
Taungdaw, 150 yards from my trench. We had been warned
of their coming and every man was crouching in his hole. The
hills forced the planes to fly down the valley from the north
and over our heads. It is easy, so we thought, for a pilot
moving at several hundred miles an hour to press the button
a second too soon. We were nervous. We heard the planes
approaching, very low (C Company must have had a grandstand view), the noise of their engines increasing swiftly to an
extreme crescendo of violence as they swept just above us,
one after the other, and at that moment started to fire their
cannons and machine-guns. The row was terrifying. For a
bonus we were showered with the empty shell cases. They
came crashing through the foliage, a hot metal hail. For
once I wished for a steel helmet.

The pilots' shooting was beautiful. Smoke and crackling
flames rose from the village, a destruction that lent us comfort.
We owed a great deal to those pilots, those and others. Months
before they had shot the Japanese air force out of Burma.
Now they gave us this wonderfully accurate close support in
our slogging tortoise land battles.

I have not so far made clear the hellish noise that can
sometimes possess a battle. The noise can be so overwhelming
as to inhibit the most elementary thought. Artillery is firing,

shells, grenades and mortar bombs are exploding, machine-guns of varying calibre are stitching their deadly patterns, rifles you can scarcely hear, and overhead perhaps aeroplanes are roaring, firing their guns, maybe dropping bombs. If there are tanks, then their engines are racing, and their guns and their machine-guns add to the inferno. All this is done by both your men and by the enemy. A soldier has to keep thinking through it. Survival depends on his acquired skill of the ear to distinguish and interpret automatically and instantly the origin and destination of every noise. It is for lack of this skill that reinforcements suffer so heavily if their early battles are tough. A soldier must know what is meant for him. One machine-gun in all that racket is perhaps streaming bullets through the leaves above his head. Where is it? Where in God's name is it? He cannot, must not, let the general noise overwhelm him.

The Platoon Commander rubs the sweat from out of his eyes. He cannot see most of his men, and he cannot see a single enemy. Shall he use his 2 in. mortar now or keep it until the enemy's positions are clearer? A Jap 75 mm shell whip-cracks over his head and explodes fifty yards behind in a shower of earth and metal and splintered foliage. This gun fires every minute or so and the next time could be too close. Lance-Naik Sarbarsing is firing his bren-gun again. What can he see? Without warning, three mortar bombs explode in quick succession just ahead, fortunately short. Cannot hear them dropping in this din. The crack of bullets through the air is almost continuous—the Japs are firing high, as usual—and his own men reply. A plane roars overhead. Can't see it for the trees. Should he tell Ratnabahadur's section to advance to that hedge while the others give covering fire? Before he can decide, Ratnabahadur and his men are on their feet and running and the noise of firing redoubles. Two men fall. *Hat tire ma chickne sala ko bachha.* Crack-whoam! That 75 mm again. He runs forward twenty yards to crouch behind the trunk of a palm tree and tries to make sense of the new scene and of the battering noise.

And the Company Commander, he is attempting four things at once. He is squatting beside the signaller, map spread on the earth, conducting an exchange over the wireless with the Colonel, who wants to know where he is now, how things are going, and whether he needs fire support; he is listening with quarter of an ear to a report from a platoon runner that his company subedar is attending to; he is, like everyone else, interpreting the swelling noise of battle on his own inner computer; and he is working all the time at the various permutations of future action that seem possible so that he can choose the best at a given moment. The 75 mm shells are closer to him, very distracting. Bullets whine and crack overhead, smack into tree trunks, ricochet past with weird wails. He can see even less than the platoon commanders. For perhaps twenty seconds there is an inexplicable pause and the sudden absence of noise is disturbing. Somewhere a man screams. There is a burst of the slow tac-tac-tac of a Jap machine-gun, and the noise is back. 'The one unforgivable sin is inaction,' a voice whispers at the back of his mind. But also he knows that battles are lost by commanders whose nerves fail, who give unnecessary orders because they have not the patience to wait. Through the centre of this infernal row he walks a mental tightrope, performing prodigies of balanced calculation, and scarcely has the time to remember that his own extinction threatens.

Fortunately, when the Hurricanes roared above our heads on this occasion, showering us with their glittering shellcases, we did not have to act. This strafing of Taungdaw village was simply part of the general slaughter of the enemy by any means to hand wherever they were spotted. C Company had seen the Japanese in the village but were too short of mortar bombs to intervene. So the planes were called in. Then it was dusk again, and we settled down to another night of siege.

It was a gloomy evening. Mike was dead. Several of the wounded with C Company had died. Peter Myers feared for others. Ken Bark was still alive, just. Shortage of food was a worry (though not to me; I was able to eat very little). The possibility of dropping tea and rice from light aircraft was considered, but was rejected in case it should reveal to the Japanese the extent of our plight. Then it started to rain heavily. And after the rain the vegetation steamed, as though we were living in some monstrous Turkish bath. There is a distressing inevitability about the seasons in the tropics. With this first rain we knew that soon we should have to live with it day and night for week after week. There was no escape. When it rained we would get wet. When the rain stopped we would begin to dry. For both sides it was a misery. And more immediately, the rain could soon reduce the tracks to un-negotiable mud; it could reduce or blot out visibility for our artillery observers; it could cut down or eliminate air support. Prolonged rain would level the odds towards equality with our enemy. There had to be a resolution to our situation tomorrow. The whole Battalion sensed this.

And back in Naini, I now read, this day, 14 May, had been declared 'Victory Day' and a general holiday, and my father lit the first of the six bonfires on the peaks round the lake at 9.15 p.m. The family took up a supper picnic, and oddly enough, the party included a major from 7th Division, who was able to tell my father of our recent movements. They stayed on their peak until 10.30, watching the celebratory fireworks rising from the lakeside two thousand feet below.

We had another quiet night. Pressure up on the col and from the north had certainly drawn off the pressure from us. We faced the dawn stand-to on the 15th comparatively refreshed, to begin another morning in our passive role of anvil, while out of sight others who were the hammer sweated into the attack.

But in battle the outlook can change with bewildering rapidity. Half the picture is always missing. The enemy suffers. His condition deteriorates. He becomes exhausted, makes mistakes, underestimates our worries and overestimates our strength. The pressures on his dwinding resources grow. If anything is to be saved, perhaps now is the time to cut losses and move on. So it must have been with the Japanese during the night. By ten o'clock that morning D Company had climbed the ridge behind the Japanese defending the track over the col. When they reached the top without opposition the Colonel knew that the battle was probably ours. They moved quickly south along the ridge, killed a few

Japanese left near the col, and joined with A Company. The
road to us was clear. At the same time Denis sent Jemadar
Manbahadur's platoon into Taungdaw village, who found it
empty where it had been full. The Japanese had given up.

We had forced them to abandon their trucks, their guns,
their stores. Now they must reach the Irrawaddy, cross it,
slog through the inhospitable hills to the east to reach the
Sittang river, and cross that, with only what they carried,
and could borrow or steal. The dead might clothe the living,
but without guns, wireless sets, a commissariat, without
reserves of ammunition, the living could be no more than of
nuisance value, guerillas on the run, hunted everywhere.
They were soldiers of Japan, so they would fight when
cornered. They were a long way from home, but still enriched
by that incredible spirit which never seemed to break. They
would not surrender. Nevertheless, we could boast that they
were another defeated group of a defeated army.

As for us, we could not quite believe that it was over, that
the artillery would not begin to thunder, the machine-guns
to stutter, the shadows to shift with menace. It takes time,
days, for such tensions to disperse. I walked out of our perimeter to the place where three days before C Company's
mortars had caught the Japanese gathering to attack us. If
there is a visual nobility in death, it is a fleeting business in
the tropics. These human beings were already half returned
to the hungry earth, obscenely bloated, each body a slow-
shifting sea of maggots, repelling all pity with its stench.

The first to reach us from outside was a company from
our friends the 1/11th Sikhs who had come down the valley
from Welmathe in the north. They had found seventy-five
lorries and many bullock carts abandoned on the blocked
track. Those bearded, turbaned, grinning Sikhs were a wonderful sight to us. An hour later D Company appeared out of
the forest at the foot of the ridge, led by Geoffrey Bull in a
jeep as though he was heading a cavalry charge. With him
was Peter Wickham, genial as ever, sleek and glossy from his
leave in England, and behind them the Colonel, and behind
the Colonel the Doctor, anxious about C Company's wounded.
The Colonel was holding out for me a wrapped-up tin of

fifty cigarettes which had just come with an air-drop. My parents' supply line had worked even to this remote corner.

The Colonel seemed pleased with us. He was an extra-ordinary man, and I use the word extraordinary with care. He was extra ordinary. I knew how I longed for sleep, how my own nerves were worn thin, like an over-used truck tyre, how almost everybody was to a greater or lesser extent suffering in the same way. I also knew that Walter Walker took less sleep than any of us, could never relax, was for all of every day and much of most nights thinking, planning, encouraging, prodding, looking ahead both in time and space, whether on the move or chained to his command post, never inactive. Yet now, as he came briskly across from his jeep with the package for me in his hand, smiling, he seemed much the same as ever. The shadows about his eyes were perhaps deeper, the bones on his face a little more prominent. He was certainly living on his nerves, he must have been, but it hardly showed.

The Taungdaw battles had proved to be another success, and once again our casualties were light compared with those of the enemy. We lost ten killed and thirty-three wounded (none of them in B Company), and in return counted 218 dead Japanese; there would have been more from artillery-fire and air strikes, torn bodies hidden by the torn jungle. Despite our anxieties and whatever the apparent risks—and I was not the only one to fear disaster—the Colonel had put us into a major battle and brought us out again with remark-ably little damage. This time the whole Battalion had got sucked into the fighting, leaving nothing in reserve, which must have given him acute anxiety. But his nerve held (as did the Brigadier's); it was the Japanese who broke. That was why we trusted him, and I was glad to see him, and despite my waning courage, I would have tried to do anything he asked.

So we marched back to Shandatgyi, a few fewer, a lot wearier. There was no lingering at the scene of our trials. There was nothing to hold once the enemy had gone. We trudged over the col which Mike had died to reach, and had no time, nor any real desire, to digress to see the ground. But for Ken Bark, the artillery lieutenant with the sniper's bullet in his stomach, relief came too late. He had clung to life so long it seemed doubly sad that he could not have lasted a little longer.

There were decorations. Peter Myers got a second M.C. Peter was the most efficient and professional of our company commanders; it had been a comfort to know that he was on the hill above us during the battle. An M.C. went to Jemadar Padamsing of 9 Platoon, the platoon which had taken the weight of the attacks against C Company. There were other well-deserved awards. But the most delicate and pleasing citation to be drafted was for a Victoria Cross. This was on behalf of 87726 Rifleman Lachhiman Gurung of Padamsing's platoon. Lachhiman had been severely wounded and was already on the move back to the hospitals of India. Few knew him; he had served with the Battalion for only two months. He had been in one of the forward trenches of 9 Platoon, exposed by the nature of the ground to the first fury of most of the enemy's attempts to capture the position. The whole platoon had fought well, but Lachhiman's courage in continuing to fight after receiving his wounds was seized upon by Peter Myers and the Colonel, and in went the citation for a V.C.

The possibility of a V.C. in the Battalion was a tonic. We should have to wait some time to know whether the application would be approved. There was no guarantee of success. What proportion of recommendations are turned down I do not know; I had heard of several. Meanwhile, to remember that we were in the running was invigorating. Perhaps soldiers should not need to take so much account of medals, but they do.

At Shandatgyi it rained again and the tracks became almost unnegotiable for motor traffic, but I was in a house and there were no Japs about and I did not care. I found Bill reinstalled as Intelligence Officer (to his disgust), and Bob Findlay returned from the wound he had received in our first action. That seemed a century back and another world, when we had been fresh and anxious to prove ourselves. Three months ago, even two months ago, I would have judged this siege at Taungdaw exhilarating, would have rejoiced in victory. Instead it had defeated me. 'Courage,' Slim has written, 'is expendable.' I had expended mine. I needed a time for restocking.

XX

INTERLUDE

After Taungdaw the Battalion motored down to the Mindon–
Thayetmyo road (see Map 4, page 190), and in patrol actions
which did not fall to me a handful of enemy stragglers were
killed and at last one captured, a man drunk on local alcohol.
The remaining Japanese west of the Irrawaddy had moved
south, and other units of our Division were after them. I was
thankful to be out of the storm centre. I did not understand
what was happening to me, and did not dare talk about it
to anybody, but I carried in my head now what I can only
describe as a black lump of wet putty: I conceptualised it
as black and wet and malleable. When there were hours free
from the chance of fighting, and from extra responsibility,
this weight in the head diminished, was not too oppressive.
So soon as we moved—for movement brought the need for
planning and the risk of meeting opposition—the weight
grew, exerted a steady pressure through which thought and
action must struggle towards a consummation. Fortunately,
for I suppose that I may have been close to some kind of
mental breakdown, on 23 May we moved to the riverside port
of Thayetmyo, and there settled in the promise of a rest that
would continue until August.

Five months earlier, almost to the day, we had left the
last rest area in Kohima. During the interval we had lost
thirty-four dead and 112 wounded. We had killed and counted
508 enemy dead, with other dead and many wounded un-
counted. We had been lucky in our battles, but we deserved
a respite. 'Rest' was the customary euphemism for retraining
and re-equipping. Yet I cared not how hard we worked so
long as food and sleep came regularly, and the enemy were

miles away and someone else's responsibility. We could speculate on our destination—Malaya perhaps, Sumatra, Thailand—for the fighting in Burma must be almost done. But August was far ahead. Two months! Till now the future had extended for no more than a day or so. Our private time-scale was suddenly enlarged, like a view of the plains from round the last corner of a mountain defile.

Thayetmyo is, or was, a pleasant spot. It is in the dry zone, and gets a light monsoon. Between the second and third Burmese wars, between say 1852 and 1886, it was a frontier station. Lower Burma had been annexed by Britain, and Upper Burma was still controlled by the Burmese kings. When all Burma became a province of British India, Thayetmyo developed as a river port: a local centre for a considerable hinterland, and a staging post on the Irrawaddy that lay roughly halfway between Mandalay and Rangoon. To judge from the acres of spacious bungalows and gardens along the river bank north of the Burmese town, Thayetmyo must have held a considerable European population until 1942. Many of the bungalows were burned, their lawns and flower-beds overgrown, but it was among them that we settled. Enough buildings with roofs intact were found to house us, and out came the whitewash, so we must be due for a long stay. There were lakes, and flowering trees. Between thunderstorms the weather was unpleasantly sticky, but this was now a minor discomfort. We did not have to search for Jap snipers beneath the dripping bushes, nor crouch in waterlogged trenches. We abandoned the evening and the dawn stand-to. We could smoke a cigarette standing openly under the stars. Food came regularly, and was hot. If we did get wet, there were dry clothes back home. We began to eye the shapely Burmese girls with more than a tired and fleeting abstract pleasure.

The cessation from battle after long immersion provides so unique and basic a revolution for the mind that probably no one who has not personally experienced it can fully understand. It is a much more sharply felt change than the original baptism of fire, for which a soldier has been training for months, usually years. The only parallel that I can imagine must be the feelings of a man condemned to death and then

reprieved. Dangerous sport gets near, but that is voluntary
and of short duration. A man in battle, whether volunteer or
conscript, cannot escape except through death, wounds, sickness
or a depth of disgrace that only the desperate contemplate; and
he cannot control or foretell how long his ordeal may last.

In Burma the tensions that ruled existence between actions
were hardly less than those at the height of them. During
the advance down Burma there was no safe area behind the
lines. There were no lines. And to particularise these general
statements, there was only one period in the five months
since Kohima when our Battalion could have been said to be
'resting': that was in March at Nyaungla, which for me was
a period of unusual strain, the period when Scotty and I
alternated in command of our isolated patrol base across the
Irrawaddy, and undertook some of our most strenuous and
nerve-wearing patrols. Some men withstood these conditions
with extraordinary toughness. I did not. Over twenty years
later the sound of the name 'Thayetmyo' still symbolises for
me those compound feelings of physical satisfaction (sleep,
food, comfort) and dawning mental relief that every battle-
weary soldier will recall. There is no joy. That is a positive
emotion, and perhaps our emotional life had been too bludgeoned for it. Relief and easement of the mind predominated.
The lump of putty in my head began slowly to diminish, as
though with each routine day that passed a little of it was
washed away by the thunderstorms.

Another symbol of relief for me was the river. Streams and
rivers have this power: occasionally they terrify; more often
they soothe, they mesmerise. The Irrawaddy at Thayetmyo
was a great river, at that season undivided by sandbanks.
Twice further north we had crossed as a battalion. I had
crossed with my patrols many more times. I had bathed in it.
On or near its banks we had lived and fought for half of
February, all of March and April, and parts of May. We had
watched its waters swell from their considerable dry weather
volume, blue between yellow sandbanks, to this full, swirling,
undivided, muddy expanse. Strategically and tactically the
river had been perhaps the only feature of our landscape that
was of unvarying importance. It had meant much in our

lives, and I could understand why peoples in other times and places worshipped rivers as gods. The Irrawaddy was a god, for what is a god if he or it is not a focus for the awe that a man can feel for the mysterious.

I used to watch the country boats gliding swiftly downstream, frail high-sterned craft, silent, peaceful, undestructive, and envied those who rode them, envied their beautiful country and their charming philosophy. It was tragic that we should rampage across the land with our guns and explosives. Though our chief aim was to kill each other, we of the warring nations, which no doubt the Burmese did not mind, we left much of the country a ruin of burned-out villages, slaughtered livestock and dead civilians. Crops were not sown, or went unharvested. The delicate irrigation systems of the rice fields were wrecked. Fishermen's boats were sunk, bridges blown. But worse, the social fabric of the community was uprooted, for both sides fought for the allegiance of souls as well as for territorial gain. Men were often forced to take sides, and some chose the Japanese, some the British and some changed sides as the fortunes of war changed. We were leaving behind us a wrack of enmity, suspicion, hate; chasms of mutual hostility that only time might bridge. It is seldom the soldiers who suffer longest.

At Thayetmyo our Officers' Mess was complete. It had not been so for months. The evenings were gay. It was good to have everyone together, close-knit after difficult times. I missed Mike, lying back there somewhere in the forest. I wished he had not been killed. But already those days were acquiring the cloak of unreality that so swiftly clothes the past. Whatever the truth, whatever actually happened, no single one of us knew more than a segment, and what we knew at once began to lose focus, to fade and shift like those Burmese morning mists. I would never be able to comprehend our collective experience, nor even perhaps my own.

Scotty taught us to play Red Dog, a card game of extreme simplicity which we played for hours and high stakes. I am a cautious card player, and neither gain nor lose much. Geoffrey Bull played cards as he fought battles, with calm impetuosity, and he lost handsome sums.

Then on 1 June seven of us officers were sent on leave to
India. We had little warning, but were used to that. All of
us were going who had served continuously through this last
campaign, except for Denis Sheil-Small and the Doctor.
Their turn would come when we returned. This left Watson-
Smyth in charge, and the five others who had recently joined
or returned from leave or hospital. For refitting and recouping
health this was just sufficient. I arranged for Nandalal and
Tulbir to join Jemadar Manbahadur's platoon for the month
I should be away. Manbahadur promised to polish up their
infantry training and I felt a little guilty, knowing how such
polishing might be carried out. I felt guilty, too, at taking
leave when so few of the men would get away. Leave for them
meant an absence of four or five months, and not many could
yet be spared that long.

But as we flew across the jungle-covered hills of the Arakan
Yomas to Chittagong, I forgot my conscience. Here was a
true liberation, a throwing-off of cares like the schoolboy
expels education on the last day of term. Bill, Scotty, Tommy
Login and I were together, an ill-favoured lot, inelegantly
dressed, mepacrine yellow and worn fine by the campaigning.
We spent the night in Chittagong, then got another air-hike
to Calcutta. Here we split, I for Naini Tal and the others
for Bombay. The reputation of Bombay's beaches and high-
class courtesans drew to it many officers on leave from Burma,
even though this meant a tedious train journey across the
width of India. In some ways I would have liked to go with
them, and, as things turned out, it might have been better
for me if I had. I should have liked to abandon virginity in
the arms of some Egyptian, French or Chinese beauty. It
seemed a waste of the gift of life to die and never to have
lain with a woman. Calcutta was apparently little good for
this; a fellow had to be desperate with lust or boredom to
sample that city's back-street prostitutes. I met an officer
who had tried. He told me how with difficulty he had achieved
the privacy of a small room in an obscure house in a poor
district somewhere east of Chowringee, and how, fearful all
the time of robbery instead of dalliance, and of disease instead
of pleasure, he had scarcely begun to disrobe before his girl

when bedlam broke out below, with whistles, cries of 'police', and the shrill wailing of innumerable semi-naked females. He found himself scudding out through a back entrance, holding up his trousers with one hand, in company of a small host of other alarmed, ill-clad and furtive males, mostly English. After one or two such tales I found myself sufficiently fastidious to prefer continence. But in Bombay, if reports were true, waited concubines of splendid physique and tested health, the top trollops of a dozen nations, in an establishment that was more a hareem than a brothel, where neither liquor nor a girl's time were rationed—if a man could pay. We could pay: months of accumulated rupees lay in our banks.

In Naini there would be no wenching. An occasional meeting with a 'nice' girl would give no chance to a backward Don Juan of my temperament and upbringing. I once worked with a lieutenant from a station in Ceylon who claimed to have deflowered thirty virgins or more, mostly young middle-class nurses from England. He may not have been exaggerating too much, for he was handsome and confident, and Ceylon was an island crammed with Combined Headquarter and naval personnel; it was well known that only in such centres for gold braid were there significant clusters of nubile women. The point is that he had the time, and he was not living with his parents. 'Don't foul your own doorstep' is a sound precept, one of the few not attributed to George Washington. But I wanted to go to Naini; I wanted the comforts of the home I knew; and my parents would be hurt if I did not see them; so I abandoned debauch.

Calcutta in June was the same Turkish bath I remembered from the year before. I stayed one night, long enough to collect money and send a telegram to Fern Cottage. Then I went to Dehra Dun to pick up a trunk of clothes from the 3rd Gurkha Centre.

I stayed in Dehra for a day, then left for Naini. It was now the 9th of June and I had been travelling for eight days. In Naini I found a telegram from my mother. She was in Kashmir. My father was on a long-planned and eagerly awaited six-week trip to the Valley of Flowers, the Bhyundar valley deep in the higher Himalayas, and did not hear of my arrival until after I had left. My mother suggested that I come to Kashmir. I wish that I had. But I remember the utter weariness that enveloped me. Kashmir meant another three or four days of travel, and then the return journey. I should only have a week there. I could not face it, and sent a telegram to say so. My mother then nobly set out to reach me, but did not arrive until the 19th, in time for the last five days of my leave. It was all very unsatisfactory, and I might as well have gone with the others to Bombay. Drink, sex and trusted companionship might have done more good for me than communing with myself among the hills round Naini.

I cannot remember what I did on this visit. Fern Cottage was not empty. Although my parents were away, and my two sisters had sailed for England, various friends were living there. It was the monsoon, and clouds would have been low on the hills for much of the time, and pouring rain upon us. I suspect that I was there with only half myself. The other half was shackled to the Battalion. Anyone who has stayed long with a fighting unit in time of war will know what I mean. Life in a fighting battalion was all-engrossing. It took everything. People and work outside were neither important nor quite real. The Battalion was a family. The men were our children, the officers were my brothers. I did not love them all equally, and some I did not love at all, but they were each of them of the family. We might criticise each other to each other, but resented the outsider who criticised. It took weeks to adjust to another life, maybe months. A short leave certainly was not long enough. In Naini on this occasion I suffered from mental astigmatism.

This was brought home to me as I was returning from leave. I reached Calcutta on 26 June. There was no ship for Rangoon until the 29th. When we boarded her she stayed in the river for three more days and we did not reach Rangoon until 4 July. Over all these nine days I heard with a growing certainty, though never with complete reliability nor any detail, that the Battalion, instead of enjoying its promised rest in Thayetmyo, was back in the fighting somewhere in south-east Burma.

The rumours came first in that crucible of gossip, Calcutta's Grand Hotel. I was aghast. The temporarily banished fear returned at once, that sick weight locked into the centre of the brain. I was riven by contradictory appetites: I had to reach the Battalion which was my family and was in trouble; simultaneously I wanted never to go near another battle. My leave hardly seemed to have begun to repair the battered mind. Yet I was so tied to the Battalion that I could be considered simply a limb of it, with perhaps no more independence of will than a jeep or a rifle, and like them destined to serve until smashed or condemned as unfit.

At Rangoon the rumours proved correct. The Division was in action east of Waw, in the bend of the Sittang river, where until 1942 the railway to Moulmein had crossed (Map 6, page 230). And the fighting, if even half of what we heard was true, was desperate. The war in Burma was not over.

Bill Blenkin and I got out of Rangoon on the third day in a jeep sent down for us by the Battalion. We travelled through country that was often flat and flooded, through unceasing rain and much mud. In the flat parts only the road, the railway and the villages were above the floods, islands connected by causeways. Between them lay expanses of water, just water. It was a drowned land, and depressing.

Travelling slowly in a long line of vehicles our jeep rammed the back of the suddenly halted lorry ahead. I was in the front passenger seat, and got off with a cut and a large bruise on the forehead. So I reached the Battalion's rear echelon at Waw with my crown inside a first-aid dressing, with a splitting headache and a very stiff neck, the wounded hero.

Now that I was among my own again I felt better, despite the head. But the situation for the Battalion was grim. Somewhere across a watery waste of flooded paddyfield, miles away, and surrounded by Japanese, they were crouching in the rain, waiting for darkness. They were to break out that night. They would have to wade through waist-high water between enemy-held villages. Nobody knew how many would reach safety. Even the optimists expected considerable losses. Looking at the map, I could see why. There was nothing we could do but wait.

XXI

LAST ACT

Four of us waited. Scotty Gilmore and Tommy Login had joined Bill and me. Of what had been going on we had only the sketchiest details, and all of them sounded unpleasant. We were acutely anxious, frustrated by our inability to help, depressed by the dreary rain.

I heard that B Company had suffered casualties, and that it was commanded by Subadar Thamansing Thapa. Denis had been evacuated to India from Thayetmyo. He had begun to have unpredictable lapses of memory. The campaign must have exhausted his physical and nervous energy too, though he had managed to conceal it very well. He had all my sympathy. I heard that Quentin Kennedy, first wounded, had then been killed next day by shells that hit the Doc's aid post. The Doc had also been wounded, though not too seriously. Quentin had been among the three officer reinforcements who joined us in early May. Douglas Farnbank had been wounded at Taungdaw. So of these three only Peter Dickenson remained out there to the east among the flooded paddyfields.

It seemed that the Battalion had been placed in an unsound tactical position, scattered in company and platoon packets along the railway embankment to the Sittang Bridge (blown up during the retreat of 1942) and in neighbouring villages. This area of Burma was as flat as a table-top, hardly raised above sea-level, its chaungs tidal, and only the villages, the railway, and a very few tracks showed above the monsoon floods. The floods covered the land with from two to three feet of water. The Sittang river itself, broad and swift, formed the eastern limit of our territory. In the hills beyond the remaining Japanese were recovering. And still on this side, cut

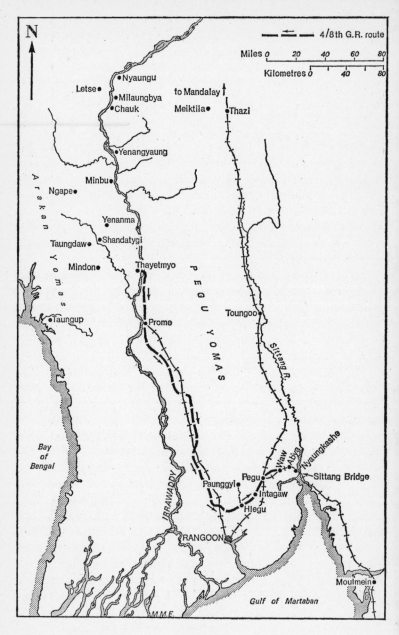

Map 6 Thayetmyo to south Burma

off in the Pegu Yomas to the north-west, were more than
eighteen thousand Japanese; it was to help block their escape
that our Division had been hauled from its rest.

And it was to aid their escape that the Japanese across
the Sittang began, in early July, to slip more and more troops
into the villages on our side which the Battalion did not have
the strength to occupy, until they were able to cut the railway
embankment, the only land communication above water, and
to surround the bulk of our men who had concentrated in a
village called Nyaungkashe (Map 6). Even in Nyaungkashe
there were not enough of our men to defend the full area of
the village; parts that were not held by Gurkhas were taken
up by Japanese. One company, A Company under Bob
Findlay, had been forced to withdraw towards Brigade HQ,
and B Company was on its own, defending a troop of 25-
pounder guns in a copse about half a mile from Nyaungkashe.

We heard that the shelling had been worse than anything
the Battalion had previously experienced, and its results
more severe, for in this flooded landscape trenches could not
be dug down. Defences had to be built up, were easy to see
and were vulnerable.

We heard that the Battalion had now been cut off for four
days, unable to evacuate casualties, relying on air supply, and
that tonight they were to withdraw. They would have to
carry the wounded and much else over several miles of flooded
plough and kaing grass, across at least one deep chaung, in the
pitch blackness of a monsoon night, guided only by compass,
and round, through or over any Japanese they might encounter.

It is hard to explain the quality of the anxiety we felt.
Perhaps it was something like the worry of parents for their
children, instinctive, not to be reasoned with, and wholly
consuming. And when next morning the men came into Waw
without, so we learned, losing a single body during their
night's retreat, an almost miraculous outcome to such a
hazardous operation, our relief was shot with guilt because
throughout their ordeal we had been at ease in India.

It seemed to be taken for granted that I would command
B Company. Indeed there was no one else, and I had learned
one lesson in the army: accept orders with outward confidence

and, if necessary, ask someone else afterwards how to carry them out. But I had little immediate joy of my command, for I began to hear of the casualties. Subadar Thamansing looked his usual gentle self. Manbahadur looked haggard. His platoon, which I had thought the best in the Battalion, was broken. He had been given the defence of an isolated bridge on the railway embankment about a mile from Nyaung-kashe, between that village and Brigade Headquarters in Abya. The first attack on this bridge came in at 7.30 p.m. on 3 July, when his platoon had twenty-six men. He left the position at 3.30 a.m. on the 6th with seven men, four of them wounded. Throughout this time his platoon had been cut off and exposed to close-range sniping, machine-gun-fire, heavy shelling, and a series of hand-to-hand encounters each night. They had been unable to sleep, or cook or bury the dead, or communicate with anyone; they had run out of ammunition and in the end, drunk with fatigue, sleeplessness, lack of food and shell-shock, armed only with bayonet and kukri, they could do no more. The surviving seven slipped off the embankment and into the water as the Japanese concentrated for what must have been the final attack.

Before this epic, so I now learned, the whole Company had taken the major part in an attack on one of the island villages near Nyaungkashe, and of the eleven men killed and eighteen wounded, most had been in the Company. So far as I could make out—and even now it is impossible to reconcile the differing accounts of the number of casualties—of the Battalion's sixty or seventy men killed, wounded and missing during late June and early July, about thirty were from B Company. This was perhaps a third of its strength at that time. By comparison with some battles these were not severe casualties. But they were heavy compared with those of the rest of the campaign. I could not dismiss them with an objective shrug of the shoulders. I knew most of these men by sight and name, knew some of them better than I knew my own family. Many of them were friends who had shared with me the tiring and dangerous days by the Irrawaddy. Dalbahadur, Chandra-bahadur, little Antare, Singbahadur, Juktabahadur, Kalba-hadur, and so many others, I should not see them again.

More were in hospital, some irreparably maimed. Perhaps my reaction was greater because I had not lived through the battles in which these casualties had been suffered, because I heard about them simultaneously afterwards.

Worst of all, among the missing was Nandalal, my orderly. Tulbir was safe. Nandalal had been with a section of Manbahadur's platoon which had been on its own on the west side of the railway bridge, and this section had been overrun on the first night of the battle. Some were known to have been killed; the fate of the rest was not known.

Day after day I hoped that he might walk in, as three of them did (two with serious wounds). He never came. Somewhere in that watery wilderness his body was rotting like all the other bodies I had seen. I hated to think of it. I felt somehow responsible. If I had not been on leave he would not have been with a rifle platoon. I grieved for him more than for any other death that year.

So this return from our leave proved a gloomy business. The weather continued to be terrible. Nandalal was gone, and I missed his quiet reassuring presence whenever I returned to my billet. I was depressed by a visit to the wounded in a hospital in Rangoon. I did not much like or respect Watson-Smyth, who now commanded us. I dreaded the resumption of active campaigning, which must come soon.

But I was kept busy. There was little time to mope and I soon ceased to do so. I had to learn to be a company commander at a time when my reduced command had lost almost everything they owned, or should have owned, except the clothes they wore on the march out from Nyaungkashe and the weapons they carried. The Battalion had to be made whole again, closing in on the gaps, knitting over the wounds. We spent a week at Hlegu, on the main road between Rangoon and Pegu, checking endless lists, cleaning, sewing, eating, sleeping. My own kit, such as it was, had gone with the rest, and I was given a claim form on which I filled in the objects I had really lost together with a few more which I might be assumed to have lost. Eventually the Command Pay Office, way back in Meerut, allowed me 150 rupees in compensation, £11.5.0. They were a mean lot. The Battalion was billeted in houses and was able to keep dry. The barn I slept in was also home for a number of large rats. They ran over my mosquito net at night.

I worried about the citations for B Company. I wanted to recommend Manbahadur for a Victoria Cross. I had not, of course, read any connected account of the battle. Yet all that I heard from him and others, and the analogy with what I knew of the citation for Lachhiman, made me think that Manbahadur's effort was the equal, probably the greater; it had lasted for much longer. But I had not been near the battle, no officer had personally witnessed it, and Watson-Smyth was in hospital for an operation on a badly poisoned leg. He was ill and dead tired. The officiating Commandant, Geoffrey Bull, had been on leave. Manbahadur was put in for a Military Cross. I could not help feeling that had Walter Walker* been with us we could have got him a V.C. Perhaps I ought to have been more insistent. But I had little influence and was feeling too low to push hard at obstacles. We all were.

There were other B Company citations; not enough, I thought. Defeat, if honourable, was bitter. Everybody was depressed that this rain-sodden dregs-end of a successful campaign should have killed and maimed so many.

Gradually the natural buoyancy of our Gurkhas overcame post-battle depression. Food and sleep were the best tonics until morale went soaring with an unofficial notification that Lachhiman had got his V.C. The procedures had taken nine weeks. There was no doubt that the men were pleased. It is a great thing for a unit to own a man who is awarded the V.C. The outside world thinks only of the individual; his unit regards the medal as partly theirs, as parents take pride and

* On his return from leave Walter Walker was posted to the Divisional staff, and Watson-Smyth was officially appointed Commandant of the Battalion. Although as a junior officer one never knows the truth of these matters, it has always seemed to me unlucky and relevant that in the weeks just before the unfortunate and probably unnecessary battle of Nyaungkashe much of our experienced command structure had changed. The Divisional Commander was on leave. Our Brigade Commander had been promoted to the command of 17 Division and his successor had not yet arrived. Our Colonel was on leave and so were about half our officers, among them some of the most experienced.

some credit for the achievements of their children. This was the first V.C. to be won by the 8th Gurkhas since 1904, and there was more than pride, there was a considerable dash of triumphant vanity that it should be a war-raised battalion, the youngest of the regiment, that had gained it.

Pride in one's own unit is a useful and proper thing that certainly has survival value in war; and if we felt a little jealous and suspicious of the regular battalions, it did them no harm. That I felt proud of the 4/8th is evident from a letter to my parents. 'The Battalion is getting quite a name for itself,' I wrote. 'Apart from the V.C., we've got nearly fifty other decorations, which is far above the average for one battalion.' This last statement does not seem to be true. I can now compare the figures for the four battalions of the 8th Gurkhas, since they are listed in the Regimental History, for the 1/11th Sikhs of our Brigade, and for the 4/1st Gurkhas of 33 Brigade. The totals for the four battalions fighting in Burma are remarkably similar. And I hasten to add that the lesser totals for our 1st and 2nd Battalions are unlikely to reflect a disparity of courage, but almost certainly a disparity in opportunity to display courage, which depends upon so many variable factors that any kind of generalisation would be most unwise.

	1/8th	2/8th	3/8th	4/8th	1/11th Sikhs	4/1st Gurkhas
V.C.					1	1
D.S.O.	2	2	1	1	3	1
Bar to D.S.O.	1	1				1
I.O.M.	1	1	2	2	5	1
M.C.	4	8	12	12	15	11
Bar to M.C.			3	1	1	
I.D.S.M.	9	3	5	12	8	7
M.M.	9	13	23	22	19	28
Bar to M.M.			1			1
O.B.E.	1	2	2		1	
M.B.E.	2	2	1	1		
American Bronze Star		2				
TOTAL	29	34	50	52	53	50

The 4/8th also had thirty-nine Mentions in Dispatches (the Sikhs had forty-five and the 4/1st fifty-one) and six Certificates of Gallantry.

The citation for Lachhiman's V.C. read as follows:

At Taungdaw in Burma, on the west bank of the Irrawaddy, on the night of 12th/13th May 1945, Rifleman Lachhiman Gurung was manning the most forward position of his platoon. At 0120 hours at least 200 enemy assaulted the company's position. The brunt of the attack was borne by Rifleman Lachhiman Gurung's section, and by his own post in particular. This post dominated a jungle path leading up into the platoon locality.

Before assaulting, the enemy hurled innumerable grenades at the position from close range. One grenade fell on the lip of Rifleman Lachhiman Gurung's trench; he at once grasped it and hurled it back at the enemy. Almost immediately another grenade fell directly inside the trench. Again this Rifleman snatched it up and threw it back. A third grenade then fell just in front of the trench. He attempted to throw it back, but it exploded in his hand, blowing off the fingers, shattering his right arm and severely wounding him in the face, body and right leg. His two comrades were also badly wounded and lay helpless in the bottom of the trench.

The enemy, screaming and shouting, now formed up shoulder to shoulder and attempted to rush the position by sheer weight of numbers. Rifleman Lachhiman Gurung, regardless of his wounds, loaded and fired his rifle with his left hand, maintaining a continuous steady rate of fire. Wave after wave of fanatical attacks were thrown in by the enemy, but all were repulsed with heavy casualties. For four hours after being severely wounded, Rifleman Lachhiman Gurung remained alone at his post, waiting with perfect calm for each attack, which he met with fire at point-blank range from his rifle, determined not to give one inch of ground. . . .

Here in July and in the south Burma monsoon Taungdaw seemed a long way back, both in space and time. I had not

seen the citation before, and now that I had, found it difficult
to believe that it related to any experience of mine, that I
had been so close to Lachhiman, he in his trench among the
trees on the ridge, I in mine in the valley, both of us cloaked
in a darkness that was filled with Japanese intent upon our
deaths. The words of the citation, by their confident clarity,
seemed to me to fictionalise the battle. But I kept this feeling
to myself. Only Lachhiman knew what had happened to him.
I believed that he had certainly shown exemplary courage;
I guessed that the confusions and uncertainties of war could
not be reproduced in citations.

Lachhiman lost his right hand and the sight from his left
eye, and never came back to us. But for long after the war
he continued to serve with the 8th Gurkhas, now part of
India's army, and was a havildar when I last heard of him.
If he thinks in terms of bargains he may well feel pleased,
for beyond the pension which the V.C. carries, his valour
must have brought him daily and lasting prestige. In India
the warrior ranks high, a man's past is not forgotten and
increasing age wins increasing respect. I read recently that
the Battalion celebrates Taungdaw Day each year, and that
in 1966 (and no doubt in other years), Havildar Lachhiman
Gurung (now nearing fifty) was guest of honour.

With the main deficiencies of equipment remedied, we
moved on 17 July to Intagaw, and became responsible for
several bridges and track junctions along the main road and
in the bordering areas. The Japanese trapped in the hills to
the north-west (among them the remnants of our opponents
at Taungdaw and Milaungbya) were expected to attempt
their breakthrough soon. They would have to cross the open
country on either side of the road, the road itself, and then
the flooded Sittang river. At this season there were not many
tracks from west to east that could be used by large bodies of
men, many of them wounded, the majority sick and under-
nourished. Most of these unfortunate Japanese, whose code
spurned surrender, were known to be further north, but it
was thought that small parties might try to infiltrate our way.
I was on my own. I and B Company dug in where one of the
few tracks out of the hills passed over rising ground just west

of the main road. We had tents, so we cannot have expected serious activity from the Japanese, and in fact saw none. I was not sorry.

When their break-out began, far to the north, it was butchery; 'a monotonous tale of ambushes, killings, pursuits, drownings' between mid-July and early August. One almost felt sorrow, but not quite. According to one source, of the eighteen thousand or so Japanese who attempted to escape, barely six thousand reached the east bank of the Sittang, starved, diseased, exhausted. Between one and two thousand more too sick to move were left behind to die. There were 740 prisoners, an unprecedented number for Burma. Allied casualties were 95 killed and 322 wounded.

This battle was the climax to two years of continuous fighting that had inflicted on the Japanese armies perhaps the worst defeat in their country's history. According to the Japanese, they lost 190,000 dead in Burma. We had beaten them not by greater numbers—for they almost always had more troops in Burma than we had, even in 1945—but by better generalship, a richer administration, by a marked superiority in air and armoured power, and by an increasing skill at arms that became most evident in 1944 and 1945. Slim later wrote of us:

> My Indian divisions after 1943 were among the best in the world. They would go anywhere, do anything, go on doing it, and do it on very little.
>
> (*Defeat into Victory*, pp. 538–9.)

We were proud of this.

All that I now remember of the eleven days we spent on Point 158 is that I here found a successor to Nandalal. My runner, small Tulbir, had been trying to cope, but was not a success. He had gained in confidence but not in intelligence. I asked Subadar Thamansing to find me someone less time-consuming. The answer was a young gangling Gurkha called Sarbajit. He was a Roka, a clan of the Magar tribe. When first he walked up with Thamansing to my small tent, he was shy and nervous. So was I. And for some time I was no more than politely interested in him, being charged with memories.

Sarbajit was tall and clumsy and knew little. I almost lost patience, nearly changed him, but hesitated because Thamansing had told me that he had asked to be my batman. Of course I got used to seeing him around, began to like him, and he discovered what to do. Like Nandalal he was even-tempered and hard-working. He did not make bright conversation, or feel impelled to tell me what I should wear.

Sarbajit was no fool. Initially Tulbir took charge of him. I listened to Tulbir giving Sarbajit minute instructions in his thin young voice as to how much milk the Sahib liked in his tea, or how his bed should be constructed. By the time Tulbir went on leave two months later (to get married, he confessed rather shamefacedly), Sarbajit was in firm control. Tulbir's knowledge had been absorbed and Tulbir's indifferent skill outstripped.

We returned to Intagaw and Battalion Headquarters on 28 July. I was sad to lose independence. Those first three weeks of company commanding had reminded me of what every junior officer learns, that it is much pleasanter to be away from headquarters, and the further away the better. I had a lot to discover about administering a rifle company; I had been with one for only seven weeks before going on leave. I preferred to discover and make my mistakes away from the direct gaze of commanding officer, quartermaster and adjutant.

The Battalion stayed at Intagaw until 9 August, then returned to our old billets in Hlegu. There were the usual rumours about our future. We knew that the troops for the invasion of Malaya had already been withdrawn and were training somewhere in India. Presumably we were not destined for Malaya. But there was plenty of Asia beyond Malaya. With command of the air and sea, hops of several hundred miles had become routine; and with the facilities hitherto enjoyed by Europe in transfer to aid us, we could expect movement to become even more ambitious. Some predicted that we must soon fight among snow-covered mountains. We had campaigned in the desert and dry heat of central Burma. We had fought among jungle-covered hills and plains. We had fought most recently more or less afloat in the monsoon floods. All that remained, they argued, was ice and snow. Oddly enough, tired and weary and glad of rest though most of us were, I do not believe that many would have preferred to stay as garrison troops in Burma.*

Three days later B Company was off on a wild-goose chase. We motored up a rough track to a village called Paunggyi, and from there next day I took a platoon on foot further into this inaccessible land to search for a small party of sick Japanese who were supposed to be lying up in a certain village. The land was inaccessible because of water. This was well-wooded country, but still flat and dissected by numerous waterways. We walked and waded to our objective without much bother, although our cautious encirclement of the village netted nothing except amused villagers who had not heard of the Japanese. Then there was a prolonged and blinding rain storm. Streams that had been easily navigable a few hours before became dangerous torrents. There was one which we had crossed in the morning by a log bridge with a flimsy handrail, and now the logs were two feet under swirling water and the handrail was left thrumming just above the surface. Most Gurkhas are poor swimmers, or non-swimmers. We rigged up a rope, stationed guards downstream on either bank armed with long branches, and one by one got each man safely over. It rained hard all the way back, the kind of rain that overwhelmed the defences of our monsoon capes in a few minutes. When it was not raining, I should add, the atmosphere was so close that one oozed sweat relaxing in a chair. A curious effect of this heat and humidity was that the stubble on my chin appeared twice as fast, like a bulb forced for Christmas flowering in a hot-cupboard.

At Paunggyi, under cover again, we stripped to under-clothes and dried off. We had housed ourselves in the village houses. The houses, or huts, were up on stilts, as usual, to cheat the rains. We took the front rooms and the villagers squashed into the back. Paunggyi was a dirty village with dirty villagers, who were obviously poor and probably suffering

* According to General Slim, our 7th Division *was* earmarked for Malaya (*Defeat into Victory*, p. 523). We were to sail there from Rangoon, presumably among the follow-up troops.

in ways which we could not imagine from the dislocations caused by war. They were patiently resigned to our presence and showed no hostility.

Despite the discomforts I enjoyed myself. These were the conditions and situations for which I had trained. I understood them, and was happier than when spitting and polishing in some more civilised station. Commanding a company, with total responsibility for others and little time to think of self, did banish much of my mental unease. Whether this return towards sanity would have continued under the stress of further battle I do not know. For here at Paunggyi, on Wednesday, 15 August, I heard in a wireless talk with Battalion Headquarters that the war was over. Some kind of super-bomb had been dropped on Japan, and the Japanese had surrendered unconditionally.

I do not remember feeling very much at first. I was more impressed by the news next day of my promotion to major. The end had come so swiftly, without warning. The rain still streamed down, and there were still Japanese in Burma who could know nothing of this decision by their government on those far-off mythical islands. When I talked with some of the others we agreed to be sceptical, for we knew the Japanese, and we thought it very probable that many of them would not surrender, would prefer to die fighting, and that we should have to do the fighting. We did not know the Japanese. Gradually, as the days passed, it grew clearer and clearer that this extraordinary people were to be as punctilious to surrender as till now they had been punctilious to fight. The battles were finished. We could dare to think of a personal future.

Then I felt relief, not joy; and a sadness for those who had not survived. None of us suggested formal celebrations. The dead from the Nyaungkashe battles were in our minds: they had so nearly made it to the end. They had mothers and fathers, wives, children, sweethearts, who would not be celebrating. The relief seeped in quietly; it spread slowly to the inner recesses of the mind and the body until the fact that the war was over became real. A sudden and nasty death might still lie round the corner—no one can foresee the manner of his end—but the odds on such a death were now so small they could be disregarded. We had to adjust to a new time scale, one that looked at the future as months, years, not hours, days. Tomorrow could be 1946 as well as Friday. We had to think of a life outside the army. Everything seemed suddenly very uncertain.

XXII

IN THE END IS THE BEGINNING

More than perhaps any campaign in the Second World War, save the Russians' defence of Stalingrad, the Burma campaign has the elements of a great Homeric saga. It took place in a fantastic terrain, isolated by great mountains and jungles from any other theatre. It went on unbroken for three years and eight months. It covered vast areas. It sucked into its maelstrom nearly 2,000,000 men. It encompassed great disasters and ended in great triumphs. It produced prodigies of heroism, patience, resolution and endurance. It brought about great suffering, but fascinated and enthralled those taking part in it, both victors and losers. It was like no war that had ever been in the history of conflict.
Arthur Swinson in Purnell's *Illustrated History of the Second World War.*

The stage was a true stage. From somewhere Chandru the Subadar-Major had won planks and had raised them a couple of feet from the earth. Behind the stage was a dressing-room for the actors and dancers, walled with green blankets. The roof was a tarpaulin, and two more tarpaulins covered space for the spectators. But the monsoon was dying, and with luck the audience could continue to spread far beyond the covered area. Some hundreds of men were standing or squatting, chattering to each other, smoking, their round and oval brown faces often smiling. From the dressing-room an occasional burst of drumming heightened the excitement. Someone had fixed up electric lights, and their novel brilliance was another item that marked this as an 'occasion'. For this was part of Dashera, a thanksgiving for the blessings of the past year, a supplication for future prosperity, a commemoration of the victory of good over evil, in the hills a time for family reunions and a gathering of the clans; this was Dashera, the

R

most important festival of the Gurkhas' year, a soldier's festival
in honour of Durga, Goddess of War; and if none of these,
it was still a controlled blind.

When it was time the British officers trooped over from
their Mess to the front rows of chairs and benches. These
front rows were provided with rough tables before them, and
on the tables were bunches of leaves and flowers in tins. We
were no sooner seated than men with jugs of rum and empty
glasses descended upon us. The Gurkha officers sat inter-
spaced between us. I had Jemadar Manbahadur to my left.

'Heh Kabiram, rum for the B Company Commander.'

'Careful! Not too much! But you may fill the glass of the
Jemadar Sahib. He has a head of iron.'

Kabiram grinned and took little notice. I had to tilt up
the jug to leave room in my glass for water. I should have won
approval by doing without, but knew that disaster lay down
that road. Kabiram was short and dark, with bright eyes and
a nose that scarcely broke the surface of his face. He was a
Pun from the high Himalayas. Two months ago the sole reason
for his existence in my eyes had been his ability to feed magazines to the No. 1 on his bren-gun. But that was another life.
What should I and young Kabiram do in a world at peace?
Drink, of course. I raised my glass to Manbahadur and took
a brave sip and shuddered. Manbahadur was made in a sterner
mould. He lowered his neat rum by an inch and stroked his
moustache sensuously.

Jitbahadur, the commander of my 6 Platoon, and recently
promoted subadar, was on the stage announcing the evening's
programme. He spoke first in English, fluent but inaccurate,
then swiftly in Gurkhali, raising laughter from the crowd.
There then followed a series of acts, mostly burlesque, mostly
lewd, some with wonderfully pointed take-offs of us officers.
Orderlies brought on food, plates piled with hot rice and
vegetables and curried goat. To remain conscious over the rum
it was necessary to eat well. We tucked in with fingers (right
hands only) that had long since grown adept at this job. The
food was delicious, though a little spoilt for me because for the
past week I had occasionally wrestled with one of these Dashera
goats and now was not too keen to think I might be eating him.

Jitbahadur joined us for a few minutes. He was part performer, part stage-manager, part producer. He had just done
a sketch in which he was clearly anxious to violate a pretty
girl. I could not follow all the dialogue, for on this sort of
occasion vocabulary strayed beyond the simpler military usage
to which I was confined. Jitbahadur said in English 'Down the
'atch, cock.' Who had taught him that? More rum. It did not
taste so harsh now.

There was a pause on the stage. Then on filed four women
and two men dancers in costume, several drummers, and
behind them to line the back of the stage, a chorus. The drummers, after an experimental bang or two with their hands,
went into a steady rhythm. The chorus started a song, and the
dancers began—their skirts and robes made a sudden swirling
and changing pattern of bright colour in contrast to the sober
jungle-green battledress of the chorus. These were the religious
dances of the Gurkha Hindu festivals, slow and dignified,
rhythmic, attractive to our Western ear and eye. They would
continue for hours.

The four men who were dressed as women, the *marunis*, had
bodices and long skirts of brilliant purples, blues, scarlets and
black. Shawls of coloured silk covered their heads and hung
down their backs. They wore ear-rings and necklaces. On their
ankles and wrists there were bangles that clashed softly with
each movement. The two men were dressed in jackets and
flowing robes of white, with white turbans and sashes of scarlet.
All six circled together, advanced and retreated in line, sank
to their haunches, feet stamping, wrists and arms undulating
in time. Sometimes the drummers moved with the dancers,
sometimes they revolved across the stage in a pattern of their
own. Their fingers evoked complicated double and treble
rhythms from the long two-ended drums. The chorus stood in
the background singing, swaying, clapping their hands. The
whole formed a curious blend of gaiety and gravity.

Behind me the audience had not ceased to laugh and talk,
to form ever-shifting groups. Some of the men clapped softly
with the music and shouted comments on the dancing. Others
were absorbed in conversation, and in drinking the night's
ration of rum. Jock Purdon, our present Quartermaster, had

collected 150 gallons of it, but this had to last several hundred
men for three or four days. Probably only a handful of them
would drink enough to get drunk. Anyway, Gurkhas are not
often drunk. It was we British officers who were in gravest
danger, for we were guests and, alas, off ration.

Outside the area of light and noise dimly seen tents ranged
back into the night. Above us, I knew, the stars shone with
that tropical clarity that was always a wonder. How had I
got here into southern Burma? That was another wonder.
Already the immediate past was becoming unreal, the vivid
dream foredoomed to fade. This inevitable fading seemed a
betrayal. The dead had no life but in us who survived. If we
forgot, they were nothing. If we forgot, where lay all the
effort and courage of their lives and ours?

> Time hath, my lord, a wallet at his back
> Wherein he puts alms for oblivion,
> A great-sized monster of ingratitudes:

So Shakespeare makes Ulysses speak to Achilles skulking in
his tent.

I knew we should forget. There is an unreality to one's own
past that surpasses the unreality of the worst novel. A novel is
organised, can be swallowed whole, can be re-read, the 'facts'
revised. One's own life is ephemeral, slipping back and back,
always back, old days crowded out by new without remission,
and most of them unrevisable. Thus are we cheated of our
past, the one possession that is unique to each of us. There was
nothing I could do, except perhaps cultivate with Alun Lewis
'a robustness in the core of sadness'.

'Drink up, Sahib. You are not drinking.' It was Manbahadur.
I simplified my thoughts.

'I was thinking of Nandalal. And of the others.'

Manbahadur understood at once. 'It is easy to forget. And
for him it was so near the end of the war.' He was silent, perhaps
remembering his platoon as it had been before Nyaungkashe.
In the silence I noticed Kabiram with his jug, and was in time
to save my glass from more rum.

'You keep away from me, Kabiram.'

'When is the Sahib going to dance?'

'Never, if he can help it.'

'Eh, but you must, Sahib. For the honour of B Company.'

'Not for the honour of all the kings and rajahs in the world. You know that I am an ignorant Englishman. You like to see me look foolish.'

Kabiram grinned. 'Every recruit makes mistakes. How else shall he cease to be a recruit?'

'Well, we shall see. Perhaps when the Colonel has gone and the rum has given me courage.' This was a tactical error, for I was then made to swallow more rum, to the unconcealed pleasure of the men behind, and my glass was refilled.

'Be off with you, Kabiram. You'd like me unconscious. Go and tease the Adjutant. He is a serious man.'

On stage the dance was gaining momentum, and the noise was considerable. Impervious now to their surroundings the dancers revolved, advanced, retreated, crouched and rose with a fine swirl of skirts and jangling of trinkets. The sweat glistened on their faces. Prolonged concentration within a ceaseless rhythm of sound and movement brought them to a kind of intoxication. So long as there was singing and drumming they seemed unconscious of fatigue.

The chorus was less constant. Their numbers fluctuated as men walked off to rest and drink and talk with friends. From the dressing-room behind the stage came laughter and occasional stanzas of unscriptural song. And from the mass of men in the audience rose an increasing hubbub.

This Dashera was both an end and a beginning. It marked the end of Burma, where we had made war, for in three days (17 October) we were to fly to Siam. Already there had been change, as there always is. People were changing. Geoffrey Bull was in England, on long leave; Scotty Gilmore had left for good, demobilised more or less at his own command and married to Peggy, a British girl; Walter Walker, as I have related, was no longer our Colonel; a lot of men had gone on leave to Nepal, and new faces had come in who had never done this terrible thing, who had never hunted a living human being or been hunted by one—they were divided from us by all the spaces of the universe.

In September our mules were taken away to a remount

depot in Rangoon. People became attached to mules and felt their loss deeply. I was not one of these, for I had never worked closely with them, but I missed the swishing tails, the clink of harness, the muley smells, the solid patient bulk of the animals about the place.

Of all that was changing our work had changed most. We did not have to fight tomorrow. There was the beginning and end of it. In Siam it would be ceremonial and police work. Equipment which we had deliberately dulled for survival's sake we now burnished. Drill supplanted fieldcraft. We, who had marched across half Burma, now played basketball to keep fit. Some jobs were transformed in spirit as well as in kind. The Quartermaster had been our friend for nine months, killing himself to beg and steal what we needed for our fighting. Now suddenly he was a miser to whom the loss of a bayonet scabbard was a major crime, whose aim was to retain his stores for ever. The Adjutant was transformed from a useful co-ordinator at headquarters into a form-disbursing, fault-finding overworked martinet. The new Colonel, whose reputation now rested upon the degree of smartness with which a guard might present arms, and no longer upon battle plans and an ability to go without sleep, discharged his eye for country, resorbed his eye for a knife-edge crease and the angle of a felt hat upon a shaven skull. Big fish feed upon little fish, and little fish upon the minnows. We company commanders also worried about creases and polish and mislaid scabbards; and below us the men had to worry about them. I, who was a child of the army at war, was new to this game, and found it trying.

Thus the change was also a beginning. A different kind of life lay ahead, a life in which we still seldom stayed long in one place, but which was to see us guarding suspected Japanese war criminals in a jail outside Bangkok, which gave us Christmas in Malaya, and the summer fighting in Java (back out of storage had to come the old skills, the old fears), another Christmas in Malaya, and for me the final goodbye in April 1947. But that is another story.

Mine had been an easy war. I fought no hand-to-hand encounters. I never had the set-piece attack on a well defended position, nor the rushed attack that failed. The gun-fire and mortaring to which I had been subjected were desultory. I was not bombed, nor lost, nor ambushed, nor really hungry; I did not have to go on fighting when exhausted, desperate and defeated. When I read of what happened to others I recognise my luck. War is unpredictable and will destroy a fine unit in an hour and let others go unscathed for years.

During the D-Day landings in Normandy on 6 June 1944, the two American infantry regiments on Utah beach lost twelve men killed. Fifteen miles away on Omaha beach a thousand men died. In the Kohima battles of 1944 the 2nd British Division towards the end had battalions shrunk to the size of companies whose men were weak with exhaustion, battle fatigue and illness. The same and worse was the fate of many units in the two Chindit expeditions. As for the Japanese, their trials were still greater, for their supply systems were elementary and their medical services often non-existent. Yuji Aida describes how, between the spring of 1944 and July 1945, his Division (which was not involved in the Imphal battles) was reduced from twenty thousand to less than three thousand men, and these mostly second-line troops, all of them with fever, scabies, athlete's foot, many with dysentery and other serious diseases. His Company was down to ten men with their rifles and one light machine-gun. For over a year they had been issued with nothing, and had to forage and barter for food, and replace equipment from the dead.

Our casualties were never on this scale and we had never been short of a piece of equipment for long. From October 1943 when the Battalion first saw action in the Arakan, to August 1946 (when two months of mild fighting in Java were finished) we lost 165 killed, 12 missing and 376 wounded, a total of 553. A larger number went sick, especially in 1944, but a lot of these returned, as did many of the wounded. These figures are not negligible (the total theoretical strength of a battalion at that time was 866), but spread over so long, with various breaks, they were bearable. Individually each dead man was a tragedy; in total the killing did not affect our morale.

Now the war was over. And although mine had been an easy war, it took me a long time to unwind—five or ten years perhaps; perhaps only now, as I write.

'What a pity that killing spoils an otherwise energetically exciting experience.' I do not know who wrote this, but it does sum up our schizophrenic attitude to war. War is energetic. It is exciting. There can be a closeness of human friendship and trust seldom achieved in peace. Yet the energy and excitement are there only at the start. At some point fatigue, under-nourishment and strain take over the body, and ultimately the mind; the fear which at first adds an edge to excitement gradually permeates everything, like a spreading cancer, and degrades what it overwhelms. And the killing is essential to the excitement: without the chance of death to oneself, without the element of hunting others, the quality of the excitement would be fundamentally changed, just another soccer match. Even the friendship is ephemeral—the incompatible made compatible by the urgency of outside pressures. It is a common experience to find that five years later you have nothing to say beyond platitudes to your former companions in battle.

Sometimes I would like to be persuaded that those war years held some meaning. On the national and international level it is easy to produce meanings: the military defeat of an aggressive Japan; the reconquest of Burma for the British and the salvage of British imperial prestige (and the loss of both despite victory), and so on. But for me, what?

I wrote earlier in this story (page 19) that I was drawn towards the war as surely as driftwood to the centre of a whirlpool. Now I had been spewed out, a bit ragged, but still afloat. I am glad that I went to the war and that I reached the sharp end in time for one campaign. I am glad that the Bomb confined my war, for after one campaign I wanted no more of it. Was there any meaning for me?

Perhaps I would have endorsed Wingate's statement, if I had known it: 'Our aim is to make possible a Government of the world in which all men can live at peace with equal opportunity of service.' (From his Order of the Day to the first Chindit expedition, February 1943.) But that seems a little remote, detached from the ordinary experience of the fighting soldier.

After the war for a little while we soldiers were in credit with our neighbours, especially those of us who had fought in

Burma. That credit has long since been consumed. Now our children question the purpose of the war and what was then so black and white now seems a shifting grey. It is almost as though we who fought were criminals. Perhaps we were, though there seemed no other way, and still does not. Like the doomed protagonists in a Greek tragedy, we were bound to fight. The world changes quickly these days. Twenty years is long enough to give our past the quality of history where once fifty or a hundred were required. And in the perspective of the historian most wars are folly. Ours did not seem so at the time.

Sociologists distinguish between the purpose that an individual has of his own accord and the purpose that others may try to induce him to have. When a man goes to war, to put his life at risk, these two purposes must be reconciled. If they are not he will make an indifferent soldier. In me, and for many of my countrymen, they were reconciled. My co-operation in the purposes of my country had been voluntary; conscription was unnecessary.

Patriotism is a portmanteau word, swollen with emotional elephantiasis. It needs careful handling. My generation had been reared on the literature of the First World War. At the most impressionable age we had absorbed something of the horror and futility and waste and incredible courage of the Western Front, and of the reaction of the survivors against the generous yet uncritical patriotism with which they had started. The two were somehow connected. The patriotism had led to the horror perhaps? We were fascinated yet repelled. I do not think anyone in 1939 could have been patriotic in the sentimental 1914 way.

Nevertheless we believed that nations which tried to dominate other nations by force ought to be resisted. It seemed clear to me then that the Germans and the Japanese had attempted such domination, and accompanied their attempt with extraordinary brutality. It did not follow that we 'believed' in the British Empire, in 'my country right or wrong', in 'God save the King' and 'Britannia rule the Waves'. Mine was a qualified patriotism. Whatever the historical reasons for Britain's accession of empire—and they were complex and only sometimes ignoble—I was not fighting to retain dominion over palm and pine exactly as it had reigned in 1939. I was not expecting a bright new world at the end of my sweat and fear. I was a subdued patriot.

This qualified patriotism should have made us poor fighters. But war imposes its own brutal logic. 'If you must go to war,' said Montgomery, 'and war is something you should always try to avoid—if you must go to war, you must win.' This applies to individuals as to nations. If I was to be a soldier, I had to be a good one so that my chances of survival and those of others who depended on me would be at their highest. Listen. I am crouched behind a tank near Milaungbya. That Japanese first-class private among the trees at the edge of the village will not refrain from squeezing the trigger because I recognise the right of Asians to rule in their own countries. Maybe he too does not swallow his government's propaganda, deplores the years of conquest in China, longs to return to his wife and to his mountain farm, is sick of hunger, fatigue, danger and the blows from his platoon commander. But he will shoot when he sees me. And I can know nothing of his doubts; I too must shoot.

In that same earlier passage I mentioned that some kind of image of the heroic was partly behind my wish to reach an active battalion. How did this image weather exposure to reality? On the whole, well. I was not disillusioned. War is sometimes exhilarating, often frightening, often horrible. The men who were in it with me, British and Gurkha, an ordinary sample of regular and war-time soldiers, survived or died with honour. The reader should remember that until the war ended almost every action of every waking hour in our Battalion was consciously directed towards achieving battle. In those battles which we strove to achieve the price for both success and failure was death. We knew this very well. It seems to me remarkable that a man can so repeatedly overcome his natural fears that he goes through this process time after time. It seems to me remarkable that the breaking-point for most men (and there is a breaking-point for every man) was so distant that few reached it. I do not believe that one man in a thousand enjoys war after his initial exposure, should that exposure continue for several weeks. The glamour disperses as the tensions prolong, and it is then that ordinary men come close to the heroic. Anyone can be brave once.

But death did not threaten now. The skills so painfully acquired were not needed. Courage would lose its primacy. We wartime temporary officers would be demobilised. The Battalion itself, a war-raised unit, my home, would be unlikely to survive for long.* Whatever lay ahead could scarcely require or receive the quality of dedication that war demands as it fastens upon its devotees like the leeches of Assam and drains them of all they can give. We should have to find other occupations, other interests, thankful that we lived to do so.

Outwardly I made no attempt to stay in the army. I some-times thought about it, if only because I did not know where to move next. I had nothing in particular to go back to in England: neither wife nor sweetheart, neither job nor even an adult experience of my own country. I had been too long away during impressionable years. There were parts of this great spacious eastern world that belonged to me far more intimately than England seemed to do.

When an organisation so embracing as the army has held a man for the first four years of adult life, he grows into it and dependent upon it. He is not so free as he thinks. The army is a vocation, like the priesthood, and asks much of those who profess it. In return the army looks after the primary needs of life: food, clothing, shelter and a place in society. To leave it for the unknown is not so easy. And when I left no one would know what I had achieved. The break would be absolute, like a birth. Who cares what embryos have been up to in the womb?

But the more I thought about staying, the more I realised that for me to stay would be a mistake. Though there is room in the army for a wider spectrum of talents and types than I realised then, there would not have been room for me. I was not really a leader; I was only a passable counterfeit. Soon it would be time for me to disband my constructed identity, to shed the skin of authority, to end this particular pilgrimage

* It still exists. After serving in Siam, Java and Malaya until December 1947, it returned to India and became part of the regular army of inde-pendent India.

and to look for another. There was plenty of time. I was still four months short of twenty-one when the Bomb was dropped.

So we come back to that Dashera, which was both an end and a beginning. Here was pleasure uncomplicated by the past or the future. The war was over. The peace had not begun to intrude. We lived for the moment.

At midnight when the Colonel left the proceedings grew less serious. His departure released an obvious tension. British and Gurkha officers settled more comfortably into their seats and sipped their rum with greater abandon.

'Now we can begin,' said Chandru, the Subadar-Major. His large round face, like Humpty Dumpty's, creased into tiny wrinkles as he smiled. He clapped his hands and without warning announced that some of the British officers would dance. His eye ranged along us. God knows what we looked like, though our faces must have been so familiar to him as to be long past criticism. To myself I cursed him. I am not one of those who spring easily into the limelight.

'The Adjutant and the Company Commander Sahibs will commence,' said Chandru.

There was no point in arguing. We rose, a little unsteadily, faces flushed, and accompanied by encouraging shouts and some clapping, climbed on the stage. Chandru said something which I did not catch and immediately the drums broke into a wild rhythm, a popular hill dance, while the dancers lined us up and told us what to do. They were smiling through the rivulets of sweat on their faces, unworried by our sudden presence. I found it good to be standing. Now that I was on the stage, embarrassment vanished. When the singing started I recognised the tune and had a fair idea of the movements.

Soon the stage held a whirlpool of circling bodies and at least half the audience seemed to be singing and beating the time. Others were pirouetting on their own in the semi-darkness outside. Comments floated up.

'That C Company Sahib knows how to dance.'
'. . . it is the energy of rum.'
'When they dance it is good. Sometimes they fall down.'

'See how the perspiration runs. Soon they will . . .'

In the first row below the stage the Subadar-Major smiled benignly. It was bad when the officers sat drinking for the whole evening. They were unhappy in the morning and angry with the men. Now they would sweat out the rum and wake up in excellent health.

On and on went the singing. Round and round, down and up went the dancers. We forgot the audience, forgot time and place. Every faculty was concentrated on the swinging rhythm and the need to make limbs conform. Dancing became the only world; life was contained in and supported by music. When at last the music ceased I felt dazed, woken from a vivid dream. I leaned against a post while others argued over which dance should come next. They were hot and short of breath but still enthusiastic. Jitbahadur from in front shouted another suggestion, several agreed, the drummers gave a thud or two, and we were off again to a slow, sad little tune, endlessly repeated.

'Come on, Sahib.' It was Dhaniram, one of my old Intelligence Section riflemen. I had seen him in the chorus. To restart movement was an effort, but once started and the same fascination took charge.

'Watch me, Sahib. This one is more difficult.' Dhaniram turned slowly round, his arms, wrists and fingers gesturing in time to the rhythm of his feet and the precise sway of his body. There was a smooth grace to his movements that even the green battledress could not hide. Down on the haunches we went, round, up and down again, now fast, now slow, as the singing swelled to a quick chorus, then faded to a thin solo, as the drums beat out a crescendo of rhythm, then a gentle background throb. This was living. We were made for this. Forgotten was the sweat of war, the anxiety and the fear and the craving for sleep, forgotten the niggling discipline of guard duty and drill. Here was the marrow of creation, expressing a satisfaction that transcended race and rank. Round and round, up and down, the never-ceasing drums, a sea of faces, the full chorus, the solo again, laughter, the bright electric light, darkness beyond. At heart I am an egalitarian and would have all men treated equal. Round and round, up and down. I *will* get that rising twist perfected. I will not stop. It is fine to be living and to be strong and to go on dancing.

Some of the officers had given up and were resting, others had joined in, others had gone to bed. The audience was thinning. Still the dance continued, and did not end until someone tripped over a hurricane lamp and burning oil spread across the earth near the stage. The dancers rested, exhausted, while others dealt with the flames.

Behind stage, where a number of bodies lay curled in corners asleep or in stupor, they were brewing tea. Sarbajit, my orderly, appeared with a mug-full. It was thick, sweet and refreshing. I sat down on the edge of the stage to drink.

'Sarbajit.'

'Yes, Sahib.'

'You are not waiting up for me?'

'Yes, Sahib.'

'There is no need.'

'No, Sahib.'

I smiled. 'There are no Japanese here.'

We sipped tea in silence while around us a companionable hum of talk went on among the singers and dancers and the remnant of the audience. Without the drums and the singing and the clapping the night was very peaceful, like that palpable tranquillity that follows the suspension of a ship's engines in port. By an unspoken harmony of feeling we were all aware that the dancing was finished. I thought that I ought to be saying something but really did not want to. I looked for Jemadar Manbahadur. He had gone. Then I wondered if I ought to have stayed so long, whether the men would have preferred to continue on their own. Subadar Jitbahadur, squatting close by, who could never keep quiet, might have divined this thought.

'It is good for the British officers to learn our dances. It makes us happy.' There was a general rumble of assent. Perhaps it was as simple as that. Gurkhas held to the direct view.

'It was fine dancing,' I said. 'A proper farewell to Burma. And are you prepared for Bangkok? I hope that your defences for the new enemy are understood and ready.'

There was a roar of laughter. The first brigade of our

Division to fly into Siam in September had succumbed in appalling numbers to venereal disease; for that pleasant eccentricity by which almost all the girls of Siam love almost all men (or so it seemed) was marred by a legacy of disease left by our predecessors, the Japanese. Gurkhas too have a reputation for the kind of dalliance that has little time for holding hands on a park bench. So it was that a few days previously I had lain on my bed in my tent one sticky afternoon while B Company held a parade from which I was debarred. I could hear most of what was going on. Somehow one volunteer from each company had been persuaded to act as demonstrator for the proper fitting of the army-issue condom to the penis. The army, quite rightly, was leaving nothing to the imagination. But what started as a serious lecture from Subadar Thamansing ended in gales of laughter.

'If we fall to that enemy there will be no medals.'

'Eh, but what a pleasant way to be wounded.'

'Is it really true about these women of Siam, Sahib?'

'So it is said by 114 Brigade. Even Purné the cook must take care.' Purné was often compared by his friends to the backside of a mule. I stood up with difficulty. '*Aré*, I'm tired! It is the moment for bed. Tomorrow comes. *Salaam, salaam*. It has been a good evening.'

I was reluctant to leave, but such moments cannot last and squeezing to the final drop can spoil them. I walked slowly through the lines towards my tent. The night air was cool, refreshing. A quarter-moon lit the way. Moonlight is calm, impersonal, unlike the sun that warms with friendship or burns with enmity. From some of the tents as I passed, the canvas white in the moonlight, voices in conversation still murmured. It was two o'clock. I had slept and marched and crawled under eight successive moons without a roof to hide me. I felt I knew the moon. Beyond the tents there was the silhouette of a small pagoda, too distant to have colour, but graceful as always. The pagodas of Burma, white or gold, set on hill-tops or rising from a green-tree circle, had been an abiding pleasure, symbols of a time and a religion and a way of life that seemed halcyon compared with our own.

Out of the corner of one eye I caught a movement and

turned instinctively. There was something familiar about the
figure stepping lightly between the two tents.

'Sarbajit!'

'Sahib?'

'There was no need. You are a stubborn fellow. But thank
you.'

'*Salaam*, Sahib.'

'*Salaam*, Sarbajit. Sleep well.'

This was probably the first occasion when Sarbajit saw me
home. It was not to be the last. I might forbid him to wait for
me and he might pretend to obey, but somewhere he was
around. He had a settled idea of his responsibilities. I might
enlarge but could not diminish them.

And perhaps Sarbajit, and Tulbir my runner who was on
leave, and Nandalal and Jemadar Manbahadur, and all the
others, but especially these, form the heart of my memory
of that time, and of any meaning it has for me. As I have said,
a man can become what he is expected to be. Our Gurkhas
expected as much of us as of themselves. We grew better for
being with them. Whatever first drove us all to war, it was
friendship, trust and loyalty to one another that kept us at it
long after we might have preferred to be elsewhere.

It is here that I will leave them, with the young moon
shining white on the tents, and the melodies of the Dashera
dance haunting the mind.

XXIII

AFTERWORD 1985

The reviews of the original edition of this book were mostly kind. This was pleasing, but what was heart-warming and fascinating were the letters that arrived, sometimes years later. They were written by both men and women, and from remarkably varied backgrounds; re-reading them now at a gulp, instead of one at a time as they came in, I am awed by the power of words to reach from one human being to another.

Most of the letters came from *British* officers and other ranks who had been in the 14th Army in Burma. Although it is estimated that nearly 2,000,000 men and women served during the three years and eight months of the Burma campaign, the majority were not English-speaking and many were barely literate. Thus fewer books in English have appeared compared with those on other theatres of fighting in the Second World War. Not many Gurkhas, Indians, East Africans, West Africans, Chinese or Burmese are likely to have written of their war, nor are many of them likely to read a book such as this. Little of the Japanese writing on Burma has been translated into English.

Gunners serving with our Seventh Indian Division were particularly active in writing to me. Artillerymen providing close support to infantry are blind without Observation Posts, and these OPs were usually manned by a Gunner officer and two or more men with a wireless. They sat with the infantry in the most forward positions, often accompanied them on patrols, and so came to know some of us, and we some of them, very well. Our Gunners were 136th Field Regiment, Royal Artillery. Here is the first to write:

'Well, here we are; middle-aged, and with descendants. Were they really us, the men who did and saw those things? I can believe it now only with difficulty but (like you) it took me a decade to get it out of my system. I'm glad I did. Yet I don't regret those years, or feel them wasted—just that they belonged to another existence in which the central figure was not wholly the man who is writing this letter...

'Your story, and the similarity of our reactions to comparable experiences, has made me think more of these things in the last few days, recalling part-forgotten names and faces. The other night, at dusk, I was in my garden in Wiltshire when a radio in a nearby cottage played "Bless this house". This was always our sign-off at battery sing-songs when "resting". It made a respectable aftermath to the One-Eyed Riley, the Bloody Great Wheel, etc., and it was always sung first solo by a gunner to whom God had given a superb baritone voice, and then in chorus by all present; but all present would by then be invisible in the shadows, detectable only by the red glow of their cigarettes contrasting with the greenish light of fireflies overhead. I was completely overwhelmed by this evocation, and wept...'

That was Wilson Stephens, who 'did OP more or less continually from January 1944 until repatriation in April 1945', mostly with our sister 33 Brigade.

There is Eric Williams, now running kennels in Norfolk, who was an OP signaller with 136th Field Regiment in support of us throughout the 1945 campaign. 'I was much nearer than you could imagine, and reading your account from Kohima to Nyaungkashe was as if following footprints in the snow.' And 'others who have not lived with Gurkhas have lost out on life; no doubt you, as myself often, when quite alone reflect on how lucky we are. I have no regrets, I learned to share and in man there is no colour...' Eric is a remarkable man who has been closely involved with the Gurkha Welfare Appeal, has been out to Nepal and there met our VC, Lachhiman Gurung (pp. 220, 236).

There is Gerry Gorman, who was the Gunner with the company of the 1/11th Sikhs that was the first to reach us after the Taungdaw battle (p. 218). He had spent the previous day in a light plane with an American ambulance pilot, Sergeant Oakapple, bringing down artillery fire on the Japanese and their transport to our north. 'Your account of the fighting along the Irrawaddy north of Chauk brings back the feel and the atmosphere of those days as though it were only yesterday.' He had come on this book in his local library. 'I could hardly believe my eyes when I glanced through it—those Burmese villages and small towns known only to those few of us who passed that way came back to life again. It completely covered the one bit of active service I had during the war.' He too has no regrets. 'Thank heaven, those days and experiences have gone for ever from us, and one sincerely hopes, for our children too, though I must also say it is part of my life I would not exchange for a load of gold, or even want to have altered very much—except perhaps here and there a happier ending for some of our friends.'

Finally there is Gilbert Gentle, the Forward Observation Officer cut off with us at Taungdaw (pp. 203, 211). He wrote 'It was very flattering of you to describe me as a young lieutenant—I was in fact in May 1945 a fairly senior captain and rising 29! Apart from that, I cannot fault you in any detail, and it was beyond my most remote expectation that this episode, and others before it with which I was concerned . . . would ever be recorded.'

This is another reminder of the fallibility of memory, about which I wrote in Chapter IX and elsewhere. Most of the facts I recorded were checked by reference to our periodic battalion newsletters, to the regimental, divisional and campaign histories, to scattered notes in diaries and to a few surviving Battalion Routine Orders and personal letters. The typescript at one stage or another was read by five of my fellow officers in the 4/8th Gurkhas. But I had no contact with the Gunners and no written record of Gilbert's age and rank; relying on memory, I got it wrong.

Some of those with me at Mhow (Chapter II) wrote in, among them Derek Norris (p. 211). 'I do want to send you my best congratulations on an extemely good account of your experiences so many of which were similar to those of us ECOs [Emergency Commissioned Officers] who served with the wonderful Gurks. Reading it revived many memories of Mhow and afterwards. You have done a great job in expressing truly what we all felt and recording for posterity what no one had done before. Previously, as far as I know, including John Masters, there had never been a real expression in writing. And after all if these things are not recorded then people don't know about them.'

And Michael Hardwick, Officer Cadet A773, presently a freelance writer, reminded me of one incident which I had forgotten: 'I went up to the attics and rummaged out the two photographs of A Company, No 3 Wing, and now, of course, I can place you as A759, recipient of that marvellous threat of Q.M.S. [Quartermaster Sergeant] Eley's, which I have always remembered: "Seven Foive Noine, Oi'll come over to you, Seven Foive Noine, Oi will!"'

A number of those who wrote echoed the words of Victor Sack, a Sapper officer commanding a Forward Airfield Platoon: 'You have put into words many of the thoughts and deeds of those days in Burma which many of us who were there have forgotten.' This pleases me the most, for it was always my hope that what had to be a personal account might turn out to mirror the general experience.

Relatives and friends discounted, several women wrote in. Most touching was a letter from the mother of a young tank officer killed near Minbu in May 1945. 'I have just finished reading your enthralling and compelling book which I have had on loan from my local library and must return, but feel I can hardly part with it … for every word I read I felt it was my son Peter talking to me and telling me so many of the things I wanted to know, and in some strange way it was a comfort to me.' Peter Rogers was with the 3rd Carabiniers, who lost several tanks at this time in support of our sister 114 Brigade.

For many correspondents, reading *A Child at Arms* released a profusion of memories, and it is sad that shortage of space has to restrict quotation.

What has happened to the 4/8th Gurkhas (now Gorkhas)? It still exists, indeed flourishes, and I was particularly pleased to receive letters from both the Commanding Officer, Lieutenant-Colonel Ranjit Majumdar, and the Second-in-Command, Major B. Bhole, in the year of publication, 1970. Taungdaw Day, 13 May, when Lachhiman won his VC, is still celebrated each year.

As for the 'characters' in my story, I have kept in touch with some and have had indirect news of others. Walter (now Sir Walter) Walker, after winning further renown in Malaya and Borneo, retired in 1972 as a General, Commander-in-Chief, Allied Forces Northern Europe. He has had a book written about him, *Fighting General: the Public and Private Campaigns of General Sir Walter Walker*, by Tom Pocock (Collins, 1973). Peter Myers retired as a Brigadier, having spent most of his dis-

tinguished post-war service in South-East Asia. Peter
Wickham has retired from the BBC, which he joined soon after
demobilisation. Bob Findley has just sold his ancestral home
on the shore of Loch Lomond and lives nearby with his
Finnish wife.

Denis Sheil-Small lives in Natal with his second wife; Sally,
his first (p. 76), died tragically in 1978. Denis published his
own war memoirs *Green Shadows* (William Kimber 1982), an
exciting read which covers some of the same ground as this
book. He had written several other books with a Gurkha
theme while working at his job in insurance. Scott Gilmore
still works in New York, but is easing up. He too has written an
account of his war that is looking for a publisher. It may be
some sort of record that three officers out of a group which
seldom numbered more than twelve at any one time, and
which perhaps totalled forty over three years, have written up
their experiences.

Bill Blenkin has been in Canada since the 1950s, battling
with real estate and the switchback fortunes of the Canadian
economy. Doc Dalton is still healing bodies and minds in
north London. Peter Dickenson was a Lieutenant-Colonel in
the Army Educational Corps when last I heard of him. I have
had no news of Tommy Login since the mid-sixties. Ian Crew,
my room companion at Mhow, works in California.

I am more conscious than ever that *A Child at Arms* is an egocentric account: I could not and did not attempt to tell the
whole story of the 4/8th Gurkhas during that 1945 advance
across Burma. I would like to have mentioned so many others,
given them life through description and anecdote, but the
random ravages of memory let me down. Indeed, like Wilson
Stephens quoted above, I can now hardly believe that the
events chronicled happened to me, and I have to re-read my
own book to be reminded of the detail. For those who would
like an overall account of the Burma campaign, an excellent
one has recently appeared. Louis Allen's *Burma, the Longest War
1941–45* (Dent, 1984) is unlikely to be soon superseded, and has
the great advantage of telling the story from the records of both
sides.

In the winter of 1981 I returned to Burma. The country is
under what might be described as a mild military dictatorship.
For the foreigner travel is restricted, partly because the moun-

tainous periphery to the great central Irrawaddy basin is in a state of intermittent unrest, partly because, outside a few centres, facilities for visitors are not developed. In so many ways I did not feel a foreigner and found these limitations sad.

Fortunately one of the tourist centres is Pagan, that extra-ordinary city of ruined pagodas which we had skirted in February 1945 (p. 132). For thirty-six years Pagan had haunted my imagination. From there my wife and I hired a jeep and travelled south along the still-atrocious sandy track to the Milaungbyas, Singu and Chauk (Chapters XIV–XVII). Much of the land was transformed by the green crops of December in place of the parched barrenness of February, and by the spread of toddy palm plantations where I thought I remembered bare slopes. I did, however, immediately recognise the crossing of the Pyinma Chaung where I had crouched that warm night in March (p. 151) with the line of cliffs guarding the oil town of Chauk towering above us, the Japanese close by on both sides, and 'home' four hours to the north.

In the wider perspective Burma has changed remarkably little. The country became independent in 1948 and left the Commonwealth. For the last several decades the Government has deliberately minimised contacts with the outside world, repelling West and East even-handedly. In Mandalay and Rangoon there are no high-risers, no hamburger joints, no strip clubs. There is decay but no visible sign of starvation. The intelligentsia are probably frustrated, the restless hill tribes are in sporadic opposition (as they always have been), but the bulk of the population seems contented. The country is self-sufficient in basic foods and oil.

One change was the arrival of the wireless and the loud-speaker in the villages. Most often you can no longer hear that lovely sound of the breeze tinkling the bells of the pagoda spires.

It is now forty years since the atom bomb reprieved our lives in Burma, and nearly twenty years since I wrote most of *A Child at Arms*. I stand by the quotation that heads the last chapter: 'More than perhaps any campaign in the Second World War ... the Burma campaign has the elements of a great Homeric saga ...' Those of us who were in it still think that we are underrated and 'forgotten'. But history, like life, is not fair. Why should it be?